always up to date

The law changes, but Nolo is always on top of it! We offer several ways to make sure you and your Nolo products are always up to date:

1 **Nolo's Legal Updater**
We'll send you an email whenever a new edition of your book is published! Sign up at **www.nolo.com/legalupdater**.

2 **Updates @ Nolo.com**
Check **www.nolo.com/update** to find recent changes in the law that affect the current edition of your book.

3 **Nolo Customer Service**
To make sure that this edition of the book is the most recent one, call us at **800-728-3555** and ask one of our friendly customer service representatives. Or find out at **www.nolo.com**.

7th edition

IRAs, 401(k)s,

& Other Retirement Plans

Taking Your Money Out

**by Twila Slesnick, Ph.D., Enrolled Agent
& Attorney John C. Suttle, CPA**

NOLO

Seventh Edition	JANUARY 2006
Editor	AMY DELPO
Cover Design	TERRI HEARSH
Book Design	TERRI HEARSH
Production	MARGARET LIVINGSTON
Proofreading	ROBERT WELLS
Index	ELLEN SHERRON
Printing	DELTA PRINTING SOLUTIONS, INC.

Slesnick, Twila.

 IRAs, 401(k)s & other retirement plans : taking your money out / by Twila Slesnick & John C. Suttle ; edited by Amy DelPo.-- 7th ed.

 p. cm.

 ISBN 1-4133-0402-8 (alk. paper)

 1. Individual retirement accounts--Law and legislation--United States--Popular works. 2. 401(k) plans--Law and legislation--Popular works. 3. Deferred compensation--Law and legislation--United States--Popular works. I. Title: IRA's, 401(k)s, and other retirement plans. II. Suttle, John C. III. DelPo, Amy, 1967- IV. Title.

KF3510.Z9S55 2006

343.7305'233--dc22

2005054707

Acknowledgments

Thanks to Nolo editor Robin Leonard for her intelligent and skillful editing on the first edition—and for adding a dose of levity to the entire process. For all other editions, thanks to Nolo editor Amy DelPo for her keen eye and clear thinking. We are also grateful to attorney Charles Purnell for reading the entire manuscript more carefully than we had any right to expect. His suggestions were valuable and much appreciated. Thanks also to Robert and Joan Leonard, and Gail Friedlander, for reading parts of the manuscript. And finally, a special thanks to Durf, partner extraordinare, and to Jack and Betty Suttle who have made it possible to balance single parenthood and a profession.

Table of Contents

3 Early Distributions: Taking Your Money Out Before the law Allows

4 Substantially Equal Periodic Payments

5 Required Distributions: Taking Money Out When You Have To

6 Required Distributions During Your Lifetime

7 Distributions to Your Beneficiary If You Die Before Age 70 1/2

8 Distributions to Your Beneficiary If You Die After Age 70 1/2

9 Roth IRAs

Appendixes

A IRS Forms, Notices, and Schedules

B Life Expectancy Tables

Index

How to Use This Book

This is not a mystery novel. It is a book about how to take money out of your retirement plan. We are not promising that you will stay up all night breathlessly turning each page to see what happens next. Nonetheless, you will find this book useful—perhaps even surprising.

Let's start with the basics. There are many kinds of retirement plans and many possible sources for owning one. You might have a retirement plan at work, an IRA that you set up yourself, or a plan or IRA you've inherited. Or you might have all three. You might still be contributing to a plan, or you may be retired. No matter what your situation, you will find information in this book to help you through the minefield of rules.

There are many reasons to take money out of a retirement plan. You might want to borrow the money for an emergency and pay it back—or not pay it back. Maybe you quit your job and you want to take your share of the company's plan. Perhaps you're required by law to withdraw some of your retirement funds because you've reached a certain age.

Whatever your situation, you probably have a lot of questions about your plan—and how to take money out of it. This book can answer:

- How do I know what kind of retirement plan I have? (See Chapter 1.)
- Do I have to wait until I retire to get money out of my plan or my IRA? (See Chapter 3.)
- Can I borrow money from my 401(k) plan to buy a house? (See Chapters 3, 4, and 5.)
- What should I do with my retirement plan when I leave my company or retire? (See Chapter 2.)
- When do I have to start taking money out of my IRA? (See Chapter 5.)
- How do I calculate how much I have to take? (See Chapter 6.)
- Can I take more than the required amount? (See Chapter 6.)

- What happens to my retirement plan when I die? (See Chapters 7 and 8.)
- Can my spouse roll over my IRA when I die? (See Chapters 7 and 8.)
- What about my children? Can they put my IRA in their names after I die? Do they have to take all the money out of the account right away? (See Chapters 7 and 8.)
- If I inherit a retirement plan, can I add my own money to it? Can I save it for my own children, if I don't need the money? (See Chapters 7 and 8.)
- Am I allowed to set up a Roth IRA? Should I? (See Chapter 9.)
- Can I convert my regular IRA to a Roth IRA? Should I? (See Chapter 9.)

To help you answer these and other questions, we include many examples. They guide you through the decision making process and take you through calculations. You will also find sample tax forms that the IRS requires, along with instructions for how to complete them.

This book contains tables to help you calculate distributions. It also contains sample letters and worksheets you can use to communicate with the IRS or with the custodian of your IRA or retirement plan. We've even included some important IRS notices so you can read firsthand how IRS personnel are thinking about certain critical issues.

The tax rules for pensions, IRAs, 401(k)s, and other types of retirement plans are notoriously complex, which can be all the more frustrating because they are important to so many people. The good news is that help is here: This book makes the rules clear and accessible.

Icons Used Throughout

At the beginning of each chapter, we let you know who should read the chapter and who can skip it or read only parts of it.

Sprinkled throughout the book are planning tips based on strategies that other people have used successfully.

We include several cautions to alert you to potential pitfalls.

Types of Retirement Plans

Who Should Read Chapter 1

Read this chapter if you aren't certain which types of retirement plans you have—either through your employer or as a self-employed person. Also read this chapter if you have an IRA but aren't sure which type.

*H*ow many people have warned you that you'll never see a penny of the hard-earned money you've poured into the Social Security system and that you'd better have your own retirement nest egg tucked away somewhere? Perhaps those doomsayers are overstating the case, but even if you eventually do collect Social Security, it is likely to provide only a fraction of the income you will need during retirement.

Congress responded to this problem several decades ago by creating a variety of tax-favored plans to help working people save for retirement. One such plan is set up by you, the individual taxpayer, and is appropriately called an individual retirement account or IRA. Another, which can be established by your employer or by you if you are self-employed, is referred to by the nondescript phrase, a qualified plan. A qualified plan is one that qualifies to receive certain tax benefits as described in Section 401 of the U.S. Tax Code.

There are other types of retirement plans, too, which enjoy some of the same tax

benefits as qualified plans but are not technically qualified, because they are defined in a different section of the Tax Code. Many of these other plans closely follow the qualified plan rules, however. The most common of these almost-qualified plans are tax-deferred annuities (TDAs) and qualified annuity plans. (Don't be thrown by the name. Even though it may be called a qualified annuity plan, it is not defined in Section 401 and therefore is not a qualified plan in the purest sense.) Both of these plans are defined in Section 403 of the Tax Code. Because many of the rules in Section 403 are similar to those in Section 401, TDAs and qualified annuity plans are often mentioned in the same breath with qualified plans.

All qualified plans, TDAs, and qualified annuity plans have been sweetened with breaks for taxpayers to encourage them to save for retirement. And working people have saved, often stretching as far as they can to put money into their retirement plans. But saving is only half the equation. The government also wants you to take money out of the plan and spend it chiefly on your retirement. For that reason, the government has enacted a series of rules on how and when you can—or, sometimes, must—take money out of your retirement plan. (When you take money out, it's called a distribution.)

What does this mean for you? If you or your employer has ever put money into a retirement plan and received tax benefits as a result, then you cannot simply take

Helpful Terms

Adjusted gross income (AGI). Total taxable income reduced by certain expenses such as qualified plan contributions, IRA contributions, and alimony payments.

Beneficiary. The person or entity entitled to receive the benefits from an insurance policy or from trust property, such as a retirement plan or IRA.

Deductible contribution. A contribution to a retirement plan that an employer may claim as a business expense to offset income on the employer's tax return. You may know it as simply the employer's contribution. In the case of an IRA, a deductible contribution is one that an individual taxpayer may use to offset income on the individual's tax return.

Distribution. A payout of property (such as shares of stock) or cash from a retirement plan or IRA to the participant or a beneficiary.

Earned income. Income received for providing goods or services. Earned income might be wages or salary or net profit from a business.

Eligible employee. An employee qualifies to participate in the employer's plan because he or she has met the eligibility requirements (such as having worked for the employer for a specified number of years).

Nondeductible contribution. A contribution to a retirement plan or IRA that may not be claimed as a business expense or used as an adjustment to offset taxable income on an income tax return.

Nondiscrimination rules. The provisions in the U.S. Tax Code that prohibit certain retirement plans from providing greater benefits to highly compensated employees than to other employees.

Participant, or active participant. An employee for whom the employer makes a contribution to the employer's retirement plan.

Tax-deductible expense. An item of expense that may be used to offset income on a tax return.

Tax deferral. The postponement of tax payments until a future year.

Vested benefit. The portion of a participant's retirement plan accumulation that a participant may keep after leaving the employer who sponsors the plan; or the portion that goes to a participant's beneficiary if the participant dies.

the money out whenever you want, nor can you leave it in the plan indefinitely, hoping, for example, to pass all of the funds on to your children.

Instead, you must follow a complex set of rules for withdrawing money from the plan during your lifetime, and your beneficiaries must follow these rules after your death. These rules are called distribution rules, and if you or your beneficiaries don't follow them, the government will impose penalties—sometimes substantial ones.

This first chapter identifies and briefly describes the types of retirement plans to which these distribution rules apply. If you have a retirement plan at work or if you have established one through your own business, you should find your plan listed below. Also, if you have an IRA, you will find your particular type among those described below.

There is also an entire category of plans known as nonqualified plans to which distribution rules do not apply. Such plans are used by employers primarily to provide incentives or rewards for particular—usually upper management—employees. These plans do not enjoy the tax benefits that IRAs and qualified plans (including TDAs and qualified annuities) do, and they consequently are not subject to the same distribution restrictions. Although this chapter helps you identify nonqualified plans, such plans have their own distribution rules, which fall outside the scope of this book.

Identifying your particular retirement plan probably won't be as difficult as you think. This is because every plan fits into one of four broad categories:

- qualified plan
- IRA
- plan which is neither an IRA nor a qualified plan, but which has many of the characteristics of a qualified plan, or
- plan which is neither an IRA nor a qualified plan, and which does not have the characteristics of a qualified plan.

A. Qualified Plans

A qualified plan is a type of retirement savings plan that an employer establishes for its employees and that conforms to the requirements of Section 401 of the U.S. Tax Code. Why is it called "qualified"? Because if the plan meets all of the requirements of Section 401, then it qualifies for special tax rules, the most significant of which is that contributions the employer makes to the plan on behalf of employees are tax deductible. Probably the best-known qualified plan is the 401(k) plan, discussed below in Section 1.

The advantages to you, the employee, working for an employer with a qualified plan, are not only the opportunity to accumulate a retirement nest egg, but also to postpone paying income taxes on money contributed to the plan. Neither the contributions you make nor any of the investment returns are taxable to you until you take money out of the plan. In tax jargon, the income tax is deferred until the money is distributed and available for spending—usually during retirement. Congress built in some safeguards to help ensure that your plan assets are around when you finally do retire. For example, the assets are required to be held in trust and are generally protected from the claims of creditors.

In return for these tax benefits, the plan must comply with a number of procedural rules. First, the plan must not discriminate in favor of the company's highly compensated employees. For example, the employer may not contribute disproportionately large amounts to the accounts of the company honchos. Also, the employer may not arbitrarily prevent employees from participating in the plan or from taking their retirement money with them when they leave the company. Finally, the plan must comply with an extremely complex set of distribution rules, which is the focus of this book.

Seven of the most common types of qualified plans are described below.

1. Profit Sharing Plans

A profit sharing plan is a type of qualified plan that allows employees to share in the profits of the company and to use those profits to help fund their retirement. Despite the plan's title and description, an employer doesn't have to make a profit in order to contribute to a profit sharing plan. Similarly, even if the employer makes a profit, it does not have to contribute to the plan. Each year, the employer has discretion over whether or not to make a contribution, regardless of profitability.

When the employer contributes money to the plan on behalf of its employees, the contributions are generally computed as a percentage of all participants' compensation. The annual contribution into all accounts can be as little as zero or as much as 25% of the total combined compensation of all participants. For the purposes of making this calculation, the maximum compensation for any individual participant is capped at $210,000. (The $210,000 increases from time to time for inflation.) No individual participant's account can receive more than $42,000 in a single year. (There is an exception to the $42,000 limit for individuals who are older than 50 and who contribute to a 401(k) plan.)

> **EXAMPLE:** Joe and Martha participate in their company's profit sharing plan. Last year, the company contributed 25% of their respective salaries to the plan. Joe's salary was $120,000 and Martha's was $190,000. The company contributed $30,000 for Joe (25% x $120,000). The company's contribution for Martha was limited to the $42,000 ceiling, however, because 25% of Martha's salary was actually $47,500, which is too much.

This year, however, the company's profits tumbled, so the company decided not to make any contributions to the profit sharing plan. Thus, the company will not contribute any money to the plan on Joe or Martha's behalf.

a. 401(k) Plans

A special type of profit sharing plan, called a 401(k) plan, is named imaginatively after the subsection of the Tax Code that describes it. All 401(k) plans allow you to direct some of your compensation into the plan, and you do not have to pay income taxes on the portion of your salary you direct into the plan until you withdraw it.

The plan may or may not provide for employer contributions. Some employers make matching contributions, depositing a certain amount for each dollar the participant contributes.

> **EXAMPLE:** Fred participates in his company's 401(k) plan. His company has promised to contribute $.25 for each dollar of Fred's salary that he directs into the plan. Fred's salary is $40,000. He directs 5% of his salary, which is $2,000, into the plan. The company matches with a $500 contribution (which is $.25 x $2,000).

Other employers contribute a fixed percentage of compensation for each eligible employee, whether or not the employee chooses to contribute to the plan.

> **EXAMPLE:** Marilyn's salary for the current year is $60,000. Her company has a 401(k) plan which does not match employee contributions. Instead, the company contributes a flat 3% of each eligible employee's salary to the plan. Marilyn is saving to buy a house, so she is not currently directing any of her salary into the 401(k) plan. Nonetheless, the company will contribute $1,800 (which is 3% x $60,000) to the plan for Marilyn.

b. Roth 401(k) Plans

Beginning in 2006, employers will be allowed to establish a new type of 401(k) called a Roth 401(k). This new plan will be similar to traditional 401(k)s in that it will allow employees to defer salary into the plan. The difference will come in the tax treatment. Whereas contributions to traditional 401(k)s are tax deductible, contributions to Roth 401(k)s will not be. Rather, the tax benefits for Roth 401(k)s will come when you take distributions, which will be tax free as long as you meet certain requirements. Although the IRS has not yet finalized these requirements, a distribution likely will be entirely tax free if it occurs after you reach age 59½ and if you have had the plan for at least five years.

2. Stock Bonus Plans

A stock bonus plan is like a profit sharing plan, except that the employer must pay the plan benefits to employees in the form of shares of company stock.

> EXAMPLE: Frankie worked for the Warp Corp. all her working life. During her employment, she participated in the company's stock bonus plan, accumulating $90,000 by retirement. When she retired, Warp Corp. stock was worth $100 per share. When the company distributed her retirement benefits to her, it gave her 900 shares of Warp Corp. stock.

3. Money Purchase Pension Plans

A money purchase pension plan is similar to a profit sharing plan in the sense that employer contributions are allocated to each participant's individual account. The difference is that the employer's contributions are mandatory, not discretionary. Under such a plan, the employer promises to pay a definite amount (such as 10% of compensation) into each participant's account every year. In that sense, money purchase pension plans are less flexible for employers than are profit sharing plans.

As with a profit sharing plan, the maximum amount that an employer can contribute to the plan for all participants combined is 25% of the total combined compensation of all participants (although each participant's compensation is limited to $210,000 for purposes of making this calculation).

The maximum that the employer can contribute to any given participant's account in a year is either $42,000 or the participant's compensation—whichever is less.

(The $210,000 and $42,000 caps increase from time to time for inflation.)

> EXAMPLE: Sand Corp. has a money purchase plan that promises to contribute 25% of compensation to each eligible employee's account. Jenna made $45,000 last year and was eligible to participate in the plan, so the company contributed $11,250 (25% x $45,000) to her account for that year. This year, the company is losing money. Nonetheless, the company is still obligated to contribute 25% of Jenna's salary to her money purchase plan account for the current year.

4. Employee Stock Ownership Plans (ESOPs)

An employee stock ownership plan, or ESOP, is a type of stock bonus plan that may have some features of a money purchase pension plan. ESOPs are designed to be funded primarily or even exclusively with employer stock. An ESOP can allow cash distributions, however, as long as the employee has the right to demand that benefits be paid in employer stock.

Because an ESOP is a stock bonus plan, the employer cannot contribute more than 25% of the total compensation of all participants and no more than $42,000 into any one participant's account.

5. Defined Benefit Plans

A defined benefit plan promises to pay each participant a set amount of money as an annuity beginning at retirement. The promised payment is usually based on a combination of factors, such as the employee's final compensation and the length of time the employee worked for the company. If the employee retires early, the benefit is reduced.

> EXAMPLE: Damien is a participant in his company's defined benefit plan. The plan guarantees that if Damien works until the company's retirement age, he will receive a retirement benefit equal to 1% of his final pay times the number of years he worked for the company. Damien will reach the company's retirement age in 20 years. If Damien is making $50,000 when he retires in 20 years, his retirement benefit will be $10,000 per year (which is 1% x $50,000 x 20 years). If he retires early, he will receive less.

Once the retirement benefit is determined, the company must compute how much to contribute each year in order to meet that goal. The computation is not simple—in fact, it requires the services of an actuary, who uses projections of salary increases and investment returns to determine the annual contribution amount. The computation must be repeated every year to take into account variations in investment returns and other factors and then to adjust the amount of the contribution to ensure the goal will be reached.

Even though, under certain circumstances, defined benefit plans permit much higher contributions than other qualified plans, they are used infrequently (especially by small companies) because they are so complex and expensive to administer.

6. Target Benefit Plans

A target benefit plan is a special type of money purchase pension plan that incorporates some of the attributes of a defined benefit plan. As with a money purchase plan, each participant in a target benefit plan has a separate account. But instead of contributing a fixed percentage of pay to every account, the employer projects a retirement benefit for each employee, as with a defined benefit plan. In fact, the contribution for the first year is computed in the same way a defined benefit plan contribution would be computed—with the help of an actuary. The difference, though, is that after the first year, the contribution formula is fixed. While a defined benefit plan guarantees a certain retirement annuity, a target benefit plan just shoots for it by estimating the required annual contribution in the employee's first participation year and then freezing the formula. The formula might be a specific dollar amount every year or perhaps a percentage of pay.

If any of the original assumptions turn out to be wrong—for example, the investment return is less than expected—the retirement target won't be reached. The employer is under no obligation to adjust the level of the contribution to reach the original target if there is a shortfall. Conversely, if investments do better than expected, the employee's retirement benefit will exceed the target, and the increased amount must be paid to the employee.

EXAMPLE: Jack is 35 when he becomes eligible to participate in his company's target benefit plan. Jack's target retirement benefit is 60% of his final pay. Assuming Jack will receive wage increases of 5% each year and will retire at 65 after 30 years of service, Jack's final pay is projected to be $80,000. His target retirement benefit, then, is $48,000 (60% of $80,000). In order to pay Jack $48,000 a year for the rest of his life beginning at age 65, the actuaries estimate that the company must contribute $4,523 to Jack's account every year. The company will contribute that amount, even if Jack doesn't receive 5% raises some years, or if other assumptions turn out to be wrong. Thus, Jack may or may not receive his targeted $48,000 during his retirement years. It might be more or it might be less.

7. Plans for Self-Employed People

Qualified plans for self-employed individuals are often called Keogh plans, named after the author of a 1962 bill that established a separate set of rules for such plans. In the ensuing years, Keoghs have come to look very much like corporate plans. In fact, the rules governing self-employed plans are no longer segregated, but have been placed under the umbrella of the qualified plan rules for corporations. Nonetheless, the Keogh moniker lingers—a burr in the side of phonetic spellers.

If you work for yourself, you may have a Keogh plan that is a profit sharing plan, money purchase pension plan, or defined benefit plan. If so, it will generally have to follow the same rules as its corporate counterpart, with some exceptions.

B. Individual Retirement Accounts

Most people are surprised to learn that individual retirement accounts, or IRAs, exist in many forms. Most common is the individual retirement account or individual retirement annuity to which any person with earnings from employment may contribute. These are called contributory IRAs. Some types of IRAs are used to receive assets distributed from other retirement plans. These are called rollover IRAs. Still others, such as SEPs and SIMPLE IRAs, are technically IRAs even though their rules are quite similar to those of qualified plans. Finally, Roth IRAs combine the features of a regular IRA and a savings plan to produce a hybrid that adheres to its own set of rules. You can learn more about each type of IRA in the following sections.

1. Traditional Contributory IRAs

If you have income from working for yourself or someone else, you may set up and contribute to an IRA The IRA can be a special depository account that you set up with a bank, brokerage firm, or other institutional custodian. Or it can be an individual retirement annuity that you purchase from an insurance company.

You may contribute a maximum of $4,000 for 2005 ($4,500 if you will reach age 50 by the end of the year). If you are not covered by an employer's retirement plan, you may take a deduction on your tax return for your contribution. If you are covered by an employer's plan, your IRA might be fully deductible, partly deductible, or not deductible at all depending on how much gross income you have.

For example, in 2005, if you are single and covered by an employer's plan, your contribution is fully deductible if your adjusted gross income, or AGI, is less than $50,000 and not deductible at all when your AGI reaches $60,000. Between $50,000 and $60,000 the deduction is gradually phased out. For married individuals, the phaseout range is from $70,000 to $80,000, if the IRA participant is covered by an employer plan. For an IRA participant who is not covered by a plan but whose spouse is covered, the phaseout range is $150,000 to $160,000.

EXAMPLE 1: Jamie, who is single and age 32, works for Sage Corp. and participates in the company's 401(k) plan. In 2005, he made $20,000. Eager to save for retirement, Jamie decided to contribute $4,000 to an IRA. Since his income was less than $50,000, Jamie may take a $4,000 deduction on his tax return for the IRA contribution, even though he also participated in his employer's retirement plan.

EXAMPLE 2: Assume the same facts as in Example 1 except that Jamie's salary was $70,000 in 2005. Although Jamie is permitted to make an IRA contribution, he may not claim a deduction for it on his tax return because his income was more than $60,000.

EXAMPLE 3: Assume Jamie made $75,000 in 2005, but Sage Corp. did not have a retirement plan for its employees. Because Jamie was not covered by an employer's retirement plan, his $4,000 IRA contribution is fully deductible even though he made more than $60,000.

Dollar amounts change yearly. The dollar amounts for contributions, as well as the phaseout ranges, increase every year. IRS Publication 590 has the details. You can obtain it by calling the IRS at 800-829-3676, by visiting the agency's website at www.irs.gov, or by visiting your local IRS office.

2. Rollover IRAs

If you receive a distribution from a qualified plan, you might decide to put some or all of it into an IRA. (See Chapter 2, Section C, for information about how and why you might do this.) The IRA that receives the qualified plan distribution is called a rollover IRA.

Although rollover IRAs used to have some special features, the 2001 pension law eradicated most of the differences between contributory and rollover IRAs.

3. Simplified Employee Pensions

A simplified employee pension, or SEP, is a special type of IRA that can be established by your employer or by you, if you are self-employed. Designed for small businesses, SEPs have many of the characteristics of qualified plans but are much simpler to set up and administer.

Under a SEP, each participant has his or her own individual retirement account to which the employer contributes. The contributions are excluded from the partici-

pant's pay and are not taxable until they are distributed from the plan. If you are self-employed, you may set up a SEP for yourself, even if you have no employees.

The advantage of a SEP over a regular IRA is that the contribution limits are higher. The contribution can be as much as 25% of your annual compensation, up to a maximum contribution of $42,000.

The disadvantage of a SEP, from an employer's perspective, is that the participation and vesting rules for SEPs are less favorable than those for qualified plans. Participation rules determine which employees must be covered by the plan and must receive contributions to their plan accounts. Vesting rules determine how much an employee is entitled to if the employee leaves the job or dies. An employer who establishes a SEP is required to make contributions on behalf of virtually all employees. Furthermore, the employees must be 100% vested at all times, which means that they must be allowed to take 100% of their plan account with them when they leave the company, no matter how long they have been employed there. Those can be costly requirements for small employers whose staff often includes many short-term, part-time employees. By contrast, 401(k) plans (and other qualified plans) can stretch the period before an employee is fully vested to as long as six or seven years.

4. SIMPLE IRAs

A simplified incentive match plan for employees, or SIMPLE IRA, is yet another type of IRA designed specifically to make it easier for small employers (those with 100 or fewer employees) to establish a retirement plan. A SIMPLE IRA is a salary reduction plan that, like a 401(k) profit sharing plan, allows employees to divert some compensation into retirement savings.

As with a SEP, contributions to a SIMPLE IRA are deposited into a separate IRA for each participating employee. The participant may select any percentage of compensation to defer into the plan—even zero—but the total dollar amount cannot exceed $10,000 for 2005 ($12,000 if you are at least age 50 by the end of the year).

 Dollar amounts change yearly. These dollar amounts increase every year. See IRS Publication 590 for details. You can obtain it by calling the IRS at 800-829-3676, by visiting the agency's website at www.irs .gov, or by visiting your local IRS office.

Unlike the employee, the employer is absolutely required to make a contribution. The employer has two options:

- It can match the employee's contribution up to 3% of the employee's compensation. (Under certain circumstances, the employer may match less than 3%, but never more.)
- As an alternative to matching, the employer may contribute a flat 2% of compensation (up to a maximum compensation of $210,000) to the accounts of all eligible employees, whether or not the employee directs any salary into the plan.

EXAMPLE 1: Tabor Corp. has four employees, who earned the following salaries:

Jane	$25,000
Jake	$20,000
Bree	$35,000
Holly	$50,000

Tabor's SIMPLE IRA offers to match employees' contributions up to 3% of compensation. All four employees are eligible to participate. Jane and Jake each direct $9,000 of their salaries into the plan, while Bree and Holly direct none of their salaries into the plan. Tabor Corp. contributes $750 (which is 3% x $25,000) for Jane and $600 (3% of $20,000) for Jake. It contributes nothing for Bree or Holly.

EXAMPLE 2: Assume the same facts as in Example 1 except that instead of matching contributions, Tabor's plan requires a contribution of 2% of compensation to the accounts of all eligible employees. So, Tabor contributes $500 for Jane (which is 2% of $25,000) and $400 (2% of $20,000) for Jake. It also contributes $700 (2% of $35,000) for Bree and $1,000 (2% of $50,000) for Holly, even though Bree and Holly did not direct any of their salaries into the plan.

5. Roth IRAs

At first glance, a Roth IRA looks a lot like a traditional contributory IRA because annual contribution limits are the same. Beyond that, though, the similarities are more difficult to see. For one thing, none of your contributions to a Roth IRA are ever deductible on your tax return. Furthermore, your ability to make a Roth IRA contribution begins to phase out when your AGI exceeds $150,000 (for joint filers) or $95,000 (for single filers). And you are not permitted a contribution at all when your AGI exceeds $160,000 (for joint filers) or $110,000 (for single filers). (Recall that with a traditional IRA, you may make a contribution even if your income is high and you are covered by an employer's plan. You might not be able to deduct the contribution on your tax return, however.)

The big advantage of a Roth IRA is that if you qualify to make contributions, all distributions from the IRA are tax free—even the investment returns—as long as the distribution satisfies certain requirements. Furthermore, unlike traditional IRAs, you may contribute to a Roth IRA for as long as you continue to have earned income. (In the case of traditional IRAs, you can't make any contributions after you reach age 70½.)

Although Roth IRAs belong to the IRA family and are subject to many of the IRA rules, the abundant exceptions and variations in treatment make it difficult to rely on what you know about traditional IRAs when trying to figure out what to do with a Roth IRA. Consequently, we devote all of Chapter 9 to Roth IRAs. In that chapter, we point out the distinguishing characteristics of the Roth IRA and identify which of the distribution rules in this book apply to it and which do not. Before you take any action on a Roth IRA based on what you know about the traditional IRA rules, be sure to read Chapter 9.

C. Almost-Qualified Plans

Tucked into the voluminous Tax Code are a number of hybrid plans that are not strictly qualified plans, but that share many of the benefits and restrictions of qualified plans. The two most common, and the two that most closely mirror the qualified plan rules, are qualified annuity plans and tax-deferred annuities.

1. Qualified Annuity Plans

The rules for qualified plans require that the assets of the plan be held by an administrator in a trust. Congress carved out an exception to this rule by adding Section 403(a) to the Tax Code. Section 403(a) allows employers to use contributions to purchase annuities for employees directly from an insurance company. This alternative to holding the contributions in a trust can simplify administration. In almost every other respect, the rules and regulations that apply to qualified plans also apply to qualified annuity plans.

2. Tax-Deferred Annuities

If you are a university professor or an employee of a public school, odds are that you are covered by an annuity plan of a public charity or public school, more commonly referred to as a tax-deferred annuity, or TDA. TDAs, defined in Section 403(b) of the Tax Code, are typically funded with individual annuity contracts purchased from an insurance company. When you retire, your benefits are usually paid to you as a monthly annuity for the rest of your life, although some TDAs offer other distribution options, such as a lump sum payment.

TDAs are not qualified plans and do not track the qualified plan rules as closely as qualified annuity plans do. For example, distributions from TDAs are not eligible for special tax options, such as averaging and capital gains treatment. (See Chapter 2 for more information about tax options.) However, the vast majority of the distribution rules that apply to qualified plans also apply to TDAs. The exceptions are noted where relevant.

D. Nonqualified Plans

Big business being what it is—subject to the sometimes wise and sometimes questionable judgment of the boss—many companies offer special incentives and compensation packages to key employees. The incentives might come in the form of deferred cash bonuses, stock certificates, or stock options. Very often, the boss doesn't offer the same deal to everyone.

Because the incentives are not available to everyone, such plans generally do not satisfy the nondiscrimination requirements of qualified plans and are therefore called nonqualified plans. Because they are nonqualified, they are not subject to the same rigorous vesting, participation, and distribution requirements.

Nonqualified plans have some additional distinctive features: an employer may not deduct contributions to the plan, assets of the plan are not required to be held in trust, and the assets of the individual participants are not protected from the claims of creditors. Because nonqualified plans are not subject to the same distribution rules as IRAs, qualified plans, qualified annuities, and TDAs, they are not covered in this book.

Creditor and Bankruptcy Protection

Corporate retirement plans have long been safe from creditors, thanks to the Employee Retirement Income Security Act of 1974, commonly known as ERISA. Unfortunately, that law does not protect retirement plans for self-employed individuals, nor does it protect IRAs of any kind.

Protection for those plans came in 2005 through a new law titled The Bankruptcy Abuse Prevention and Consumer Protection Act. That law provides debtors in bankruptcy with an exemption for retirement assets in qualified plans, qualified annuities, tax-sheltered annuities, and self-employed plans.

In addition, the law exempts all assets in an IRA that are attributable to rollovers from a retirement plan described above. If you happen to have a traditional IRA or Roth IRA containing assets that are not attributable to a rollover from some other type of retirement plan, (for example, the assets are from amounts you contributed directly to the IRA), then you will also be allowed an exemption of up to $1 million total for the assets in those contributory IRAs.

Key Tax Code Sections

§ 401(a)
Qualified Plans in General (including Keoghs): profit sharing, stock bonus, money purchase pension, defined benefit plans.

§ 401(k)
Cash or Salary Deferral Plan: A special type of qualified plan. Can be profit sharing or stock bonus plan.

§ 403(a)
Qualified Annuity Plan: Plan established by employer that is not a public charity or public school. Funded by the employer with purchased annuities.

§ 403(b)
Annuity Plan of Public Charity or Public School: Commonly called tax-deferred annuity or TDA. Usually funded with purchased annuities owned by the employee.

§ 408
IRAs: Contributory, rollover, SEP, SIMPLE.

§ 408A
Roth IRAs.

An Overview of Tax Rules

Who Should Read Chapter 2

➡️ Everyone should read this chapter. It describes the basic tax rules that apply to your retirement plan when you leave your job. (Chapters 3-6 contain more specific rules.) If the only retirement plan you have is an IRA, you can skip Sections C and D of this chapter.

*O*ur tax laws provide both incentive and opportunity to sock away significant sums for retirement. The combination of an up-front tax deduction for contributions to retirement plans, years of tax-deferred growth, and eventual taxation at relatively low rates (such as during retirement) can produce dramatic returns on retirement savings.

A. Taxation Fundamentals

To reap maximum benefit from your retirement plan, you must contribute as much as you can through the years, and you must adhere to certain guidelines when you draw money out. Keep in mind that your financial goal should be to maximize your after-tax wealth. It won't do you much good to accumulate a comfortable nest egg if you lose the bulk of it to taxes. As you pursue this goal, the following fundamentals will serve you well when you are not sure how to proceed.

1. Defer the Payment of Tax

When you have a choice, it is usually best to delay or defer the payment of income tax for as long as possible. During the deferral period, you will have the use of money that would otherwise have gone to taxes; if you invest it, that money will help generate more tax-deferred income. The easiest way to defer the payment of tax is by deferring the receipt of income. For example, if you have the option of taking a distribution from your retirement plan this year or next, it is often better to wait. As the tables below show, even a one-year delay can be beneficial. Your money grows while the tax man waits.

Many people vastly underestimate the benefits of tax-deferred compounding of investment returns inside a retirement plan account. Take a look at Tables I and II below. Both cases assume a simple 8% return on your investment and a flat 28% tax rate. Table I shows what happens if you take $10,000 out of your IRA, pay tax on it and invest the remainder for 15 years. Because the investment is outside your IRA, each year you will pay tax on your interest, dividends, and capital gains.

Now look at Table II, which shows what happens if you leave the $10,000 inside the IRA. The table projects the value of your investment after one year, two years, or more. After 15 years, the total value of your IRA will be $31,722, almost twice as much as the balance shown in Table I after 15 years. If you take the money out and pay

Helpful Terms

After-tax dollars. The amount of income left after all income taxes have been withheld or paid.

Amortization. The reduction of a debt through periodic payments of principal and interest.

Basis. An amount treated as the purchase price or cost of an asset for purposes of determining the taxable gain or loss when the asset is sold.

Custodian. A person or entity who is in possession of property belonging to another. For example, the custodian of an IRA is the institution that holds the stocks, bonds, cash, or other property of the IRA, even though the assets actually belong to the individual who established and funded the IRA.

Distribution. A payout of property (such as shares of stock) or cash from a retirement plan or IRA to the participant or a beneficiary.

Fair market value (FMV). The price at which an item could be sold at retail by a willing seller to a willing buyer.

Net unrealized appreciation. The amount by which an asset has increased in value before it is sold.

Nondeductible contribution. A contribution to a retirement plan or IRA that may not be used as a business expense or an adjustment to offset taxable income on an income tax return.

Pretax dollars. Total taxable income before income taxes have been paid.

Pro rata. Proportionately. For example, an amount distributed pro rata over four years is distributed evenly over those four years. Property that is distributed pro rata to its owners is distributed according to the percentage of each owner's interest.

Tax bracket or marginal tax bracket. The rate at which each additional dollar of income will be taxed. Under the Internal Revenue Code, a certain amount of income is taxed at one rate, and additional income is taxed at another. Therefore, it is possible that if you have one more dollar of income it will be taxed at a different rate than the previous dollar. Your marginal rate is the rate at which your next dollar of income will be taxed.

Trustee. A person or entity who holds legal title to the property in a trust. For example, a qualified retirement plan is a trust that is administered by a trustee who manages the trust property for the plan participant.

Table I

Withdraw from IRA: $10,000
Pay income tax: $2,800
Invest remainder: $7,200
Investment return: 8%
Tax Rate: 28%

Year	Initial Investment Beginning of Year	Interest Earned	Current Year Tax on Interest	Total Investment Year End
1	$ 7,200	$ 576	$ 161	$ 7,615
2	7,615	609	171	8,053
3	8,053	644	180	8,517
4	8,517	681	191	9,008
5	9,008	721	202	9,527
6	9,527	762	213	10,075
7	10,075	806	226	10,656
8	10,656	852	239	11,269
9	11,269	902	252	11,919
10	11,919	953	267	12,605
11	12,605	1,008	282	13,331
12	13,331	1,066	299	14,099
13	14,099	1,128	316	14,911
14	14,911	1,193	334	15,770
15	15,770	1,262	353	16,678

Table II

Leave inside IRA: $10,000
Investment return: 8%
Tax Rate: 28%

Year	Initial Investment Beginning of Year	Interest Earned	Current Year Tax on Interest	Total Investment Year End	Tax If Distributed	Net If Distributed*
1	$ 10,000	$ 800	$ 0	$ 10,800	$ 3,024	$ 7,776
2	10,800	864	0	11,664	3,266	8,398
3	11,664	933	0	12,597	3,527	9,070
4	12,597	1,008	0	13,605	3,809	9,796
5	13,605	1,088	0	14,693	4,114	10,579
6	14,693	1,175	0	15,869	4,443	11,425
7	15,869	1,269	0	17,138	4,799	12,340
8	17,138	1,371	0	18,509	5,183	13,327
9	18,509	1,481	0	19,990	5,597	14,393
10	19,990	1,599	0	21,589	6,045	15,544
11	21,589	1,727	0	23,316	6,529	16,788
12	23,316	1,865	0	25,182	7,051	18,131
13	25,182	2,015	0	27,196	7,615	19,581
14	27,196	2,176	0	29,372	8,224	21,148
15	29,372	2,350	0	31,722	8,882	22,840

*Compare last column with last column of Table I.

the tax on the distribution, your balance will be $22,840, which is still $6,162 more than you would have if you had paid the tax in year one and invested the money outside the IRA. This is true even though you start with the same amount of money, earn the same investment return, and are subject to the same tax rate in both situations.

Occasionally, it may be better not to defer distributions—if you expect to be in a permanently higher tax bracket in the future, for example. Or perhaps the income you earn outside the IRA will be taxed at a capital gains rate that is lower than your ordinary income tax rate. Bear in mind, however, that a slightly higher tax bracket or a temporary spike in your tax rate is not usually enough justification to accelerate distributions. Your tax rate would have to increase significantly to offset the enormous benefits of compounded growth.

2. Pay Tax at the Lowest Rate

Generally, your goal should be to pay tax on all of your retirement income at the lowest possible rate. But how will you know when the time is right to take the money out? Most people will be in a lower tax bracket after retirement, which provides yet another reason to defer distributions as long as possible.

3. Avoid Tax Penalties

A raft of penalty taxes awaits you if you fail to comply with the myriad distribution laws. Some penalties are designed to discourage you from withdrawing money before you retire. Others target individuals who want to leave their retirement funds to their heirs. Penalties are discussed at length in subsequent chapters, but be advised: It is rarely wise to take a distribution and pay a tax penalty, even if it seems like a small amount to you. Not only will you have to pay the penalty when you file your next tax return, but you will also have to report the distribution as income and pay regular income tax on it. When you factor in the loss of tax-deferred compounded growth, you might even be better off borrowing the money you need, rather than dipping into your retirement plan.

At some point, though, you certainly will take money out of your retirement plan, whether it is because your employer distributes it to you when you leave your job, because you need the money, or because the law requires you to withdraw it. When that time comes, you must understand how retirement plans are taxed and know your options. You will also need to be aware of potential penalties in order to stay out of harm's way.

B. General Income Tax Rules for Retirement Plans

When you take money out of a retirement plan, whether it is an IRA, qualified plan, qualified annuity, or TDA, some basic income tax rules apply. Although each rule has exceptions, expect the rule to apply in most situations.

1. Distributions Are Taxable Immediately

First and most basic: All distributions will be taxed in the year they come out of the plan. Exceptions to this rule are when you roll over your distribution into another retirement plan or an IRA within 60 days or when your employer transfers the distribution directly into another plan or IRA. In these cases, you do not pay income tax until the money is eventually distributed from the new plan or IRA. (Rollovers are discussed in Section C1b, below.)

⚠ Some money might be withheld! Beware of rules that require your plan administrator to withhold money to cover income taxes you may owe when you take money out of your retirement plan—even if you plan to roll it over. You can avoid the withholding by having your employer transfer the retirement funds directly into another retirement plan or IRA. (See Section C, below, for more information about these withholding rules.)

2. Your Basis Is Not Taxable

If you made contributions to a retirement plan or IRA for which you were not permitted to take a tax deduction on your tax return, then you have what is called "basis" in the plan. In other words, you have contributed money to a plan or IRA that you have already reported as income on your tax return. You will not have to pay taxes on those amounts a second time when you take the money out of your plan, but unfortunately, you usually don't have the luxury of deciding when to withdraw the portion of the money attributable to the basis.

If you have a regular IRA or a Keogh (see Chapter 1 for a description of these plans), your basis generally comes out pro rata, which means that every time you take a distribution, part of it is taxable and part is not. You compute the taxable and nontaxable portions of each distribution on IRS Form 8606 and submit it with the rest of your tax return at tax time. (A copy of Form 8606 is in Appendix A.) Roth IRAs are different—they have special basis rules. (See Chapter 9 for more information about Roth IRAs.) In the case of an employer plan, the contributions you made with dollars on which you already paid taxes are usually distributed as a lump sum when you retire—unless you elect to take your retirement benefits as an annuity. If so, you may have to take your basis out pro rata—a little bit with each annuity payment.

EXAMPLE: Over the years, you contributed a total of $10,000 to your IRA.
You were not permitted to claim a tax
deduction on your tax return for any of
those contributions. Thus the $10,000
is all after-tax money, or basis. On
December 31, the fair market value of
the IRA was $45,000. During the year,
you withdrew $5,000 to help cover living
expenses. Part of the $5,000 is taxable,
and part is not. To determine the tax-
free portion, use the following method:

Step 1: Add the distributions you took
during the year to the fair market
value of the IRA on December
31.

$5,000 + $45,000 = $50,000

Step 2: Divide your total basis in the IRA
by the amount from Step 1.

10,000 ÷ $50,000 = .2 or 20%

Step 3: Multiply the result in Step 2 by
the amount of the year's distribution.

20% x $5,000 = $1,000

You will not have to pay taxes on
$1,000 of the $5,000 distribution, but
the remaining $4,000 will be subject to
income tax.

Multiple IRAs. If you have more
than one IRA, all of your IRAs (including traditional IRAs, SEPs, and SIMPLE
IRAs but not Roth IRAs) are combined and
treated as one for purposes of computing
the tax-free portion of each distribution.

EXAMPLE: You have two IRAs. Over the
years, you made nondeductible contributions of $8,000 to IRA #1. All of your
contributions to IRA #2 were deductible. Consequently, your total basis for
both IRAs is $8,000. On July 19 of this
year, you withdrew $5,000 from IRA #1.
On December 31, the fair market value
of IRA #1 was $45,000 and IRA #2 was
$30,000. To determine the tax-free por-
tion of the distribution, you must follow
these steps:

Step 1: Determine the total fair market
value of all of your IRAs as of
December 31.

$45,000 + $30,000 = $75,000

Step 2: Add the distributions you took
during the year to the total from
Step 1.

$5,000 + $75,000 = $80,000

Step 3: Determine the total basis
(nondeductible contributions) for
all IRAs.

$8,000 + 0 = $8,000

Step 4: Divide the total basis from Step 3
by the amount from Step 2.

$8,000/$80,000 = .1 or 10%

Step 5: Multiply the result in Step 4 by the amount of your distribution.

10% x $5,000 = $500

You will not have to pay tax on $500 of the $5,000 distribution, but you will on the remaining $4,500.

3. You Don't Have to Withdraw Cash

Generally, when you take a distribution from an IRA, you may choose the assets you want to withdraw; you are not required to take cash. For example, suppose you want to withdraw $20,000. Your portfolio consists of $10,000 in cash and the remainder in stocks and bonds. You may take your $20,000 in any combination of cash and property you choose. You may take part of your distribution in cash and part in stocks and bonds, or even all of it in stock. If you take the distribution in property other than cash, the amount of the distribution is the fair market value of the property (such as the stock) on the day it comes out of the IRA.

EXAMPLE: You decide to take a distribution from your retirement account on June 1. On that day, the total value of your account is $50,000, of which $10,000 is in cash and the remainder in 1,000 shares of MacBlue stock valued at $40 per share. The stock was purchased in the IRA for $10 per share. You decide to withdraw all of the cash and 250 shares of MacBlue stock. The total value of your distribution for tax purposes is $20,000 ($10,000 of cash plus 250 shares of MacBlue stock x $40 per share). After the distribution, you will have no cash inside the IRA, but you will have 750 shares of MacBlue stock. The tax basis of the MacBlue stock in your hands will be $40 per share, not its original cost of $10 per share. Therefore, if you sell the stock at some time in the future, the taxable amount will be the sale price less your basis of $40.

When you receive a distribution from your employer's retirement plan, the plan itself usually dictates which assets must be distributed; you frequently have little control.

4. You May Not Claim Losses

You may not claim on your tax return losses you incur inside your IRA or retirement plan. Instead, you simply pay tax on each distribution based on the cash value or the fair market value of the property on the date it is distributed from the plan. For example, if you purchased 100 shares of LM Corp. at $12,000 and the fair market value of the stock is $5,000 when you withdraw all 100 shares from your IRA, you are not permitted to take a loss of $7,000. But before you cry foul, remember that you didn't pay tax on the money you used to purchase the stock, either. It was purchased inside your retirement plan with tax-deferred money. The value of the stock at distribution is $5,000, and that is the entire taxable amount. In fact, you will have obtained a tax benefit from the loss through the reduction of the taxable distribution.

One extremely rare exception to this rule might occur if you have made contributions with after-tax dollars and never managed to withdraw all of your basis. For example, if your basis in your IRA exceeds the fair market value of the entire IRA (or all of your IRAs combined, if you have more than one) when you take a final distribution, you may claim the loss as a miscellaneous itemized deduction on your tax return.

EXAMPLE: In 1990 you made a nondeductible $2,000 contribution to an IRA. You invested all of the money in junk bonds. Because the investment started to go bad immediately, you never made any additional contributions. Now the account is worth $1,500. If you take a distribution of the entire $1,500 and close the account, you may claim a loss of $500 on Schedule A of your tax return.

Roth IRAs are different. If you have a Roth IRA, all of your contributions (but not your investment returns) are after tax, so your basis in your Roth IRA is likely to be higher than in your regular IRA.

5. Divorce or Inheritance Doesn't Change the Basic Tax Rules

If you inherit a retirement plan or IRA, or if you receive one from your spouse in a divorce settlement, the four rules just discussed apply to you as though you were the original owner. For example, when you take money or property out of an IRA you inherited from your mother, you pay tax on the fair market value of the assets on the date of distribution. And if your mother had some basis left in the account, that remaining basis is passed on to you.

Step-up rules don't apply to retirement plans. Many assets receive what is called a step up in basis when the owner of those assets dies. In other words, the basis of the asset is deemed to be its value when the owner dies rather than what the owner originally paid for it. Because investment assets usually increase in value over time, this benefit is referred to as a step-up.

Assets in IRAs and other retirement plans are not permitted a step-up in basis. The assets in the IRA will be subject to tax at their fair market value whenever they are distributed. Death only determines who will pay the tax. The original owner pays during his lifetime; after that, the beneficiary of the plan pays the tax.

C. Income Tax on Qualified Plans and Qualified Annuities

A variety of circumstances could lead to a distribution from your retirement plan during your working years. Or you might not take money out until you actually retire. If you wait until retirement, you have many options for paying the tax on the money you receive. If you take a distribution before retirement, you will encounter a minefield of restrictions, and you might even have to pay tax penalties.

1. Options for Paying Taxes at Retirement

In general, when you receive a distribution from a qualified plan or qualified annuity, you should consider three tax options:

- You can report the distribution on your return as ordinary income.
- You can roll over the distribution into an IRA or another retirement plan, which means you can continue to delay paying taxes.
- If you qualify, you can use ten-year averaging, which is a method of computing the tax as though the distribution were spread over a ten-year period.

⚠ After-tax contributions aren't taxable. If part of your distribution includes after-tax contributions you made

to your plan, those amounts will not be taxable and should not be included when computing your income tax using any of the above methods.

a. Pay Ordinary Income Tax

Some people are tempted to choose the path of least resistance. This is true in life generally, but especially true in that part of life that requires dealing with the IRS. When taking distributions from a retirement plan, the easiest option is simply to take the money, deposit it in your regular bank account, and report the amount of the distribution as ordinary income on your tax return at tax time.

But if your retirement plan distribution is large, you ordinarily would not choose to pay tax on the entire amount unless you need the money immediately and don't qualify for any special tax options.

Another reason you might have to use the ordinary income tax option is if you made a procedural error when attempting to use one of the other tax options, which left you no choice but to use the ordinary income tax option.

i. Who Is Eligible?

Anyone who receives a distribution from a retirement plan can choose to have the distribution taxed in this way.

ii. Which Distributions Are Eligible?

All distributions you receive from a retirement plan that are attributable to pretax contributions or to investment returns may be taxed at ordinary income tax rates. This is true whether the distribution represents only part of your account or the entire balance.

 Roth 401(k)s are different. Note that in the case of a distribution from a Roth 401(k) plan, investment returns, as well as your original after-tax contributions, will not be subject to tax, provided you have met the age and holding period requirements.

iii. Advantages and Disadvantages

The advantage of this tax option is that once the money comes out of the retirement plan and you pay the taxes owed, you have unrestricted use of the funds. The money that you withdraw is no longer subject to the terms of the plan.

But that peace of mind is expensive. Paying tax at ordinary rates on the money in the same year you receive it is usually the least advantageous option—at least from a financial perspective. If your distribution is large, it could easily push you into a higher tax bracket. It's hardly cheery to think of starting your retirement by handing the government 40% or more of your nest egg.

b. Roll Over Your Distribution

Rather than paying ordinary income tax on your entire retirement plan distribution, you might consider a more versatile and attractive strategy: Rolling some or all of the distribution into an IRA or another employer's plan.

A rollover is usually accomplished by having your employer transfer your funds directly to another employer's plan or an IRA through a transaction called a direct rollover. If the funds are distributed directly to you, however, you have 60 days to deposit them into another plan or an IRA. The portion that is rolled over will continue to be tax deferred and will be subject to all the rules of the new plan or IRA. Any portion that is not rolled over within 60 days will be subject to ordinary income tax.

Rollovers into another qualified plan after retirement are unusual. This is because once a person retires, he or she probably doesn't have another plan. Distributions at retirement are usually rolled into an IRA, unless you are taking your benefits as an annuity, in which case no rollover of any kind is permitted.

i. Who Is Eligible?

Anyone who receives a distribution from a qualified plan or qualified annuity is permitted to roll it over. It doesn't matter how old you are or how long you have been a participant in the plan.

ii. Which Distributions Are Eligible?

Generally, all distributions and partial distributions from qualified plans and qualified annuities are eligible to be rolled over.

The most significant exceptions are:

- distributions that are required to be distributed to you because you have passed age 70½ (see Chapters 5-8 for information about required distributions), and
- distributions in the form of a life annuity or periodic payments that last for ten years or more.

iii. Advantages and Disadvantages

If you don't need to use your retirement money right away, rolling it over is a big advantage. It allows you to defer paying income tax until you are ready to spend the money (or until you are required to take it out by the new plan). If you take money out only when you need it, you may be able to withdraw it in small enough chunks to keep yourself in a low tax bracket. Meanwhile, whatever you don't need can be left to grow inside the new plan or IRA.

The disadvantage of rolling over the distribution is that you don't have unrestricted use of the money. As long as it's in an IRA or qualified plan, it is subject to all the rules and restrictions of the plan.

iv. Pitfalls

If you are about to receive a distribution from a qualified plan or qualified annuity and you want to roll it over into another plan or an IRA, arrange for a direct rollover. In other words, have the funds transferred directly from your old employer's plan into the new plan or IRA. If you don't and instead receive the funds yourself before delivering them to the new plan, the distribution will be subject to income tax withholding, which could cause you some serious problems. (See Section 5, below, for more information about withholding.) In addition to the withholding problem, you could encounter other traps.

Trap 1: 60-Day Rule. You have 60 days from the time you receive a distribution to roll it over into another plan or IRA, and the clock starts ticking when you have the distribution in hand. The IRS is devilishly unforgiving when it comes to enforcing this rule, so if you're on your way to the bank on the 60th day, don't stop to tie your shoes. Also, not all types of plans can be mixed. For example, if you want to roll over your Roth 401(k) plan to a new employer's plan, the new employer must have a Roth 401(k) plan. Or if you want to roll over your Roth 401(k) plan to an IRA, it must be a Roth IRA.

Trap 2: Changing Your Mind. Once you actually complete the rollover of your retirement plan into another plan or IRA, there is no going back.

For example, suppose you instruct the plan administrator of your employer's plan to transfer your retirement money directly into an IRA. A week after the money is deposited to your IRA, you decide that you really should have taken the distribution and elected ten-year averaging (see Subsection c, below). Unfortunately, you cannot undo a rollover. Once the rollover is complete, you may not pull the money out of the account and elect averaging, even if the 60 days has not yet expired.

If you do pull the money out, it will be treated as another retirement plan distribution, and you will have to pay income tax—and you might even have to pay an early distribution tax. (See Chapter 3 for information about the early distribution tax.)

Trap 3: Rolling Over Ineligible Funds. Some of the money you receive from a retirement plan might not be eligible to be rolled over. You cannot roll over annuity payments or money that must be distributed to you when you are age 70½ or older.

If you accidentally roll over ineligible funds, you have a certain amount of time to correct the problem—usually until the due date of your tax return. (That's April 15th of the following year, unless you request an extension of time for filing your return. In that case, you will have until the extended deadline.) If you do not remove the funds in time, you will have to pay a penalty for each calendar year or part of a year those funds remain in the plan or IRA. (For more about the 60-day rules, see Section E2c, below.)

Trap 4: Plan Rules Govern. Sometimes you might find that the law permits you to take certain steps with your retirement plan, but the terms of your plan are more restrictive. In that case, the plan's rules will govern. For example, the law generally allows you to roll over qualified plans and qualified annuities into almost any other type of retirement plan. Some plans, however, do not permit mixing and matching.

Qualified annuity plan administrators often will not accept rollovers from other qualified annuities. However, you can always roll over a qualified plan or qualified annuity distribution into an IRA.

c. Use Ten-Year Averaging to Compute Tax

It may be that you cannot afford to roll over all of your retirement distribution because you need the money. And if you do need the money, you don't want to give up a large chunk of the distribution to income taxes. Although there is no way to avoid paying taxes if you elect not to roll over the distribution, you may be able to compute the tax using a method called ten-year averaging, which can reduce your total bill.

i. Who Is Eligible?

You are eligible to use ten-year averaging if you satisfy all of the following conditions:

- you were born before 1936
- you have not used ten-year averaging on any distribution since 1986, and
- you participated in the plan for at least five years, which means you or your employer made a contribution to your plan account in at least five separate years before the year of the distribution.

 Figuring the length of participation. If your account is transferred from one plan to another, you don't have to start the participation clock ticking all over again. The years you participated in the old plan count toward the five-year requirement.

ii. Which Distributions Are Eligible?

Even if you are eligible, you may use ten-year averaging only if your distribution also qualifies. Your distribution will qualify only if both of the following are true:

- The distribution to be averaged must be the entire amount of your qualified plan or qualified annuity. You cannot roll over part of the distribution and you cannot have rolled over part of it in the past.
- You must receive the distribution all within one tax year, even if you receive more than one payment.

⚠ You might have two plans that the IRS treats as one for ten-year averaging. For example, money purchase pension plans and defined benefit plans must be combined and considered one plan for purposes of the ten-year averaging rules. Let's say you receive a distribution of your defined benefit plan one year and roll it over. The next year you receive a distribution of your money purchase pension plan and want to use ten-year averaging. You cannot, however, because the distributions were received in different years.

iii. How Is It Computed?

If you receive a distribution and elect to use ten-year averaging, the tax on the distribution itself is computed on IRS Form 4972 (see Appendix A) and recorded on a separate line of your tax return. You must pay that amount to the IRS even if you owe no other income taxes.

The tax is calculated as though you were a single individual (even if you are married) and as though you received the distribution in ten installments over ten years. Despite this calculation, you pay the total tax due in the year of the distribution, not over ten years. These are the steps:

Step 1: Determine the taxable amount of the distribution.

This is usually the entire amount of the distribution reduced by any after-tax contributions you made. Your employer or the administrator of the plan should provide this information.

Step 2: Determine the Minimum Distribution Allowance.

If your distribution is less than $70,000, you may exclude some of it from your income when computing the tax. The excludable portion is called your minimum distribution allowance, or MDA. To determine the MDA:

1. Reduce the taxable amount of the distribution by $20,000, but not below zero.
2. Multiply the result by 20%, or .2.
3. Subtract the result from $10,000 or from one-half of the taxable amount (the number from Step 1), whichever is less. The result is your MDA.

Step 3: Subtract your MDA from the taxable amount (Step 1 minus Step 2).

Step 4: Divide the result by 10.

Step 5: Compute the income tax on the amount from Step 4.

You must use the 1986 tax rates for a single person. (A schedule of 1986 tax rates is in Appendix A.)

Step 6: Multiply the result by 10.

> EXAMPLE: You receive a lump sum distribution of $50,000 that qualifies for ten-year averaging. You want to use the money to build your retirement dream house, so you decide to pay the tax. Here's how it is computed:
>
> Step 1: Taxable amount = $50,000
>
> Step 2: Since the distribution is under $70,000, you will be entitled to an MDA as follows:
>
> $50,000 – $20,000 = $30,000
> $30,000 x .2 = $6,000
> $10,000 – $6,000 = $4,000
> (your MDA)
>
> Step 3: $50,000 – $4,000 = $46,000
>
> Step 4: $46,000/10 = $4,600
>
> Step 5: Tax on $4,600 at 1986 single rates = $597
>
> Step 6: $597 x 10 = $5,970

Thus, you will owe $5,970 of federal income tax on your $50,000 distribution in the year you receive it. By contrast, if you simply reported the $50,000 as additional income without using the special averaging, you could owe as much as $19,800 of federal income tax on that $50,000, if you are in the top tax bracket.

iv. Advantages and Disadvantages

When should you use averaging? Although it is usually better to roll over a distribution and continue your tax deferral rather than pay a ten-year averaging tax, those guidelines go right out the window if you need the money. In such a situation, ten-year averaging could mean big tax savings.

You might also choose ten-year averaging if your distribution is small enough to be taxed at a rate lower than you are likely to see in the future. But if your distribution is large, ten-year averaging is rarely a good choice. For one thing, you give up substantial compounded growth on the money that would otherwise remain in the retirement account. But also, the tax advantages of averaging decline as the distribution increases in amount. In addition, the top tax rates in 1986 were quite a bit higher than top rates today.

> EXAMPLE: You receive a retirement plan distribution of $100,000. If you use ten-year averaging, the entire tax would be $14,470—all of it taxed at less than 15%. In contrast, if your distribution is $500,000 and you choose ten-year averaging, more than $150,000 would be taxed at rates higher than any current tax rate. In this case, you may be better off rolling over the $500,000 and spreading distributions out over your retirement years.

Bottom line: it's easy to be seduced by the lure of lower tax rates and ready money. But if your goal is to accumulate substantial sums for your retirement, you are usually better off rolling over your distribution and deferring the payment of tax.

v. Pitfalls

If you still think ten-year averaging is your best option, consider these traps.

Trap 1: One-Time Election. Ten-year averaging is a once-in-a-lifetime election. If you choose to use it on a distribution, you may never again use ten-year averaging on a future distribution from any plan.

Trap 2: Multiple Distributions. If you receive distributions from more than one retirement plan in a single year and want to use ten-year averaging, you must use it on all the distributions you receive that year. If you want to use ten-year averaging on only one distribution, you must arrange to receive the distribution you want to average in a separate year, if possible. This rule is different from the aggregation rule covered above. Under the aggregation rule, if two plans are of the same type, for example both profit sharing plans, they are considered one plan for ten-year averaging purposes. In that case, the distributions from both plans must be received in the same year or you may not use ten-year averaging on either distribution.

d. Use Capital Gain Rates to Compute Tax

If you were born before 1936 and you began participating in your employer's plan before 1974, you have another option available to you in addition to ten-year averaging: You may treat part of your distribution as capital gain subject to a flat 20% tax rate. The amount of your distribution that is eligible for this rate is computed by the plan administrator and is based on the number of years you participated in the plan before 1974. The administrator will report the eligible amount to you so that you can decide if you want to elect the 20% tax option. You may elect to use this special rate whether you choose to use ten-year averaging or ordinary income tax rates on the remaining portion of your distribution.

e. Special Rules for Employer Stock

Your retirement account distribution may include some shares of your employer's stock. If the total current value of the shares of stock purchased in your plan account is greater than the total basis, the difference is called the net unrealized appreciation.

Net unrealized appreciation is the difference between the fair market value of the stock and the stock's basis. Basis for this purpose means the cost of the stock when the plan purchased it. For example, suppose your employer contributed $1,000 to your retirement account on your behalf. The plan then used that $1,000 to purchase 100 shares of company stock at $10 per share. The stock's basis is $10 per share or $1,000 total. Many years later, when you retire, those 100 shares are worth $20,000. The net unrealized appreciation is $19,000, which is the fair market value less the plan's basis in those shares ($20,000 – $1,000).

You have several options for paying income taxes on employer stock that is part of a retirement plan distribution:

- If you elect ten-year averaging, you can exclude the net unrealized appreciation when computing the tax. In that case, you would include only the plan's basis in the ten-year averaging calculation (assuming, of course, that the stock was purchased with pretax dollars). If you use this tax strategy, you will pay tax on the net unrealized appreciation using long-term capital gains rates when you later sell the company stock.

- You can include the net unrealized appreciation when calculating your tax using ten-year averaging. You might do this if your tax rate using averaging is lower than the long-term capital gains rate.

- You can pay ordinary income tax (as opposed to using ten-year averaging) on all but the net unrealized appreciation (paying tax on the plan's basis, for example, if the stock was purchased with pretax dollars). You would use this strategy if you did not qualify for ten-year averaging but did not want to roll over all of your employer stock into an IRA. Using this strategy you would pay capital gains tax on the net unrealized appreciation only when you sell the stock.

- You can roll over your entire distribution, including employer stock, into an IRA. If you do so, the net unrealized appreciation in the stock becomes irrelevant because all future distributions from the IRA will be taxed as ordinary income, not as capital gains.

Paying taxes to preserve capital gains rates. It might well be to your advantage not to roll over all of your employer stock into an IRA. This might be true if your net unrealized appreciation is large relative to the plan's basis in the stock, because the bulk of the distribution (the net unrealized appreciation) could be taxed at low capital gains rates when you eventually sell the stock. Remember, once the stock is rolled over into an IRA, all future distributions from the IRA will be taxed at ordinary rates—not capital gains rates. Note, too, that this strategy might work for you even if you are younger than age 59½. Although the portion of the distribution that you must pay tax on at the time of distribution (typically the basis) will be subject both to ordinary income tax and an early distribution penalty, the tradeoff—taxing the bulk of the distribution at capital gains rates instead of ordinary rates—could easily offset any disadvantage. But just how large the net unrealized appreciation must be relative to the plan's basis for this strategy to work might require a calculation by you or your accountant.

⚠️ **No step-up for net unrealized appreciation.** Your inclination may be to exclude the net unrealized appreciation from your income tax and keep the stock, passing it on to your heirs when you die. You might do this if you think your heirs will obtain a step-up in the basis of the stock when you die. The step-up would allow them to avoid all tax on the net unrealized appreciation. (See Section B.5, above, for an explanation of a step-up in basis.) But this strategy won't work. The Tax Code specifically denies any step-up in basis for net unrealized appreciation in employer stock.

2. Options for Paying Taxes Before Retirement

It is quite possible that you will receive a distribution from your retirement plan before you retire. Here are some common situations in which that might occur:

- you change jobs
- your company terminates its retirement plan, or
- you are self-employed and terminate your own plan.

The retirement plan rules were written to discourage distributions before retirement. For this reason, you'll find your options for paying taxes somewhat limited if you receive a retirement plan distribution while the government thinks you are too young to be retired.

a. Pay Ordinary Income Tax

If you do not need the distribution you receive from your retirement plan for living expenses, you will almost certainly want to do something with it other than spend it or put it in a regular bank account. If you don't, you will have to report the distribution on your tax return and pay ordinary income tax on it. Furthermore, you might have to pay penalties for withdrawing the money early.

b. Roll Over Your Distribution

If you have not yet reached age 59½ and you receive a distribution from a qualified plan or qualified annuity, you can roll over the distribution into an IRA or another retirement plan to continue deferring the tax and to avoid paying an early distribution penalty.

⚠️ **Arrange a direct rollover.** If you receive a distribution from a qualified plan, intending to roll it over into another plan or into an IRA, arrange to have the administrator of your old employer's plan transfer the funds directly into the new plan or IRA instead of sending the money to you. Otherwise, the administrator of the old plan may be required to withhold money to cover taxes you might owe. (See Section 5, below, for more information about withholding.)

c. Use Ten-Year Averaging to Compute Tax

As long as you satisfy the requirements outlined in Section C1c, above, then averaging is an option for you.

3. Options for Paying Taxes on Inherited Plans

If you are the beneficiary, rather than the owner, of a qualified plan and you receive a distribution as a result of the owner's death, the rules for paying income taxes are a little different from the general rules described in Section Cl, above.

a. Pay Ordinary Income Tax

If the plan assets are distributed outright to you and you simply take the money and put it into your regular bank account, then you will have to report the distribution as income on your tax return and pay tax on it, as you might expect. You may be able to reduce the total amount of the tax or gain some breathing room in paying the tax, however, by taking the distribution in installments over a number of years.

There is a bit of good news, too. If you receive a distribution from a plan you inherited, you will not have to pay an early distribution tax, even if you are younger than 59½. The penalty is waived for inherited plans. (See Chapter 3 for information about the early distribution tax.)

b. Roll Over Your Distribution

If you inherit a qualified plan or qualified annuity, you cannot roll over the distribution into an IRA or another qualified plan, unless you were the spouse of the deceased owner. If you were not the spouse, the plan must remain in the name of the original (now deceased) owner until the assets are actually distributed from the plan.

If you were the spouse of the original owner, you can roll over the distribution into an IRA in your name or into your employer's plan.

c. Use Ten-Year Averaging to Compute Tax

If you inherit a qualified plan or qualified annuity, you can use ten-year averaging provided the distribution is a qualified distribution as described in Section C1c, above, and the original owner had satisfied all the eligibility requirements (except the five-year participation requirement) at the time of death.

Meeting the eligibility requirements. It is not you, the person who inherited the plan, who must meet the eligibility requirements for ten-year averaging, it is the original owner. It doesn't matter how old you are, nor would it matter if you had used averaging on one of your own distributions. As long as the original owner would have qualified for averaging, you qualify.

4. Options for Paying Taxes on Qualified Plans Received at Divorce

Congress has gone to great lengths to protect your qualified plan assets. The cornerstone of that protection is a provision known as the anti-alienation rule, which attempts to ensure that you cannot be forced to give away your qualified plan assets.

Divorce presents a unique problem, however. What if you want to use your retirement plan as part of a property settlement? Can you give away some or all of your plan assets in that situation? And if you can, who should be responsible for the taxes and penalties (if any) on the part you give away?

Congress addressed these concerns by giving divorcing couples a vehicle for protecting plan assets and minimizing tax penalties. It's called a Qualified Domestic Relations Order or QDRO (pronounced "Quadro"). The QDRO rules spell out the circumstances under which your qualified plan benefits can go to someone else—an alternate payee—such as your soon-to-be former spouse.

A QDRO is a judgment, decree, or order (including a court-approved property settlement agreement) that satisfies all of the following:

- It relates to child support, alimony, or the marital property rights of a spouse, a former spouse, a dependent child, or some other dependent of the qualified plan participant.

- It gives an alternate payee, such as a spouse, former spouse, dependent child, or other dependent, the right to receive all or a portion of the participant's plan benefits.

- It does not alter the form or the amount of the benefit originally intended for the participant even though the benefit might now go to an alternate payee. For example, the QDRO cannot require the plan to pay a larger annuity to the alternate payee than it would have paid to the participant.

- It contains certain language. Specifically:

  - The alternate payee must be referred to as "the alternate payee" in the QDRO.
  - The QDRO must identify the plan, as well as the amount of each payment and the number of payments to be made.
  - The QDRO must contain the name and address of both the participant and the alternate payee.

If you are in the process of divorcing and you and your spouse agree that you will receive an interest in your spouse's qualified plan, you may be able to preserve some of the tax benefits of the plan for yourself. But this is possible only if there is a QDRO in place. If you and your spouse write up your agreement but it does not meet the above four requirements and is not court-approved, then your agreement is not a QDRO. In such a situation, distributions to a spouse, former spouse, or child could be subject to penalties.

In most cases, QDRO payments are made to a spouse or former spouse as alimony or as part of a property settlement. Payments might also be used for child support. If you receive a qualified plan distribution under a QDRO, the rules for how it is taxed and what you can do with it will depend upon your relationship to the original owner or plan participant.

a. Options for a Nonspouse Alternate Payee

If the recipient of a QDRO payment is not the spouse or former spouse of the plan participant, then the plan participant must report all distributions from the qualified plan as income on the participant's own tax return and pay taxes on them. If the distribution qualifies for special tax treatment, however, the plan participant can opt for the special rules. For example, the plan participant may use ten-year averaging on a distribution to figure the tax liability, provided the participant is eligible. If you are the recipient, you would pay no taxes when you receive the distribution.

Although the tax burden falls heavily on the plan participant, a couple of special rules provide a little tax relief:

- The participant will not have to pay an early distribution tax on any QDRO distribution paid to a nonspouse recipient, no matter how old the participant is or how old the recipient is. (See Chapter 3 for more information about the early distribution tax.)

- If the participant separates the recipient's share of the plan, perhaps by rolling it over into a new IRA, the participant can use ten-year averaging on the remaining portion—provided the remaining portion would have qualified for averaging if it had been the participant's entire plan balance. The participant may not treat the recipient's portion alone as a distribution eligible for averaging, however, unless that portion constitutes the participant's entire plan balance.

b. Options for a Spouse or Former Spouse Alternate Payee

If you are a spouse or former spouse receiving a distribution under a QDRO, you are treated in almost every respect as though you are the plan participant. Specifically:

- You may roll over some or all of the distribution to your own IRA or employer plan.

- You must pay tax on the distribution if you do not roll it over.

- The distribution is subject to mandatory withholding rules as though you were the plan participant. (See Section 5, below.)

As you might expect, there are exceptions to the general rule that you are to be treated as though you were the plan participant:

- Although you may elect ten-year averaging on the distribution you receive, your eligibility for averaging depends on the participant's eligibility. In other words, if the participant was born before 1936, has not made an averaging election since 1986, and has participated in the plan for at least five years, then you may elect ten-year averaging. If the plan participant does not qualify, neither do you.

- Although you may elect averaging, you are not permitted to use the special capital gain rules for pre-1974 accumulations (see Section C1d, above), nor may you exclude from income the net unrealized appreciation in employer stock. (See Section C1e, above.)

- Any distribution you keep in a regular account instead of rolling it over will not be subject to an early distribution tax, regardless of your age or the participant's age. (See Chapter 3 for information about early distributions.)

Once you do roll over the distribution into an IRA or another retirement plan in your name, the assets become yours in every respect, as though they never belonged to the original participant.

5. Withholding Money to Pay Taxes

Congress, in its increasingly creative efforts to improve the Treasury's cash flow, passed a mandatory withholding law in 1993 for qualified plans. The law requires your plan administrator to keep 20% of all qualified plan distributions to pay federal income tax before distributing the remainder to you.

EXAMPLE: You leave your job and plan to travel around the world for six months. Your employer distributes your retirement plan to you. The total value of your account is $10,000. The plan administrator gives you $8,000 and sends the rest to the government to pay the taxes you will owe on the distribution.

a. Exceptions to Mandatory Withholding

There are some exceptions to the mandatory withholding law.

- Amounts that are transferred directly from the trustee of your retirement plan to the trustee of another plan or to the custodian of your IRA are not subject to the withholding. This is called a direct rollover and is the most appropriate action to take if your intention is to roll over your distribution.

Standard rollovers are not exempt from the mandatory withholding rule. If you take a distribution of your retirement plan—for example, you receive a check payable to you—intending to roll it over into an IRA, your employer must withhold 20% for taxes. The direct rollover exception works only if the money is delivered directly from your retirement plan trustee to the trustee of another plan or to the custodian of your IRA. (See Subsection ci., below, for more information about direct rollovers.)

- Any after-tax contributions you made to the plan are not subject to withholding when they are distributed to you.
- If you elect to receive your distribution in roughly equal periodic payments over ten or more years, those payments will not be subject to mandatory withholding.
- Small distributions of less than $200 are not subject to mandatory withholding.

b. Pitfalls of Mandatory Withholding

Unless you use a direct rollover, the withholding law can pose some serious problems for you and maybe even take a permanent bite out of your retirement nest egg.

i. Reducing Your Retirement Accumulation

If it is your intention to roll over your entire retirement plan distribution into an IRA or another retirement plan and continue the tax deferral, and you don't use a direct rollover, mandatory withholding could put a crimp in those plans. Because the withholding is usually paid out of the distribution, you will have a smaller amount to roll over.

EXAMPLE: You have just retired. You accumulated $200,000 in your employer's retirement plan. You plan to roll over your distribution into an IRA. However, when you receive the check from your employer, it is only $160,000. Because of the mandatory withholding rules, your employer was required to send 20% or $40,000 to the IRS to cover any income taxes you might owe on the distribution, even if it was always your intention to roll over the entire amount. So now you only have $160,000 in your retirement nest egg. (You may be able to replace the amount withheld, however. See Subsection cii, below.)

ii. Owing Penalties and Taxes

If your distribution was subject to withholding, you may claim a refund of the tax withheld for the portion that was rolled over. However, the portion of the distribution that was sent to the government for taxes was part of your distribution, too, and it wasn't rolled over, so it will be subject to income tax. Worse, if you are not yet 59½, you might have to pay an early distribution tax on the portion withheld for taxes, even though the withholding was mandatory. (See Chapter 3 for more information about the early distribution tax.)

EXAMPLE: You decide to retire in November of the year you turn 61. You have accumulated $300,000 in your employer's retirement plan. When you receive your distribution, the amount is only $240,000 because your employer was required to send 20% or $60,000 to the IRS for taxes. When you file your next tax return, you will report the $60,000 of withholding as tax you have already paid along with any other amounts withheld from your regular paychecks during the year.

In addition, you must report $60,000 of the retirement plan distribution as income. The $240,000 that was rolled over is not subject to tax, but the $60,000 that was sent to the IRS to pay taxes is. Even though the withholding was mandatory, it is still treated as a taxable distribution. In essence you took money out of your retirement account to pay your taxes.

On the plus side, you should be entitled to a big tax refund when you file your tax return, since you paid $60,000 (through withholding) for taxes due on your distribution, but the taxable portion itself was only $60,000. The remaining $240,000 was rolled over.

iii. Selling Assets to Pay Taxes

What happens if there's not enough cash in your account to cover the required withholding? The news is not good. The plan administrator must withhold taxes even if it means selling property in the account to generate enough cash. If you hold stock you don't want to sell, you might be out of luck—unless one of these exceptions applies:

- The plan permits you to come up with the money for withholding from sources outside the plan. This requires that you have a stash of cash.
- If your retirement assets consist solely of cash and employer securities (as opposed to other securities or property) and you don't have enough cash to cover the 20% mandatory withholding, the administrator will withhold only the cash. In other words, you are not required to liquidate employer securities in order to pay the withholding.

EXAMPLE: On the day you retire from Flush Corp., your retirement plan assets consist of $5,000 in cash and 3,000 shares of Flush Corp. stock valued at $50 per share or $150,000. The total value of your retirement plan is $155,000, which means that the mandatory withholding is $31,000 (20% x $155,000). Because you do not have $31,000 in cash and you are not required to liquidate employer stock, your mandatory withholding is limited to the amount of cash in your retirement account, which is $5,000.

iv. Repaying Loans From the Plan

If you borrow money from your plan and don't pay it all back by the time you are to receive your distribution, the unpaid loan amount counts as part of your distribution and is subject to both income tax and mandatory withholding. Again, you might need to liquidate assets (except employer securities) in order to cover the withholding.

> EXAMPLE: When you retire, you will have $10,000 of cash in your retirement plan and 5,000 mutual fund shares valued at $20 per share. The total value of your account is $110,000. However, you also borrowed money from the plan last year and still owe $20,000 on that loan. The plan will report a distribution of $130,000 to the IRS ($10,000 in cash plus $100,000 in mutual fund shares plus the outstanding loan balance of $20,000). The mandatory 20% withholding is based on the full $130,000, and therefore is $26,000. Because you have only $10,000 in cash, the plan must sell 800 of your mutual fund shares to come up with enough cash to cover the withholding. Thus, although a distribution of $130,000 is reported to the IRS, the amount you actually receive will be only $84,000, which is $130,000 reduced by the loan amount and reduced further by the 20% withholding ($130,000 − $20,000 − $26,000 = $84,000).

c. Avoiding or Correcting Mandatory Withholding

Happily, you can avoid the withholding pitfalls altogether. If you don't and instead find yourself in a quagmire, you still might be able to dig yourself out.

i. Direct Rollover

You can avoid mandatory withholding simply by requesting that the plan administrator transfer your entire distribution directly into another qualified plan or an IRA. If you never have access to the funds during the transfer, the administrator is not required to withhold any money. This solution is called a direct rollover. The rule applies even if your distribution check is sent to you personally, as long as it is payable to the trustee or custodian of the new plan, and not to you.

It is possible to elect a direct rollover for part of your distribution, saving you at least some of the mandatory withholding. Only the portion paid directly to you will be subject to mandatory withholding.

ii. Replace the Withholding Amount

If you fail to request a direct rollover and instead receive a distribution check reduced by the 20% withholding amount, you may be able to make yourself whole. If you can come up with the cash to cover the amount withheld, you can deposit it into the new plan or IRA as though you received it as part of your distribution. Then at tax time, you can claim a refund of the entire withholding amount. You avoid income taxes and penalties and manage to roll over every dollar of the distribution.

Although this approach works, you must have adequate cash on hand to take advantage of it. And of course, the government has free use of your money until you file your next tax return.

You can use a similar strategy if you have an outstanding loan from your plan. In other words, you can use cash you have outside the plan to roll over the amount of the loan into the new plan.

d. Notification of Mandatory Withholding

Are you worried that if you miss the direct rollover option you'll feel like a fool caught in a radar trap by a camouflaged cop? Take heart: It's not as easy to miss as you might think. Not only must the plan administrator give you the option to elect a direct rollover, but the administrator must notify you of the option at least 30 days (and no more than 90 days, lest you forget) before the distribution is to take place. Failure to give notice will cost the administrator $100 per incidence, up to $50,000 per year. However, once the administrator provides notice, he has satisfied his obligation. The administrator is not required to make sure you read the notice.

6. Loans From Qualified Plans

The law generally permits employees to borrow money from their qualified plans, although some plans do not allow it. Most do, however, because employees consider the ability to borrow from their retirement plan an important benefit. But the borrowing rules are stringent.

A loan from a qualified plan is considered a taxable distribution unless it satisfies certain requirements:

- The loan must be repaid at a reasonable rate of interest with well-defined repayment terms.
- The loan amount cannot exceed $50,000.
- The loan amount cannot exceed the greater of $10,000 or 50% of your vested account balance. (The vested amount is the portion you may take with you when you leave the company.) In other words, the loan is limited to 50% of your vested balance unless your account is under $20,000. Then you may borrow up to $10,000 as long as you have that much in your account and the plan allows it.

EXAMPLE: You have a vested account balance of $70,000 in your employer's retirement plan. You would like to borrow as much as you can from the plan. The loan may not exceed $50,000. But it also may not exceed 50% of your vested account balance, which is $35,000 (50% x $70,000). Thus the maximum you may borrow from the plan is $35,000.

- If you have more than one outstanding loan, the total of all loans from the plan cannot exceed $50,000 reduced by the difference between the highest loan balance for the previous 12 months and the current balance.

EXAMPLE: On January 15, your vested benefit in your employer's retirement plan is $150,000. You borrow $25,000 from the plan. On December of the same year, you realize that you need to borrow some additional money to get through the holiday season. Although you had begun to pay back the first loan, you still owe $20,000. To compute the amount you may borrow now, you begin with the $50,000 limit and reduce it by the amount of money you still owe to the plan. That reduces your limit to $30,000 ($50,000 − $20,000). The $30,000 must be reduced further by the difference between the highest outstanding balance in the last 12 months (which was $25,000) and the current outstanding balance (which is $20,000). That difference is $5,000. Thus the $30,000 is further reduced to $25,000, which is the maximum you may now borrow from the plan.

- The loan must be repaid within five years, using a level amortization schedule (like a home mortgage) with payments to be made at least quarterly. There is an exception to the five-year repayment rule if the loan is used to purchase (but not improve) a principal residence. In that case, you may simply repay the loan in a reasonable amount of time. (The Tax Code does not define "reasonable"—however, the IRS has been known to approve loans outstanding for as long as 30 years when they are used to make mortgage payments.)

As long as the above five requirements are met, the amount of the loan will not be considered a taxable distribution to you, either at the time it is made or during the repayment period.

⚠ **You may owe taxes on an outstanding loan.** If you haven't repaid your loan by the time your share of the plan assets is distributed to you, the loan amount will be subject to income tax. (See Section 5biv, above.)

7. Hardship Distributions From Qualified Plans

A special relief provision in the Tax Code allows participants in 401(k) plans and other profit sharing plans—but no other type of qualified plan—to withdraw money in the event of hardship. It is not sufficient that the law permits such withdrawals; the plan itself must specifically allow them as well.

The Tax Code defines hardship withdrawal to be a distribution because of "immediate and heavy financial need." The plan must establish objective and nondiscriminatory ways of determining whether such a need exists and measuring the amount of money necessary to satisfy that need.

The IRS provides a list of expenses that qualify as hardship withdrawals. That means that if your expenses fall into one of the listed categories and your plan allows hardship withdrawals, your distribution will generally qualify as a hardship withdrawal. The IRS expenditures are as follows:

- medical expenses for you, your spouse, or your dependents
- expenses to purchase a principal residence (but not money to make mortgage payments)
- expenses to pay postsecondary education for a 12-month period, including tuition, room, and board, and
- expenses to stave off eviction from your principal residence or to fore-stall a foreclosure.

Expenses can qualify for hardship withdrawals even if they don't fall into one of the above categories. In that case, the plan document must provide some method of determining whether an expense constitutes immediate and heavy financial need. You must also provide a statement to the IRS declaring that you have exhausted other available resources. For example, if you have a vacation home, you would be required to sell it and use the proceeds before you would qualify to take money out of your plan.

Now the coup de grace. Suppose you jump through all the hoops and are eligible for a hardship withdrawal. What you gain is access to your funds without disqualifying the plan. But a hardship withdrawal is still subject to income tax. And you will also owe a 10% early distribution penalty if you are younger than 59½, unless the withdrawal qualifies for one of the exceptions described in Chapter 3.

⚠️ **Hardship distributions are not eligible to be rolled over into an IRA or another qualified plan.** So if you take a distribution from your 401(k) plan under its hardship provisions, and then you decide you don't need the money after all, you are stuck. You cannot roll it into an IRA, nor can you put it back into the plan.

D. Special Income Tax Rules for Tax-Deferred Annuities

Although tax-deferred annuities, or TDAs, closely track the taxation rules for qualified plans, there are some important differences. (See Chapter 1, Section C2, for more information about TDAs.)

1. Pay Ordinary Income Tax

In general, distributions from TDAs will be taxed along with the rest of your income at normal tax rates unless you roll over the distribution. But you may not exclude from your income the net unrealized appreciation in employer stock, as you can with a qualified plan. (See Section C1e, above.)

2. Roll Over Your Distribution

As with qualified plan distributions, you may roll over any portion of a TDA distribution into an IRA or another retirement plan. However, if you roll over the TDA distribution into a qualified plan, you forfeit the right to use ten-year averaging on any future distribution from that qualified plan. (See Section 3, below.)

3. Averaging and Capital Gain Treatment Not Allowed

Ten-year averaging is not permitted for distributions from TDAs, nor is capital gain treatment for pre-1974 accumulations. (See Sections C1c and C1d, above.) Distributions from TDAs must be rolled over or they will be subject to ordinary income tax at the tax rates in effect in the year of distribution.

4. Special Rules at Divorce or Separation

The QDRO rules (see Section C4, above) apply to TDAs just as they do to qualified plans, except that the alternate payee is not permitted to use ten-year averaging or the special capital gain treatment.

5. Hardship Distributions

Hardship distributions from TDAs are permitted and are subject to the same rules as hardship distributions from 401(k) plans. (See Section C7, above.)

E. Special Income Tax Rules for IRAs

Unlike TDAs, which mimic qualified plans in most respects, IRAs are quite different, and in many ways more restrictive.

Roth IRAs are not standard IRAs. If you have a Roth IRA, the following rules may not apply. See Chapter 9 for a detailed description of Roth IRAs and the taxes, penalties, and distribution rules that apply to them.

1. Pay Ordinary Income Tax

All distributions from IRAs are subject to ordinary income tax unless you have made nondeductible contributions to the IRA over the years. In that case, a portion of each distribution will be tax free. (See Section B2, above, for information about computing the tax-free portion.) The fair market value of the taxable portion is simply included with your income and taxed at your normal rates. You may not use capital gain rates, nor may you claim losses.

2. Roll Over Your Distribution

You can roll IRA distributions into another IRA or even into your employer's plan—with certain restrictions.

a.   Roll to Another IRA

You may roll over an IRA or part of an IRA into a different IRA or even back into the same IRA, but you must follow two important rules:

- If you take a distribution with the intention of rolling it into a different IRA, you have 60 days from the time you receive the distribution to deposit it into the new IRA. If you miss the deadline, you will owe income tax and perhaps penalties, such as an early distribution tax. (See Chapter 3.)

 If you need a short-term loan. It is quite acceptable to take money from your IRA as long as you deposit it into another IRA, or back into the same IRA, within 60 days. Just be careful to redeposit the precise amount of cash you distributed in the first place. Don't buy stock with the distributed funds and then try to deposit the stock into the IRA in lieu of the cash. If cash came out, cash must go back in.

- You are permitted only one rollover per year from each IRA that you own. For example, if your IRA #1 has $50,000 in it and you decide to roll over $20,000 to your IRA #2, you may not roll over any other funds from IRA #1 for 12 months. (Note that the restriction is for a full 12 months, not just a calendar year.)

 The same funds can be rolled over only once in a 12-month period. For example, if you roll over $10,000 from one of your IRAs into a new IRA, you may not later roll over that same $10,000 into yet another IRA until 12 months have passed.

 The one-rollover-per-year rule applies only to rollovers. This rule does not apply to transfers that go directly from one IRA custodian to another. For example, if you want to roll funds from IRA #1 to IRA #2, you could simply ask the custodian of IRA #1 to send you a check. When you receive it, you deliver it to the custodian of IRA #2. That is considered a rollover. But if you instruct the custodian of IRA #1 to transfer funds directly to the custodian of IRA #2, so that you never personally receive the funds, that is considered a transfer. The IRS is more lenient with transfers, because you don't have access to the funds and presumably can't do anything improper. The IRS allows you to make as many transfers as you like during the year.

b.   Roll to an Employer Plan

You may also roll over some or all of your IRA distribution into your employer's plan—provided the plan permits such rollovers. Be careful, though; you are not permitted to roll over any after-tax amounts from the IRA to the employer plan. Thus, if you have made nondeductible contributions to the IRA, you cannot roll these into an employer plan.

c. 60-Day Rule

For many years, the IRS adamantly refused to entertain even the most heartbreaking excuse for why a taxpayer was unable to complete a rollover from one plan or IRA to another within 60 days. But eventually, the IRS issued a compassionate revenue procedure (Rev. Proc. 2003-16) promising to grant waivers "where failure to waive…would be against equity or good conscience." The revenue procedure lists the following circumstances under which a waiver is likely to be granted:

- financial institution error (the waiver will generally be automatic if the error is corrected within a year)
- death
- disability
- hospitalization, or
- incarceration

To obtain a waiver, the taxpayer must formally apply for one and pay a fee of $90.

3. Averaging and Capital Gain Treatment Not Allowed

Neither ten-year averaging nor capital gain treatment is permitted on distributions from an IRA.

4. Special Rules at Divorce or Separation

The QDRO rules for qualified plans (described in Section C4, above) do not apply to IRAs. It is still possible to give a spouse or former spouse an IRA or a portion of an IRA, however, as part of a marital property settlement without subjecting the distribution to current income tax or penalties. To do so, you must have a valid divorce decree, a written instrument incident to divorce, a written agreement incident to a legal separation, or a maintenance or alimony decree.

With one of those documents in place, the IRA may be transferred in whole or in part to a spouse or former spouse through one of the following methods:

- The custodian of the participant's IRA may transfer the IRA directly to the trustee of the spouse or former spouse's IRA.
- The participant may direct the custodian to change the title of the IRA to an IRA in the spouse's or former spouse's name.
- The original participant or owner may roll over the IRA into an IRA in the name of the spouse or former spouse.

Under no circumstances, however, should the spouse or former spouse initiate the transfer of the participant's IRA or take possession of the funds before they are deposited into an IRA in the spouse's name. Only the participant may direct the transfer or rollover. Once the funds are in an IRA in the name of the spouse or former spouse, the IRA is treated in every respect as though the spouse or former spouse were the original owner. When assets are later distributed, they will be subject to ordinary income tax and perhaps penalties, for which the spouse or former spouse will be liable.

⚠ You'll still owe the early distribution tax. Although there is an exception to the early distribution tax for distributions to an alternate payee under a QDRO, that exception does not apply to IRAs. (See Chapter 3.)

5. Mandatory Withholding Doesn't Apply

Distributions from IRAs are not subject to the mandatory withholding rules that apply to distributions from qualified plans. (See Section C5, above.)

6. Loans Not Allowed

You are not permitted to borrow from an IRA. There are no exceptions. If you do, the consequences are disastrous. If you borrow any amount at all, the entire IRA is disqualified and all assets deemed distributed. The distribution will be subject to income taxes and perhaps other penalties as well, such as the early distribution tax.

7. Hardship Distributions Not Allowed

There is no such thing as a hardship distribution from an IRA—any type of IRA. That's because hardship distributions are not necessary. Unlike a qualified plan, which restricts your access to funds, you can take money out of your IRA any time you want. Of course, you will have to pay income tax and, if you are younger than 59½, you'll also have to pay an early distri-

bution tax. But you always have access to the money.

F. How Penalties Can Guide Planning

In this chapter and the previous one, we have defined the most common types of retirement plans, highlighted their differences, and discussed the income tax consequences of distributions. In the remaining chapters, we discuss distribution rules that apply across the board—to qualified plans, qualified annuities, TDAs, and IRAs. Those rules come with punishing penalties for violations. The penalties are in the form of an additional tax, but are usually avoidable if you understand the rules.

The following two penalty taxes will drive many of the decisions you make about your retirement plan or IRA.

Early Distribution Penalty

You will be hit with an early distribution tax if you take a retirement plan distribution too early—usually before age 59½. This penalty is discussed in depth in Chapters 3 and 4.

Required Distribution Penalty

Once you reach a certain age, usually 70½, you will be required to take a minimum amount from your retirement plan each year. If you don't, you will be subject to a huge penalty—50% of the shortfall. Similar rules apply after you inherit a retirement plan. These required distributions are discussed in Chapters 5-8.

Permissible Rollovers	
Original plan	**New plan**
Qualified plan—401(a)	Traditional IRA
	SEP
	Qualified plan—401(a)
	Qualified annuity plan—403(a)
	Tax deferred annuity—403(b)
Qualified annuity plan—403(a)*	Traditional IRA
	SEP
	Qualified plan—401(a)
	Qualified annuity plan—403(a)
	Tax deferred annuity—403(b)
Tax deferred annuity—403(b)	Traditional IRA
	SEP
	Qualified plan—401(a)
	Qualified annuity plan—403(a)
	Tax deferred annuity—403(b)
SEP	Traditional IRA
	SEP
	Qualified plan—401(a)**
	Qualified annuity plan—403(a)**
	Tax deferred annuity plan—403(b)**
SIMPLE IRA	SIMPLE IRA
	Traditional IRA (after two years)
Traditional IRA	Traditional IRA
	Roth IRA (if certain requirements are met)
	SEP
	Qualified plan—401(a)**
	Qualified annuity plan—403(a)**
	Tax deferred annuity plan—403(b)**
Roth IRA	Roth IRA
Roth 401(k) plan	Roth 401(k) plan
	Roth IRA

* 403(a) plans often don't permit rollovers to or from any other plan even though the law itself permits it.

** Can receive pretax portion only.

Key Tax Code Sections

§ 401(a)(31)

Direct Rollover

§ 402

Rollovers; Ten-Year Averaging

§ 414(p)

Qualified Domestic Relations Orders
(QDROs)

§ 3405

Qualified Plan Withholding Rules

§ 4975

Prohibited Transactions

Chapter 3

Early Distributions: Taking Your Money Out Before the Law Allows

Who Should Read Chapter 3

➡️ Read this chapter if you are younger than 59½ and want to withdraw money from your retirement plan or IRA. If you are older than 59½, this chapter does not apply to you.

ℐf you take money out of a qualified plan, qualified annuity, tax-deferred annuity, or IRA before you reach age 59½, your withdrawal is called an early distribution, and you will have to pay a 10% early distribution tax on the money unless you can meet one of the exceptions.

This chapter describes those exceptions, and it also tells you how to calculate and report the tax just in case your distribution doesn't fit within one of those exceptions. In addition, it describes special rules for IRAs.

⚠️ **Don't forget regular income taxes**. The exceptions we describe in this chapter get you out of the early distribution tax, not income taxes.

A. Exceptions to the Early Distribution Tax

The 10% early distribution tax feels more like a penalty than a tax, and no wonder: It is the cornerstone of the government's efforts to discourage us from plundering our savings before our golden years. Fortunately, there are many exceptions to the rule.

1. Age 59½

Although it's a little nonsensical to call being 59½ an exception to the tax on early distributions (after all, if you are 59½, your distribution isn't early in the first place), the Tax Code views it as an exception, so that is the way we discuss it here.

Before taking money out, make sure you will be at least 59½ on the day of the withdrawal. Otherwise, you'll pay the tax. In other words, it's not good enough that you turn 59½ during the year of the withdrawal. You must be at least 59½ on the day that you get the funds.

⚠️ **Escaping the early distribution tax doesn't mean you get free access to your money.** Just because you have passed age 59½ doesn't guarantee that you can take money out of your retirement plan. Many qualified plans do not permit distributions before you terminate your employment. Attaining age 59½ simply ensures that if you are able to take money out, it will not be subject to the early distribution tax.

Helpful Terms

Adjusted gross income (AGI). Total taxable income reduced by certain expenses such as qualified plan or IRA contributions or alimony payments. Note: Adjusted gross income does not take into account any itemized deductions (see definition below).

After-tax contribution. A contribution to a retirement plan or IRA for which no deduction was taken on an income tax return.

Ancestor. A person from whom an individual is descended. For example, an individual's parents, grandparents, and great grandparents are among his or her ancestors.

Distribution. A payout of property (such as shares of stock) or cash from a retirement plan or IRA to the participant or a beneficiary.

Itemized deductions. Expenses, such as medical payments, mortgage interest, and charitable contributions, that may be used to reduce AGI to arrive at the total amount of income subject to tax.

Principal residence. The home in which an individual lives most of the time. ("Most" is not defined in the Tax Code. It is established by your actions.)

Separation from service. Termination of employment.

Standard deduction. A fixed dollar amount that may be used instead of itemized deductions to reduce AGI before computing tax liability.

2. Death

Another straightforward exception to the tax, albeit a less attractive one, is death. None of the funds distributed from your retirement plan after your death will be subject to the early distribution tax, as long as the account is still in your name when the distribution occurs.

If you are the beneficiary of your spouse's retirement plan or IRA, then upon your spouse's death you may roll over a distribution from your spouse's retirement plan or IRA to a retirement plan or IRA of your own. (See Chapters 7 and 8 for more information about post-death distributions.) This benefit is available only to you as a spouse-beneficiary. But once the funds have been rolled over into an IRA in your name, the post-death exception to the early distribution tax no longer applies, because the account is no longer in the deceased owner's name.

If you want to roll over a post-death distribution from your deceased spouse's retirement plan into an IRA or plan of your own, but need to hold back some of the money for living expenses, this could pose a problem. If you take a distribution from a retirement plan while the plan is still in your deceased spouse's name, the distribution will indeed avoid the 10% tax. But the IRS has ruled that when a surviving spouse invokes this exception, the spouse forfeits the option to roll over the remainder into an IRA in his or her own name. Although this conclusion arises from a private letter ruling (which means that other taxpayers may not rely on the result when planning their own tax strategies), it serves as a warning.

The logical solution to this problem is for the spouse to roll over only the amount that is not needed for living expenses, leaving the remainder in the deceased spouse's name. The remaining portion could then be tapped to pay expenses without incurring the 10% tax. The IRS has not yet ruled on such a strategy, however.

About Private Letter Rulings

Many taxpayers who are unclear about how to proceed in a murky area of the tax law and who feel they have too much at stake to take a wait-and-see posture with the IRS will request private letter rulings. These rulings are just what their title implies—private—meaning the ruling applies only to the taxpayer who requested it and only to the situation in question. The result of the ruling will not serve as precedent and cannot be relied upon by anyone else with similar or even identical circumstances. But the rulings can provide valuable insights into which way the IRS leans on a particular issue.

3. Disability

If you become disabled, you can take money out of your retirement plan without worrying about the early distribution tax.

But what does it mean to be disabled? And who decides? The law defines disabled as the inability to "engage in any substantial gainful activity by reason of any medically determinable physical or mental impairment which can be expected to result in death or to be of long-continued and indefinite duration." Is this helpful?

The key to the disability exception seems to lie in the permanence of the condition, not the severity. Disability exceptions have been denied for chemical dependence and chronic depression, even when the taxpayers were hospitalized for those conditions. It also appears that the disability must be deemed permanent at the time of the distribution, whether or not it is later found to be permanent. For example, the IRS denied the disability exception for a taxpayer, even knowing that the taxpayer later qualified for Social Security disability benefits.

Successful disability claims have included a dentist who suffered nerve damage to his thumb and who produced documents from four insurance companies declaring his disability permanent. Another successful claim involved a taxpayer who had been granted a disability retirement by his company. The IRS relied on the company's determination of the individual's disability. These cases reveal that the IRS is most concerned about the timing and the nature of the disability. Using the cases as a guide, if your disability prevents you from working and is deemed permanent at the time you take your retirement plan distribution, then you should qualify for the disability exception. But there are no guarantees in this arena.

The IRS regulations do clarify one point, however. Gainful activity refers specifically to the type of work you were doing before becoming disabled. Thus it would seem that you need not be unfit for all work—just the work you customarily do.

4. Substantially Equal Periodic Payments

The substantially equal periodic payment exception is available to anyone with an IRA or a retirement plan, regardless of age, which makes it an attractive escape hatch. Theoretically, if you begin taking distributions from your retirement plan in equal annual installments, and those payments are designed to be spread out over your entire life or the joint life of you and your beneficiary, then the payments will not be subject to an early distribution tax.

The fly in the ointment is that you are not permitted to compute payments any way you please. The payment method must conform to IRS guidelines, which sanction three computation methods. Nonetheless, the guidelines are somewhat flexible, making the exception at once versatile and complex. For these reasons, Chapter 4 is devoted exclusively to interpreting the IRS's computational guidelines and related rulings.

If you think you might need to tap your retirement plan early, this is the option that is most likely to work for you. One caveat: If you want to begin taking substantially equal periodic payments from your employer's plan, you must have terminated your employment before payments begin. If the payments are from an IRA, however, the status of your employment is irrelevant.

5. Leaving Your Job After Age 55

If you are at least 55 years old when you leave your job, you will not have to pay the early distribution tax on money that you take out of your retirement plan. This exception applies per employer, meaning that you can go to work for another employer and still meet this exception to your previous employer's plan.

This exception is relevant only if you are between ages 55 and 59½. After age 59½, the early distribution tax does not apply to any retirement plan distribution.

As with other exceptions, you must pay attention to certain details. For example, you need not be age 55 on the day you leave your job, as long as you turn 55 by December 31 of the same year. The strategy falls apart if you retire in a year that precedes the year you turn 55, even if you postpone receiving the retirement benefits until you reach age 55.

> **EXAMPLE:** You retire at age 53 and convince your employer to keep your retirement plan benefits in the plan until you reach age 55. The day after your 55th birthday, you receive $100,000 from your former employer's plan. You buy a Jaguar and spend the rest of the money on a trip around the world. At tax time, you will owe regular income tax on the $100,000 plus a 10% early distribution tax.
>
> If instead you had retired in the same year you turned 55, the $100,000 would be subject to regular income tax, but you would not have to pay an early distribution tax.

⚠ The age 55 exception is not available for IRAs. See Section C1, below, for other rules that apply only to IRAs.

6. Dividends From ESOPs

You do not have to pay the early distribution tax on distributions of dividends from employer stock held inside an ESOP, no matter when you receive the dividend. (See Chapter 1, Section A4, for more information about ESOPs.)

7. Medical Expenses

If you withdraw money from a retirement plan to pay medical expenses, a portion of that distribution might escape the early distribution tax. But once again, the exception is not as simple or as generous as it sounds. The tax exemption applies only to the portion of your medical expenses that would be deductible if you itemized deductions on your tax return. Medical expenses are deductible if they are yours, your spouse's, or your dependent's. But they are deductible only to the extent they exceed 7.5% of your adjusted gross income. Consequently, your retirement plan distribution will avoid the early distribution tax only to the extent it also exceeds the 7.5% threshold.

> **EXAMPLE:** You are single and your adjusted gross income is $50,000. You had medical bills of $6,000 during the year, which you paid with funds you withdrew from your retirement plan. For income tax purposes, you are permitted to deduct medical expenses that exceed 7.5% of your adjusted gross income. Thus,

Adjusted gross income (AGI) = $50,000

Nondeductible expenses
7.5% of AGI (.075 x 50,000) = $ 3,750
Deductible expenses
Excess (6,000 – 3,750) = $ 2,250

Although you took $6,000 from your retirement plan to pay medical expenses, only $2,250 will escape the early distribution tax. The remaining $3,750 will be subject to the 10% additional tax (unless you qualify for another exception). And don't forget that the entire $6,000 is subject to regular income tax, as well.

On the plus side, the medical expense exception is available even if you don't itemize deductions. It applies to those amounts that would be deductible if you did itemize.

EXAMPLE: As in the preceding example, your adjusted gross income is $50,000. You have $6,000 of medical expenses, which you paid with funds from your retirement plan. Only $2,250 of those expenses are deductible (as calculated above). Your deductible items for the year are as follows:

Deductible medical:	$2,250
Deductible taxes:	$1,000
Charitable contributions:	$ 500
Total	$3,750

The standard deduction for a single individual is greater than $3,750. When computing your tax liability, you are permitted to reduce your adjusted gross income by the larger of your itemized deductions or the standard deduction. In this case, because the standard deduction is larger, you will not itemize deductions on your tax return. You may still exclude $2,250 of your retirement plan distribution from the early distribution tax computation, however.

8. QDRO Payments

If you are paying child support or alimony from your retirement plan, or if you intend to distribute some or all of the plan to your former spouse as part of a property settlement, you will not have to pay an early distribution tax on any of those payments as long as there is a QDRO in place that orders the payments. (See Chapter 2, Section C4, for more information about QDROs.) A QDRO usually arises from a separation or divorce agreement and involves court-ordered payments to an alternate payee, such as a former spouse or minor child. Although the QDRO exception applies to all distributions from a qualified plan to any named alternate payee, it is critical that the payments arise from a valid QDRO, not just a private agreement between you and your former spouse.

⚠️ **The exception to the early distribution tax for QDRO payments does not apply to IRAs.** See Section D1b, below, for more information.

9. Federal Tax Levy

If you owe back taxes, you can be reasonably certain the government will try to collect them. If you have assets in a retirement plan, the government can take those assets (in other words, the IRS can put a levy on the assets of the plan) to pay your debt. If it does, then those amounts taken for taxes will not be subject to the early distribution penalty. This shouldn't be too much of a worry for you because IRS policy frowns on the government grabbing retirement plans to satisfy back tax debts unless the debtor is uncooperative and has no other assets.

10. Refunds

If you receive a refund of a contribution to your retirement plan because you contributed more than the law permits, you will not have to pay the early distribution tax on those corrective distributions.

B. Calculating the Tax

If you take money out a retirement plan before you reach age 59½ and cannot meet one of the exceptions described in Section A, above, you will have to pay a 10% early distribution tax on the money.

This tax applies to the taxable portion of your distribution only. So if you receive a distribution that includes after-tax contributions that you made to your retirement plan, the 10% tax will not apply to that portion. Similarly, if you receive a distribution of employer stock and elect to exclude the net unrealized appreciation from your taxable income, the excluded portion will not fall under the 10% tax. (See Chapter 2 for more information about employer stock and net unrealized appreciation.)

> EXAMPLE: You retire at age 51 and take $80,000 out of your retirement plan. The distribution includes $15,000 of after-tax contributions that you make to the plan over the years. The remaining $65,000 consists of employer contribution and investment returns. You plan to use the money to buy a vacation home, so you don't meet any of the exceptions to the early distribution tax. At tax time, you will owe regular income tax and the 10% early distribution tax on the $65,000 portion; you will owe not taxes on the $15,000 portion.

C. Reporting the Tax

If you take a distribution from a retirement plan during the year, the trustee or custodian of your retirement plan will send you a copy of IRS Form 1099-R, which reports the amount distributed to you. (See the following page for a sample Form 1099-R.) The trustee or custodian will also send a copy to the IRS. You don't need to attach a copy of Form 1099-R to your tax return unless income tax was withheld from your distribution. In that case, you must attach the 1099-R just as you would attach your W-2 to show how much tax was withheld.

If you are younger than 59½ at the time of the distribution, a Code 1 should appear in Box 7 of the form, indicating that the early distribution tax applies. If you are younger than 59½ but you qualify for another exception (including having left your job after age 55), Box 7 should reflect that information as well. Code 3 indicates a disability exception, Code 4 is a post-death distribution, and Code 2 is for most other exceptions.

> EXAMPLE: At age 30, Geoff Sute quit his job with Tech Inc. for a higher paying job with another company. Tech Inc. distributed $1,500 to Geoff, which represented the entire balance of his 401(k) plan account. Geoff decided to spend the $1,500 on a new suit. At tax time, Tech Inc. sent Geoff the Form 1099-R reporting the distribution. (See sample form on following page.) Note that Box 7 correctly shows a Code 1.

If the Form 1099-R is accurate, your only responsibility is to compute and pay the extra 10%. This early distribution tax is reported as an additional tax under "other

taxes" on page 2 of Form 1040, your regular income tax form. Even if you do not owe the IRS any regular income tax, you must still report the early distribution tax on your tax return and pay it at tax time.

> EXAMPLE: Using the same facts as in the previous example, Geoff should report his $1,500 distribution on Form 1040, as shown below. Then he should report the early distribution tax of $150 on page 2 of Form 1040.

If the Form 1099-R is not properly coded, you must still compute and pay the additional tax, but you must also complete IRS Form 5329 to show your computation of the tax. Include it with your other forms when you file your tax return. (A sample Form 5329 is in Appendix A.)

> EXAMPLE 1: The facts are the same as in the previous example except that Tech Inc. failed to enter Code 1 in Box 7 of Form 1099-R. As a result, Geoff must complete Part I of Form 5329 and include the form when he files the rest of his tax return. Part I should be completed as shown in Sample 1, below.

> EXAMPLE 2: Irwin retired from Tech Inc. at age 56. The company distributed $25,000 to Irwin, which represented the entire balance in his 401(k) plan. When Irwin received his Form 1099-R from Tech Inc. at tax time, the

Sample: Form 1099-R From Plan Trustee or Custodian to Report Distribution

9898	☐ VOID ☐ CORRECTED		
PAYER'S name, street address, city, state, and ZIP code Tech Inc 401(k) Plan 786 Chipstone Way Sunburn, California	**1** Gross distribution $ 1,500 **2a** Taxable amount $ 1,500	OMB No. 1545-0119 2005 Form **1099-R**	**Distributions From Pensions, Annuities, Retirement or Profit-Sharing Plans, IRAs, Insurance Contracts, etc.**
	2b Taxable amount not determined ☐	Total distribution ☒	**Copy A** **For**
PAYER'S Federal identification number 99-9999	RECIPIENT'S identification number 555-55-5555	**3** Capital gain (included in box 2a) $	**4** Federal income tax withheld $ 300	**Internal Revenue Service Center** File with Form 1096.
RECIPIENT'S name Geoff Sute	**5** Employee contributions or insurance premiums $	**6** Net unrealized appreciation in employer's securities $	For Privacy Act and Paperwork Reduction Act Notice, see the
Street address (including apt. no.) 42 Rising Ave	**7** Distribution code(s) 1	IRA/ SEP/ SIMPLE ☐	**8** Other $ %	**2005 General Instructions for Forms 1099, 1098, 5498,**
City, state, and ZIP code Sand City, CA	**9a** Your percentage of total distribution %	**9b** Total employee contributions $	**and W-2G.**
Account number (see instructions)	**10** State tax withheld $ $	**11** State/Payer's state no.	**12** State distribution $ $
	13 Local tax withheld $ $	**14** Name of locality	**15** Local distribution $ $

Form **1099-R**   Cat. No. 14436Q   Department of the Treasury - Internal Revenue Service

Do Not Cut or Separate Forms on This Page — Do Not Cut or Separate Forms on This Page

Sample: Form 1040, Page 1, to Report Early Distribution

| Form **1040** | Department of the Treasury—Internal Revenue Service **U.S. Individual Income Tax Return** | **2004** | (99) | IRS Use Only—Do not write or staple in this space. |

For the year Jan. 1–Dec. 31, 2004, or other tax year beginning , 2004, ending , 20

OMB No. 1545-0074

Label
(See instructions on page 16.)

Use the IRS label. Otherwise, please print or type.

Your first name and initial: Geoff   Last name: Sute

Your social security number: 555 : 55 : 5555

If a joint return, spouse's first name and initial   Last name

Spouse's social security number

Home address (number and street). If you have a P.O. box, see page 16.   Apt. no.

42 Rising Avenue

City, town or post office, state, and ZIP code. If you have a foreign address, see page 16.

Sand City, CA

▲ **Important!** ▲
You **must** enter your SSN(s) above.

Presidential Election Campaign
(See page 16.)

Note. Checking "Yes" will not change your tax or reduce your refund.
Do you, or your spouse if filing a joint return, want $3 to go to this fund? ▶

	You	Spouse
	☐ Yes ☐ No	☐ Yes ☐ No

Filing Status

Check only one box.

1 ☐ Single
2 ☐ Married filing jointly (even if only one had income)
3 ☐ Married filing separately. Enter spouse's SSN above and full name here. ▶
4 ☐ Head of household (with qualifying person). (See page 17.) If the qualifying person is a child but not your dependent, enter this child's name here. ▶
5 ☐ Qualifying widow(er) with dependent child (see page 17)

Exemptions

6a ☐ **Yourself.** If someone can claim you as a dependent, **do not** check box 6a
b ☐ **Spouse**
c **Dependents:**

(1) First name Last name	(2) Dependent's social security number	(3) Dependent's relationship to you	(4) ✔ if qualifying child for child tax credit (see page 18)
			☐
			☐
			☐
			☐

If more than four dependents, see page 18.

Boxes checked on 6a and 6b
No. of children on 6c who:
• lived with you
• did not live with you due to divorce or separation (see page 18)
Dependents on 6c not entered above
Add numbers on lines above ▶

d Total number of exemptions claimed

Income

Attach Form(s) W-2 here. Also attach Forms W-2G and 1099-R if tax was withheld.

If you did not get a W-2, see page 19.

Enclose, but do not attach, any payment. Also, please use Form 1040-V.

7	Wages, salaries, tips, etc. Attach Form(s) W-2	7	
8a	**Taxable** interest. Attach Schedule B if required	8a	
b	**Tax-exempt** interest. **Do not** include on line 8a	8b	
9a	Ordinary dividends. Attach Schedule B if required	9a	
b	Qualified dividends (see page 20)	9b	
10	Taxable refunds, credits, or offsets of state and local income taxes (see page 20)	10	
11	Alimony received	11	
12	Business income or (loss). Attach Schedule C or C-EZ	12	
13	Capital gain or (loss). Attach Schedule D if required. If not required, check here ▶ ☐	13	
14	Other gains or (losses). Attach Form 4797	14	
15a	IRA distributions 15a b Taxable amount (see page 22)	15b	
16a	Pensions and annuities 16a 1,500 00 b Taxable amount (see page 22)	16b	1,500
17	Rental real estate, royalties, partnerships, S corporations, trusts, etc. Attach Schedule E	17	
18	Farm income or (loss). Attach Schedule F	18	
19	Unemployment compensation	19	
20a	Social security benefits 20a b Taxable amount (see page 24)	20b	
21	Other income. List type and amount (see page 24)	21	
22	Add the amounts in the far right column for lines 7 through 21. This is your **total income** ▶	22	

Adjusted Gross Income

23	Educator expenses (see page 26)	23	
24	Certain business expenses of reservists, performing artists, and fee-basis government officials. Attach Form 2106 or 2106-EZ	24	
25	IRA deduction (see page 26)	25	
26	Student loan interest deduction (see page 28)	26	
27	Tuition and fees deduction (see page 29)	27	
28	Health savings account deduction. Attach Form 8889	28	
29	Moving expenses. Attach Form 3903	29	
30	One-half of self-employment tax. Attach Schedule SE	30	
31	Self-employed health insurance deduction (see page 30)	31	
32	Self-employed SEP, SIMPLE, and qualified plans	32	
33	Penalty on early withdrawal of savings	33	
34a	Alimony paid b Recipient's SSN ▶	34a	
35	Add lines 23 through 34a	35	
36	Subtract line 35 from line 22. This is your **adjusted gross income** ▶	36	

For Disclosure, Privacy Act, and Paperwork Reduction Act Notice, see page 75.   Cat. No. 11320B   Form **1040** (2004)

Sample: Form 1040, Page 2, to Report Early Distribution

Form 1040 (2004)   Page **2**

Tax and Credits	37	Amount from line 36 (adjusted gross income)	37
	38a	Check { **You** were born before January 2, 1940, ☐ Blind. } Total boxes	
		if: { ☐ **Spouse** was born before January 2, 1940, ☐ Blind. } checked ▶ 38a	
Standard Deduction for—	b	If your spouse itemizes on a separate return or you were a dual-status alien, see page 31 and check here ▶ 38b ☐	
	39	**Itemized deductions** (from Schedule A) **or** your **standard deduction** (see left margin) . .	39
• People who checked any box on line 38a or 38b **or** who can be claimed as a dependent, see page 31.	40	Subtract line 39 from line 37	40
	41	If line 37 is $107,025 or less, multiply $3,100 by the total number of exemptions claimed on line 6d. If line 37 is over $107,025, see the worksheet on page 33	41
	42	**Taxable income.** Subtract line 41 from line 40. If line 41 is more than line 40, enter -0-	42
	43	**Tax** (see page 33). Check if any tax is from: a ☐ Form(s) 8814 b ☐ Form 4972 . . .	43
	44	**Alternative minimum tax** (see page 35). Attach Form 6251	44
• All others:	45	Add lines 43 and 44 . . . . ▶	45
Single or Married filing separately, $4,850	46	Foreign tax credit. Attach Form 1116 if required	46	
	47	Credit for child and dependent care expenses. Attach Form 2441 .	47	
	48	Credit for the elderly or the disabled. Attach Schedule R . .	48	
Married filing jointly or Qualifying widow(er), $9,700	49	Education credits. Attach Form 8863	49	
	50	Retirement savings contributions credit. Attach Form 8880 . .	50	
	51	Child tax credit (see page 37)	51	
Head of household, $7,150	52	Adoption credit. Attach Form 8839	52	
	53	Credits from: a ☐ Form 8396 b ☐ Form 8859 .	53	
	54	Other credits. Check applicable box(es): a ☐ Form 3800		
		b ☐ Form 8801 c ☐ Specify _____ . .	54	
	55	Add lines 46 through 54. These are your **total credits**	55
	56	Subtract line 55 from line 45. If line 55 is more than line 45, enter -0- . . . . . ▶	56
Other Taxes	57	Self-employment tax. Attach Schedule SE	57
	58	Social security and Medicare tax on tip income not reported to employer. Attach Form 4137 . .	58
	59	Additional tax on IRAs, other qualified retirement plans, etc. Attach Form 5329 if required .	59 *150*
	60	Advance earned income credit payments from Form(s) W-2	60
	61	Household employment taxes. Attach Schedule H	61
	62	Add lines 56 through 61. This is your **total tax** . . . . ▶	62
Payments	63	Federal income tax withheld from Forms W-2 and 1099 . .	63	
	64	2004 estimated tax payments and amount applied from 2003 return	64	
If you have a qualifying child, attach Schedule EIC.	65a	**Earned income credit (EIC)**	65a	
	b	Nontaxable combat pay election ▶ 65b		
	66	Excess social security and tier 1 RRTA tax withheld (see page 54)	66	
	67	Additional child tax credit. Attach Form 8812	67	
	68	Amount paid with request for extension to file (see page 54) .	68	
	69	Other payments from: a ☐ Form 2439 b ☐ Form 4136 c ☐ Form 8885 .	69	
	70	Add lines 63, 64, 65a, and 66 through 69. These are your **total payments** . . . . ▶	70
Refund	71	If line 70 is more than line 62, subtract line 62 from line 70. This is the amount you **overpaid**	71
Direct deposit? See page 54 and fill in 72b, 72c, and 72d.	72a	Amount of line 71 you want **refunded to you** . . . . ▶	72a
	▶ b	Routing number _____ ▶ c Type: ☐ Checking ☐ Savings	
	▶ d	Account number _____	
	73	Amount of line 71 you want **applied to your 2005 estimated tax** ▶	73	
Amount You Owe	74	**Amount you owe.** Subtract line 70 from line 62. For details on how to pay, see page 55 ▶	74
	75	Estimated tax penalty (see page 55)	75	

Third Party Designee	Do you want to allow another person to discuss this return with the IRS (see page 56)? ☐ **Yes.** Complete the following. ☐ **No**
	Designee's name ▶ Phone no. ▶ ( ) Personal identification number (PIN) ▶ _____

Sign Here
Joint return? See page 17.
Keep a copy for your records.

Under penalties of perjury, I declare that I have examined this return and accompanying schedules and statements, and to the best of my knowledge and belief, they are true, correct, and complete. Declaration of preparer (other than taxpayer) is based on all information of which preparer has any knowledge.

Your signature	Date	Your occupation	Daytime phone number
			( )
Spouse's signature. If a joint return, **both** must sign.	Date	Spouse's occupation	

Paid Preparer's Use Only

Preparer's signature ▶		Date	Check if self-employed ☐	Preparer's SSN or PTIN
Firm's name (or yours if self-employed), address, and ZIP code ▶			EIN	
			Phone no.	( )

Form **1040** (2004)

Sample 1: Form 5329 to Report Early Distribution, No Code on 1099-R

Form **5329**	**Additional Taxes on Qualified Plans (Including IRAs) and Other Tax-Favored Accounts**	OMB No. 1545-0203
Department of the Treasury Internal Revenue Service (99)	▶ Attach to Form 1040. ▶ See separate instructions.	20**04** Attachment Sequence No. **29**

Name of individual subject to additional tax. If married filing jointly, see instructions.		Your social security number
Geoff Sute		555	55	5555

Fill in Your Address Only If You Are Filing This Form by Itself and Not With Your Tax Return

Home address (number and street), or P.O. box if mail is not delivered to your home	Apt. no.
City, town or post office, state, and ZIP code	If this is an amended return, check here ▶ ☐

If you **only** owe the additional 10% tax on early distributions, you may be able to report this tax directly on Form 1040, line 59, without filing Form 5329. See the instructions for Form 1040, line 59.

Part I Additional Tax on Early Distributions

Complete this part if you took a taxable distribution, before you reached age 59½, from a qualified retirement plan (including an IRA) or modified endowment contract (unless you are reporting this tax directly on Form 1040—see above). You may also have to complete this part to indicate that you qualify for an exception to the additional tax on early distributions or for certain Roth IRA distributions (see instructions).

1	Early distributions included in income. For Roth IRA distributions, see instructions	**1**	1,500
2	Early distributions included on line 1 that are not subject to the additional tax (see instructions). Enter the appropriate exception number from the instructions: _____	**2**	0
3	Amount subject to additional tax. Subtract line 2 from line 1	**3**	1,500
4	**Additional tax.** Enter 10% (.10) of line 3. Include this amount on Form 1040, line 59 . . .	**4**	150

Caution: *If any part of the amount on line 3 was a distribution from a SIMPLE IRA, you may have to include 25% of that amount on line 4 instead of 10% (see instructions).*

Part II Additional Tax on Certain Distributions From Education Accounts

Complete this part if you included an amount in income, on Form 1040, line 21, from a Coverdell education savings account (ESA) or a qualified tuition program (QTP).

5	Distributions included in income from Coverdell ESAs and QTPs	**5**	
6	Distributions included on line 5 that are not subject to the additional tax (see instructions) . .	**6**	
7	Amount subject to additional tax. Subtract line 6 from line 5	**7**	
8	**Additional tax.** Enter 10% (.10) of line 7. Include this amount on Form 1040, line 59	**8**	

Part III Additional Tax on Excess Contributions to Traditional IRAs

Complete this part if you contributed more to your traditional IRAs for 2004 than is allowable or you had an amount on line 17 of your 2003 Form 5329.

9	Enter your excess contributions from line 16 of your 2003 Form 5329 (see instructions). If zero, go to line 15	**9**	
10	If your traditional IRA contributions for 2004 are less than your maximum allowable contribution, see instructions. Otherwise, enter -0-	**10**		
11	2004 traditional IRA distributions included in income (see instructions)	**11**		
12	2004 distributions of prior year excess contributions (see instructions)	**12**		
13	Add lines 10, 11, and 12	**13**	
14	Prior year excess contributions. Subtract line 13 from line 9. If zero or less, enter -0-	**14**	
15	Excess contributions for 2004 (see instructions)	**15**	
16	Total excess contributions. Add lines 14 and 15	**16**	
17	**Additional tax.** Enter 6% (.06) of the **smaller** of line 16 **or** the value of your traditional IRAs on December 31, 2004 (including 2004 contributions made in 2005). Include this amount on Form 1040, line 59 . . .	**17**	

Part IV Additional Tax on Excess Contributions to Roth IRAs

Complete this part if you contributed more to your Roth IRAs for 2004 than is allowable or you had an amount on line 25 of your 2003 Form 5329.

18	Enter your excess contributions from line 24 of your 2003 Form 5329 (see instructions). If zero, go to line 23	**18**	
19	If your Roth IRA contributions for 2004 are less than your maximum allowable contribution, see instructions. Otherwise, enter -0- . . .	**19**		
20	2004 distributions from your Roth IRAs (see instructions)	**20**		
21	Add lines 19 and 20	**21**	
22	Prior year excess contributions. Subtract line 21 from line 18. If zero or less, enter -0-	**22**	
23	Excess contributions for 2004 (see instructions)	**23**	
24	Total excess contributions. Add lines 22 and 23	**24**	
25	**Additional tax.** Enter 6% (.06) of the **smaller** of line 24 **or** the value of your Roth IRAs on December 31, 2004 (including 2004 contributions made in 2005). Include this amount on Form 1040, line 59 . . .	**25**	

For Paperwork Reduction Act Notice, see page 5 of the instructions. Cat. No. 13329Q Form **5329** (2004)

Sample 2: Form 5329 to Report Exception to Early Distribution Tax

Form **5329**	**Additional Taxes on Qualified Plans (Including IRAs) and Other Tax-Favored Accounts** ▶ Attach to Form 1040. ▶ See separate instructions.	OMB No. 1545-0203 **20̅0̅4**

Department of the Treasury
Internal Revenue Service   (99)

Attachment Sequence No. **29**

Name of individual subject to additional tax. If married filing jointly, see instructions.

Irwin Hirsh

Your social security number

444 44 4444

Fill in Your Address Only If You Are Filing This Form by Itself and Not With Your Tax Return ▷

Home address (number and street), or P.O. box if mail is not delivered to your home

Apt. no.

City, town or post office, state, and ZIP code

If this is an amended return, check here ▶ ☐

If you **only** owe the additional 10% tax on early distributions, you may be able to report this tax directly on Form 1040, line 59, without filing Form 5329. See the instructions for Form 1040, line 59.

Part I   Additional Tax on Early Distributions

Complete this part if you took a taxable distribution, before you reached age 59½, from a qualified retirement plan (including an IRA) or modified endowment contract (unless you are reporting this tax directly on Form 1040—see above). You may also have to complete this part to indicate that you qualify for an exception to the additional tax on early distributions or for certain Roth IRA distributions (see instructions).

1	Early distributions included in income. For Roth IRA distributions, see instructions	**1**	25,000
2	Early distributions included on line 1 that are not subject to the additional tax (see instructions). Enter the appropriate exception number from the instructions: _01_	**2**	25,000
3	Amount subject to additional tax. Subtract line 2 from line 1	**3**	0
4	**Additional tax.** Enter 10% (.10) of line 3. Include this amount on Form 1040, line 59	**4**	0

Caution: If any part of the amount on line 3 was a distribution from a SIMPLE IRA, you may have to include 25% of that amount on line 4 instead of 10% (see instructions).

Part II   Additional Tax on Certain Distributions From Education Accounts

Complete this part if you included an amount in income, on Form 1040, line 21, from a Coverdell education savings account (ESA) or a qualified tuition program (QTP).

5	Distributions included in income from Coverdell ESAs and QTPs	**5**	
6	Distributions included on line 5 that are not subject to the additional tax (see instructions)	**6**	
7	Amount subject to additional tax. Subtract line 6 from line 5	**7**	
8	**Additional tax.** Enter 10% (.10) of line 7. Include this amount on Form 1040, line 59	**8**	

Part III   Additional Tax on Excess Contributions to Traditional IRAs

Complete this part if you contributed more to your traditional IRAs for 2004 than is allowable or you had an amount on line 17 of your 2003 Form 5329.

9	Enter your excess contributions from line 16 of your 2003 Form 5329 (see instructions). If zero, go to line 15	**9**	
10	If your traditional IRA contributions for 2004 are less than your maximum allowable contribution, see instructions. Otherwise, enter -0-	**10**	
11	2004 traditional IRA distributions included in income (see instructions)	**11**	
12	2004 distributions of prior year excess contributions (see instructions)	**12**	
13	Add lines 10, 11, and 12	**13**	
14	Prior year excess contributions. Subtract line 13 from line 9. If zero or less, enter -0-	**14**	
15	Excess contributions for 2004 (see instructions)	**15**	
16	Total excess contributions. Add lines 14 and 15	**16**	
17	**Additional tax.** Enter 6% (.06) of the **smaller** of line 16 or the value of your traditional IRAs on December 31, 2004 (including 2004 contributions made in 2005). Include this amount on Form 1040, line 59	**17**	

Part IV   Additional Tax on Excess Contributions to Roth IRAs

Complete this part if you contributed more to your Roth IRAs for 2004 than is allowable or you had an amount on line 25 of your 2003 Form 5329.

18	Enter your excess contributions from line 24 of your 2003 Form 5329 (see instructions). If zero, go to line 23	**18**	
19	If your Roth IRA contributions for 2004 are less than your maximum allowable contribution, see instructions. Otherwise, enter -0-	**19**	
20	2004 distributions from your Roth IRAs (see instructions)	**20**	
21	Add lines 19 and 20	**21**	
22	Prior year excess contributions. Subtract line 21 from line 18. If zero or less, enter -0-	**22**	
23	Excess contributions for 2004 (see instructions)	**23**	
24	Total excess contributions. Add lines 22 and 23	**24**	
25	**Additional tax.** Enter 6% (.06) of the **smaller** of line 24 **or** the value of your Roth IRAs on December 31, 2004 (including 2004 contributions made in 2005). Include this amount on Form 1040, line 59	**25**	

For Paperwork Reduction Act Notice, see page 5 of the instructions.   Cat. No. 13329Q   Form **5329** (2004)

form showed a Code 1 in Box 7, indicating that Irwin had received an early distribution. Because Irwin left the company after age 55, his distribution is not subject to an early distribution tax. He must complete and attach Form 5329 to his tax return to tell the IRS which exception applies. The instructions for Form 5329 indicate that the age 55 exception is number 01. Irwin must enter 01 on line 2 of Part I. Irwin completes the rest of the form as shown in Sample 2, above.

D. Special Rules for IRAs

The early distribution tax applies to IRAs in much the same way it applies to qualified plans, with just a few exceptions and variations described in this section. Bear in mind, however, that the Roth IRA is not a typical IRA, so the following rules do not necessarily apply to it. For a complete discussion of the Roth IRA rules, see Chapter 9.

1. Rules Applicable to All IRAs Except Roth IRAs

Six special rules apply to rollover IRAs, contributory IRAs, SEP IRAs, and SIMPLE IRAs.

a. No Age 55 Exception

As we explained earlier in this chapter, employees who are at least age 55 when they terminate their employment will not have to pay an early distribution tax on distributions from their former employer's qualified plan. This rule does not apply to IRAs, however. If you have an IRA, you must be at least 59½ to use the age exception to the early distribution tax. Of course, you may still qualify for an exception that is unrelated to your age.

b. No QDRO Exception

The special QDRO rules in the Tax Code do not apply to IRAs. This means the QDRO exception to the early distribution tax is available for qualified plan distributions, but not for IRA distributions. Even if your divorce agreement or court order mandates child support or alimony payments from an IRA, the payments will be subject to an early distribution tax unless one of the other exceptions applies. Sometimes the divorce agreement simply requires the distribution to a spouse of his or her interest in the IRA (for example, a community property interest), but in that case, too, the distribution could be subject to an early distribution tax.

There is one way around this, but it is available only to the former spouse of the IRA participant, and only if the spouse is to receive some or all of the IRA as directed by a divorce or maintenance decree or a written separation agreement. The IRA participant may direct the custodian of the IRA to transfer some or all of the IRA assets directly into an IRA in the former spouse's name. Alternatively, the participant could roll over the spouse's share into a new IRA in the participant's name and then direct the custodian to change title on the new

IRA to the spouse's name. The participant might even roll over the spouse's interest into an IRA in the spouse's name (instead of using a direct transfer). The key in each case is for the spouse not to take possession of the funds before they are deposited into an IRA in the spouse's own name.

Once the funds are in an IRA in the spouse's name, however, they belong to the spouse in every way. Thereafter, all IRA rules apply to the assets as though the spouse had been the original IRA participant. If the spouse takes a distribution, the spouse will have to pay an early distribution tax unless an exception applies.

Get it in writing! The transfer of IRA assets to an account in the name of a spouse or former spouse must be as a result of a written divorce or separation agreement. You may not transfer funds from your IRA into your current spouse's IRA simply because you want to increase the value of his or her account for some reason.

Child support cannot go into an IRA. The above transfer strategy is available only for payments that are made to a separated or former spouse. Child support payments may not be transferred to an IRA in either the child's name or the former spouse's name.

c. Health Insurance Premiums

An early distribution tax exception unique to IRAs concerns health insurance premiums. If you are unemployed or were recently unemployed and use money from your IRA to pay health insurance premiums, the IRA funds used specifically for that purpose will not be subject to an early distribution tax, as long as you satisfy the following conditions:

- you received unemployment compensation for at least 12 consecutive weeks
- you received the funds from the IRA during a year in which you received unemployment compensation or during the following year, and
- the IRA distribution is received no more than 60 days after you return to work.

EXAMPLE: You are 45. You lost your job in 2005 and began receiving unemployment compensation on September 22, 2005. You want to maintain your health insurance even during your unemployment. You pay $400 per month on the first day of each month beginning October 1. Because you are short of cash, you withdraw the $400 from your IRA each month to cover the cost of the premiums. You land a job and begin working on March 15, 2006. Unfortunately, your new employer does not provide any health benefits, so you continue to pay premiums of $400 per month, withdrawing the money from your IRA each time. Only the premiums you pay after December 15, 2005 (12 weeks after your unemployment compensation payments began), and before May 15, 2006 (60 days after you began work), are eligible for the exception to the early distribution tax. Thus your distributions of $400 on January 1, February 1, March 1, April 1, and May 1 totaling $2,000 all escape the early distribution tax. Distributions after May 15 are subject to the early distribution tax unless another exception applies.

You may also make a penalty-free withdrawal from your IRA to pay for health insurance if you were self-employed before you stopped working, as long as you would have qualified for unemployment compensation except for the fact that you were self-employed.

d. Higher Education Expenses

Distributions that you use to pay higher education expenses will not be subject to the early distribution tax, as long as those distributions meet the following requirements:

- The distributions are used to pay for tuition, fees, books, supplies, and equipment. They may also be used for room and board if the student is carrying at least half of a normal study load (or is considered at least a halftime student).
- The expenses are paid on behalf of the IRA owner, spouse, child, or grandchild.
- The distributions do not exceed the amount of the higher education expenses. Furthermore, the total expenses (tuition, fees, and so on) must be reduced by any tax-free scholarships or other tax-free assistance the student receives, not including loans, gifts, or inheritances.

e. First Home Purchase

In 1997, Congress enacted an exception to the early distribution tax to make it easier for people to buy their first homes. When the dust settled, the benefit was not as dramatic as people had hoped—not because it was difficult to qualify for, but because the lifetime distribution limit was only $10,000. Here are the details:

- The IRA distribution must be used for the acquisition, construction, or reconstruction of a home.
- The funds must be used within 120 days of receipt. If it happens that the home purchase is canceled or delayed, the funds may be rolled over into another IRA (or back into the same one) as long as the rollover is complete within 120 days of the initial distribution.
- The funds must be used to purchase a principal residence for a first-time home buyer. A first-time home buyer is someone who has had no interest in a principal residence during the two years ending on the date of purchase of the new home. If the

individual happens to be married, then neither the individual nor the spouse may have owned any part of a principal residence during the preceding two-year period.

- The first-time home buyer must be the IRA owner, or the owner's spouse, or an ancestor (such as a parent, grandparent, or great grandparent), child, or grandchild of either the IRA owner or the owner's spouse.
- The lifetime limit of $10,000 applies regardless of whose home is purchased or improved. If the IRA owner withdraws $10,000 and gives it to his or her child, the lifetime limit for the IRA owner is used up. The IRA owner may not invoke the first home exception for any future distribution even if it is to buy a house for a different relative or for himself. The $10,000 does not have to be distributed all at once or even in a single year. For example, the IRA owner could withdraw $5,000 one year, giving it to a qualified person for a home purchase, and then withdraw another $5,000 in a later year.

f.   Refunds

There is a limit to how much you may contribute to an IRA each year. If you contribute too much, then you have made an excess contribution. If you withdraw the excess by the time you file your tax return (including extensions, if you filed a request and were granted an extension), you will not have to pay an early distribution tax on the excess. You must also withdraw the income earned on the excess while it was in the IRA, however, and that portion will be subject to the early distribution tax, unless it qualifies for another exception.

EXAMPLE: You are self-employed. In January you open an IRA and contribute $3,000 for the current tax year. On December 31, when you compute your net income for the year, you discover that you only made $2,500 in self-employment income. Because your IRA contribution is limited to the lesser of $3,000 or your net income, you have made an excess contribution of $500. Also, you earned 10% on the IRA investment during the year. To correct the excess contribution, you must withdraw not only the $500, but the $50 of earnings on that excess (10% of $500) as well. If you withdraw these amounts by April 15 of the year after the excess contribution (or the due date of your tax return, if you received an extension of time for filing the return), there will be no penalty on the $500 distribution. The $50 of earnings will be subject to ordinary income tax and a 10% early distribution tax of $5.

If you fail to correct an excess contribution to an IRA by the time you file your tax return, but make a corrective distribution later, the entire amount of the distribution is subject to the early distribution tax unless it qualifies for another exception.

2. One Rule Applicable Only to SIMPLE IRAs

SIMPLE IRAs are described in Chapter 1, Section B4. All the special IRA rules discussed above apply to SIMPLE IRAs, but there is one additional rule. If you are a participant in a SIMPLE IRA and you receive a distribution within two years of the date you began contributing to it, the early distribution tax increases from 10% to 25%. At the end of two years, it falls back to 10%. Of course, if the distribution qualifies for an exception, the early distribution tax will not apply at all.

Key Tax Code Sections and IRS Pronouncements

§ 72(t)
Early Distribution Tax

§ 402(g)(2)(C)
Distribution of Excess Deferrals

§ 4972
Nondeductible Contributions to Qualified Plans

§ 4973
Excess Contributions to IRAs

§ 4979
Excess Contributions to Qualified Plans (in Violation of Nondiscrimination Rules)

Revenue Procedure 92-93
Treatment of Corrective Distributions

Chapter 4

Substantially Equal Periodic Payments

Who Should Read Chapter 4

Read this chapter if you are younger than 59½ and want to learn about using substantially equal periodic payments to escape the early distribution tax.

Chapter 3 introduced you to all of the exceptions to the early distribution tax. Here, we take an in-depth look at the most complicated of those exceptions: Substantially equal periodic payments.

As you may recall, the exception essentially means that you do not have to pay the early distribution tax on money that you take out of your plan in regular payments over either your life expectancy or the joint life expectancy of you and your beneficiary, even if you are younger than 59½.

Here are some basic rules about the exception:

- There are no age restrictions. So, for example, you could be 25 and start taking substantially equal periodic payments.
- The payments must be substantially equal, which means you cannot alter the payment each year to suit your needs, perhaps by taking a few dollars one year and a few thousand the next.

- You must compute the payments as though you intend to distribute the retirement plan over your entire life, or over the joint life of you and your beneficiary.
- Payments from your employer's plan must begin after you leave your job. (This restriction does not apply to IRAs.)
- You may not discontinue payments or alter the computation method for at least five years. And if you have not reached age 59½ at the end of the five-year period, you must wait until you do reach that age before making a change. If you modify payments too soon, the early distribution tax (plus interest) will be applied retroactively to all of the payments you have received. There is one exception to the rule that you may not modify the payments: You are permitted a one-time switch to the required minimum distribution method if you started out using another method. (See Section A, below, for a discussion of the various methods you can use to compute your payments.) (See Section C, below, for more information about modifying payments.)

To find out more. If you'd like to read more about these guidelines, refer to IRS Revenue Ruling 2002-62, which you can find in Appendix A to this book.

Helpful Terms

Amortize. To liquidate or reduce (as in the case of a debt) through periodic payments of principal and interest.

Annuity. A contract, sold by an insurance company, that promises to make monthly, quarterly, semiannual, or annual payments for life or for a specified period of time.

Distribution. A payout of property (such as shares of stock) or cash from a retirement plan or IRA to the participant or a beneficiary.

Joint life expectancy. The number of years expected to pass before the second of two individuals dies.

Recalculated life expectancy. Life expectancy that is revised each year according to statistically accurate measures of mortality.

Payments that are part of a series of substantially equal periodic payments are not eligible to be rolled over. Perhaps in your zeal to withdraw from your retirement plan precisely the amount you need and no more, you devise a plan to begin periodic withdrawals and then roll over into an IRA the portion of each payment you don't use. That strategy is creative, logical, reasonable—and prohibited. The Tax Code specifically denies rollover treatment to periodic payments. You should be able to achieve a similar result by splitting the account first before beginning periodic payments. At least that strategy is not specifically forbidden. (You can learn more about this strategy in "If You Don't Want to Withdraw All of Your Money," below.)

Periodic payments are also exempt from the mandatory income tax withholding rules for qualified plan distributions. (See Chapter 2, Section C5, for more information about withholding.) Mandatory withholding applies only to those plan distributions that are eligible to be rolled over. Because periodic payments are not eligible to be rolled over, they are not subject to mandatory withholding.

If You Don't Want to Withdraw All of Your Money

Because the methods described in Section A, below, require that the whole plan get distributed eventually, some people find that they end up with larger payments from their plan than they need. That's not a good thing, because taking more money out of your plan than is necessary means paying income tax on money when you don't really have to.

If you have two or more retirement plans, you might be able to solve your problem by taking periodic payments from one plan and leaving the other(s) alone.

But if you have only one plan, you're in a bit of a pickle. Some taxpayers split an existing plan or IRA into two accounts so that one of the accounts is the right size to produce the payment they want. They then leave the other account alone. If you choose this method, however, be warned that no one knows for certain if the IRS will routinely condone it.

A. Computing Periodic Payments

The basic requirement for periodic payments is that they be spread over your lifetime in roughly equal payments. This is trickier than it first appears. For one thing, you probably don't know how long you are going to live, and you also probably don't know how your investments are going to do over the years. If you did (and more important, if the IRS did) the calculation would be simple.

But because most of us have pretty murky crystal balls, the IRS requires us to use some generally accepted life expectancy assumptions and interest rates. Although the IRS does not hand us the numbers we are to use, the agency has put its stamp of approval on three methods for computing required distributions. These are the required minimum distribution, fixed amortization, and fixed annuitization methods. Each has its own set of guidelines for determining life expectancy and selecting an interest rate or an expected investment return.

You are permitted to use any of the methods you want, but before you choose, you should be aware of the principles that are common to all three computation methods:

- **Principle 1:** Using a joint life expectancy instead of your single life expectancy will reduce the size of your payments.
- **Principle 2:** Reducing the interest rate assumption will reduce the size of your payments.
- **Principle 3:** The IRS is more likely to object to large periodic payments than small ones.

If You Stray From the Guidelines

The computation methods outlined in Revenue Ruling 2002-62 and described in this chapter serve as safe harbors. As long as you use one of those methods, you can be certain that the IRS will not challenge you. You are free to stray from these guidelines, but if you do—by using an alternative method, for example, or by altering the variables (such as the interest rate) in one of the IRS methods—you will lose the safe harbor protection, and the IRS can challenge your method. You would then have to successfully defend your method or pay penalties. As a result, the IRS recommends that you request a private letter ruling if you will not be following one of the three methods precisely.

1. Required Minimum Distribution Method

In this relatively simple method, you determine your retirement account balance and divide it by a life expectancy factor each year. The result is your periodic payment for that year. The life expectancy factor can be plucked right out of tables provided by the IRS. (See Tables I, II, and III in Appendix B.) You don't have to worry about choosing an interest rate because your year-end account balance reflects the actual investment returns you earned during the year.

As simple as this method is, you must still decide whether to use your single life expectancy, the Uniform Lifetime Table, or the joint life expectancy of you and your beneficiary. A joint life expectancy and the Uniform Table (which assumes a joint life expectancy) will produce a smaller payment than a single life expectancy will. The size of the payment you need should be the only factor in your decision, given that your choice will affect no other aspect of your retirement plan.

After you make your decision about life expectancies, follow the steps below, to arrive at a payment.

Step 1: Determine your life expectancy factor.

If you use your single life expectancy, you will look up your age each year in Table I in Appendix B, and use the number from the table.

If you use the Uniform Lifetime Table, you will look up your age each year in Table III in Appendix B and use the number you find there.

If you have one or more beneficiaries, you may (but are not required to) use the joint life expectancy table (Table II in Appendix B) to find the appropriate factor. To use a joint life expectancy, the person whose life you use along with your own must be your actual beneficiary. If you have named more than one beneficiary, then you must use the oldest beneficiary's age for determining your joint life expectancy.

If you choose to use either the single life table or the Uniform Lifetime Table, you must use the same table in all subsequent years.

If you choose the joint life table, you must continue to use that table while the beneficiary whose life you are using remains the oldest beneficiary of the account. If during a year, a beneficiary dies, is removed as beneficiary, or is no longer the oldest (for example, if you add an older beneficiary), do not change the calculation for the year of change. For the next year, however, you must use the oldest beneficiary's life when determining your joint life factor. If you have no beneficiary in that next year, you must use the single life table.

Step 2: Determine your account balance.

IRS guidelines state that the account balance you use to calculate your payment "must be determined in a reasonable manner." That statement in and of itself is not terribly useful. But fortunately, the statement is followed by an example in which the IRS makes it clear that using the account balance as of December 31 of the year before periodic payments are to begin is reasonable. And, according to the IRS, it is also reasonable to use the account balance for any date "within a reasonable period before the distribution." For example, if you take your first distribution on July 15, the IRS says it would be reasonable to choose an account balance as of any date between December 31 of the previous year and your distribution date.

Step 3: Calculate the payment.

Divide the account balance by the factor you determined in Step 1, above. The result is the amount that must be distributed during the first year. For the second year, you follow a similar procedure, using the account balance either as of December 31 of the first payment year or as of a date within a reasonable period of your next distribution.

> **EXAMPLE:** You quit your job last year and rolled over your retirement plan into an IRA. The balance of your IRA at the end of the year you retired was $100,000. This year, you will turn 50. You need to draw on the IRA to help make ends meet, so you plan to begin periodic payments.

Year 1

Step 1: From Table I you see that your single life expectancy (for age 50) is 34.2 years.

Step 2: Your December 31 balance for the year before payments are to begin was $100,000.

Step 3: Your first annual periodic payment is $2,924, or $100,000 divided by 34.2.

Year 2

Assume that the balance of your IRA at the end of the first year of periodic payments was $110,000. (You earned more in interest than you withdrew the first year.) Follow these steps to compute the second year payment.

Step 1: Refer again to Table I. You will turn 51 this year. Thus, your life expectancy is 33.3.

Step 2: Your account balance as of December 31 of the first year of periodic payments was $110,000.

Step 3: Your second periodic payment is $3,303, or $110,000 divided by 33.3.

Be exact. Although this method is referred to as the required minimum distribution method, the payment does not represent the minimum you must take, but the exact amount. Once you compute your periodic payment for the year, you must distribute precisely that amount—no more, no less.

a. Advantages of the Required Minimum Distribution Method

The IRS has declared that payments computed under the required minimum distribution rules will be considered substantially equal periodic payments. Nonetheless, the payments could vary significantly from one year to the next, depending on how well or poorly your portfolio performs. Thus, the advantage of this method is that it reflects your actual investment returns. And if your intention is to spread payments over your lifetime, this method can accomplish your goal. Not to be overlooked is the fact that this calculation method is simple and straightforward. And if you choose it, the IRS is unlikely to challenge your payment size or your methodology.

b. Disadvantages of the Required Minimum Distribution Method

Although this method might accurately reflect your investment returns, it is the least flexible. Except by choosing to use a joint life expectancy or the Uniform Lifetime Table, there is no way to tweak payments to produce the distribution you want. And because of market fluctuations, you might find your payments too large one year and not quite large enough the next. Even without market fluctuations, this method will tend to skew payments so that they are small in the early years and larger in later years. That's fine if you expect to need more income later, but if you need more now, there's no way to skew payments in the other direction.

2. Fixed Amortization Method

This method is favored by many taxpayers because it is flexible enough to produce a range of payments, and the computation is straightforward. Once you compute your annual payment, the payment remains fixed for all subsequent years. To compute your payment under this method, you must first decide which table you will use: the single, joint life, or Uniform Lifetime Table. (Remember, a joint life expectancy produces lower payments.) Then you follow these steps.

Step 1: Choose an interest rate.

This is where most of the flexibility comes in, although your choice isn't completely open-ended. IRS safe-harbor guidelines (in Revenue Ruling 2002-62) state that you may use any interest rate that does not exceed 120% of the federal midterm rate for either of the two months before the month distributions begin.

You can find federal mid-term rates at www.irs.gov/taxpros/lists/0,,id=98042,00 .html. Because the payments must be made at least annually, you may use the "annual" interest rate found at this site.

Remember, the IRS guidelines provide a safe harbor, but nothing in the law prohibits you from using a higher rate. (Higher rates produce higher payments.) However, as mentioned above, the IRS recommends—but does not require—that you obtain a private letter ruling if you stray from the guidelines.

In past private letter rulings, the IRS has approved rates that range from 5% to 10.6%. However, those private letter rulings were issued before the safe harbor guidelines in Revenue Ruling 2002-62.

Step 2: Determine your life expectancy.

You may choose to use the single life table (Table I) or the Uniform Lifetime Table (Table III). If you have one or more designated beneficiaries of your account, you may use a joint life expectancy (Table II) with the oldest beneficiary.

Step 3: Determine your account balance.

As is the case with the required minimum distribution method, your account balance may be determined on one of two dates: as of December 31 of the year before your first distribution or as of a date "within a reasonable period" before the first distribution. Thus, presumably, if the account balance has dropped (or increased) dramatically between the end of the prior year and the date you take your first distribution, your choice of valuation date could make a significant difference in the size of your periodic payment.

Step 4: Calculate the payment.

Amortize your account balance using the life expectancy and interest rate you have chosen. Use the same method you would use to amortize a home mortgage or other loan. You can make the computation with a financial calculator, on a computer spreadsheet, or with an amortization program that might be included with other financial software you have. Fortunately, Nolo and several financial sites on the Internet have free calculators you can use for this purpose:

- Nolo at www.nolo.com/lawcenter/ calc
- First Source Bank at www.1stsrce .com/phtml/finance/financl.htm, and
- Financial Visions at www.fincalc.com.

Enter your account balance when asked for the loan amount and your life expectancy when asked for the number of years or months you will take to repay the loan. Then enter the interest rate you have chosen. The calculator then computes the payment amount.

EXAMPLE: You have decided to start taking substantially equal periodic payments annually from your IRA beginning in the year you turn 52. Your IRA account balance as of December 31 of the preceding year was $82,000.

Step 1: You decide to use 120% of the federal midterm rate for December of the year before you begin distributions. That rate is 7%.

Step 2: You will take distributions over your own single life expectancy, which is 32.3 (from Table I) for age 52.

Step 3: Your account balance on December 31 of the year before payments are to begin was $82,000.

Step 4: Using a financial calculator, you compute your annual payment to be $6,467 ($82,000 amortized over 32.3 years at 7%). Your payment for the second and future years will also be $6,467. If you are using Hewlett Packard's

financial calculator (the HP-12C) you will reach a slightly different result: $6,620 instead of $6,467. This is because the HP-12C rounds up to the next integer when you use a fractional period (number of years) in the equation.

a. Advantages of the Fixed Amortization Method

One significant attraction of this method is its simplicity. Once you determine your payment, you never have to compute it again. No looking up numbers in tables every year or trying to remember computation formulas. You do it once and it's done.

Along with the simplicity comes some flexibility. You can choose from a range of interest rates, and you may use one of three life expectancy tables. That flexibility should get you close to the payment you want unless you need an exceptionally large amount. And if you really want to use a higher interest rate than the guidelines suggest, you can always request a private letter ruling.

b. Disadvantages of the Fixed Amortization Method

The amortization example in the IRS guidelines, as well as in most of the favorable private letter rulings, computes a fixed payment—one that doesn't vary at all from year to year. Fixed payments, by definition, do not take into account recalculation of life expectancies, actual investment returns on your account, or inflation. The payments are constant. Consequently, if inflation surges, you might find yourself stuck with a payment that is too low for your needs and that doesn't reflect either the real returns on your investments or the changing economic climate.

However, recent private letter rulings give hope to taxpayers who want to modify their payments to keep up with inflation. In one case, for example, the taxpayer amortized his account balance anew each year, using 120% of the current federal midterm rate and his updated life expectancy. The IRS took the position that although the payment changed, the method of computing the payment was exactly the same each year. If you choose to do something like this, keep in mind that it doesn't follow the method precisely and therefore does not enjoy safe harbor protection.

3. Fixed Annuitization Method

Although the underlying arithmetic in the annuitization method is essentially the same as in the amortization method, the computation is performed simply by dividing your account balance by an annuity factor. The annuity factor is derived from a formula used mostly by actuaries.

As with the amortization method, once you determine your annual payment, it should remain the same every year, if you want to stay within the safe harbor.

The factor is based on certain interest rate and mortality assumptions. Those of us who are inexperienced with these calculations rely on actuaries and other number crunchers to produce tables we can use to look up the appropriate factor.

IRS regulations state that you may use any reasonable mortality table to come up with your annuity factor. The IRS has provided a safe harbor mortality table in Revenue Ruling 2002-62. As you might expect, this mortality table produces a smaller payment than many of the mortality tables used by insurance companies or even in other sections of the Tax Code.

Step 1: Choose an interest rate.
Your criterion for choosing an interest rate should be no different for this method than for the amortization method. Higher rates will produce higher payments; but the safe harbor is an interest rate that does not exceed 120% of the federal midterm rate.

Step 2: Find your annuity factor.
Although the IRS provided a safe-harbor mortality table, it didn't go so far as to actually compute the factors for us. Does that mean you need to hire your own actuary? Fortunately, at least one website, www.72t.net, has popped up to fill in this gap. When you go to the website, click on the tab "72(t) Distributions" then choose "Calculators" and then "72(t) Calculator." The calculator that comes up will not only calculate your payment under the annui-

tization method, but it will also allow you to choose another safe harbor method and compare the payment sizes.

Step 3: Determine your account balance.
You use the same guidelines for determining your account balance under the annuitization method as you would under the amortization method. You may use the balance as of December 31 of the year before the first distribution or you may use the balance as of the date within a reasonable period before the date of your first distribution.

Step 4: Compute the payment.
Divide the account balance by the annuity factor to arrive at your payment.

> EXAMPLE: You will turn 52 this year. You decide to begin substantially equal periodic payments from your IRA, and you plan to use your own single life expectancy. Your IRA account balance as of December 31 of the preceding year was $82,000.

> Step 1: You choose an interest rate of 7%, which is 120% of the federal midterm rate.

> Step 2: You use the annuity factor calculator you downloaded to come up with an annuity factor of 13.031.

> Step 3: Your account balance on December 31 of last year was $82,000.

> Step 4: Your periodic payment for this year, your first payment year, is $6,239 (Step 3 divided by Step 2; or $82,000 divided by 13.031).

 Only fixed payments are officially approved by the IRS. Bear in mind that although some private letter rulings sanction variable payments under the annuity factor method, only fixed payments have been approved officially by the IRS.

a. Advantages of the Fixed Annuitization Method

The only substantive difference between this method and the amortization method is that this method allows you to use mortality figures other than those provided by the IRS. Thus, theoretically, you have the flexibility to choose a table that accurately reflects your situation or produces a payment that better suits your needs.

If you choose a mortality table other than the IRS's, however, you fall outside the safe harbor.

b. Disadvantages of the Fixed Annuitization Method

The disadvantages of this are the same as those under the amortization method: Because your payment is fixed (if you use the safe harbor), it will not reflect a changing economy or the actual performance of your investments.

B. Implementing and Reporting Your Decision

Once you have selected your computation method, prepare a worksheet illustrating the computation. (See sample, below.) Keep it with your other important tax papers in case the IRS should ever ask you to explain the methodology you chose. Next, arrange with your plan administrator or IRA custodian to begin periodic payments. After that, your only remaining task is to report the payments on your tax return.

Sample Worksheet for Your Tax Files

Computation of Substantially Equal Periodic Payments Using Amortization Method
Annual distributions to be made each January 1, beginning in the year 2005.
December 31, 2004, value of IRA Account # 01234: $100,000.
My single life expectancy at age 52 in the year 2005 (from IRS Publication 590, Appendix C, Table 1): 32.3 years.
120% of the federal midterm rate for December 2004: 4.28%.
Annual payment ($100,000 amortized over 32.3 years at 4.28%): $5,770.

After the end of the year, you will receive a Form 1099-R from either the trustee of your plan or the custodian of your IRA. This form will report the total amount of distributions you received during the year. If the form shows a Code 2 in Box 7, you do not need to file any special forms with your tax return. (Code 2 means that the distribution qualifies for an exception to the early distribution tax.) You will simply report your periodic payments as ordinary income on your tax return. (See Chapter 3, Section B, for more information about Form 1099-R codes and the reporting requirements for IRA and qualified plan distributions.)

If Box 7 of Form 1099-R does not show Code 2, you must complete Part I of Form 5329 and file it with the rest of your tax return. Part I of Form 5329 asks you to report the total amount of your early distributions (on line 1) and the distributions that are eligible for an exception to the early distribution tax (line 2). Line 2 also provides a space for you to write in the exception number. The exception number for substantially equal periodic payments is 02. You can find exception codes in the instructions for Form 5329, which is in Appendix A.

EXAMPLE: At age 52, you began receiving substantially equal periodic payments of $2,000 per month from your IRA. After the end of the year, you receive your 1099-R from your IRA custodian, reporting distributions of

Sample: Form 5329 to Report Incorrectly Coded 1099-R

Form **5329**	**Additional Taxes on Qualified Plans** **(Including IRAs) and Other Tax-Favored Accounts**	OMB No. 1545-0203
	▶ Attach to Form 1040.	**2004**
Department of the Treasury Internal Revenue Service (99)	▶ See separate instructions.	Attachment Sequence No. **29**

Name of individual subject to additional tax. If married filing jointly, see instructions.	Your social security number

Fill in Your Address Only If You Are Filing This Form by Itself and Not With Your Tax Return	Home address (number and street), or P.O. box if mail is not delivered to your home	Apt. no.
	City, town or post office, state, and ZIP code	If this is an amended return, check here ▶ ☐

If you **only** owe the additional 10% tax on early distributions, you may be able to report this tax directly on Form 1040, line 59, without filing Form 5329. See the instructions for Form 1040, line 59.

Part I   **Additional Tax on Early Distributions**

Complete this part if you took a taxable distribution, before you reached age 59½, from a qualified retirement plan (including an IRA) or modified endowment contract (unless you are reporting this tax directly on Form 1040—see above). You may also have to complete this part to indicate that you qualify for an exception to the additional tax on early distributions or for certain Roth IRA distributions (see instructions).

1	Early distributions included in income. For Roth IRA distributions, see instructions	**1**	24,000
2	Early distributions included on line 1 that are not subject to the additional tax (see instructions). Enter the appropriate exception number from the instructions: _02_	**2**	24,000
3	Amount subject to additional tax. Subtract line 2 from line 1	**3**	0
4	**Additional tax.** Enter 10% (.10) of line 3. Include this amount on Form 1040, line 59	**4**	0

Caution: *If any part of the amount on line 3 was a distribution from a SIMPLE IRA, you may have to include 25% of that amount on line 4 instead of 10% (see instructions).*

Part II   **Additional Tax on Certain Distributions From Education Accounts**

Complete this part if you included an amount in income, on Form 1040, line 21, from a Coverdell education savings account (ESA) or a qualified tuition program (QTP).

5	Distributions included in income from Coverdell ESAs and QTPs	**5**	
6	Distributions included on line 5 that are not subject to the additional tax (see instructions) . .	**6**	
7	Amount subject to additional tax. Subtract line 6 from line 5	**7**	
8	**Additional tax.** Enter 10% (.10) of line 7. Include this amount on Form 1040, line 59	**8**	

Part III   **Additional Tax on Excess Contributions to Traditional IRAs**

Complete this part if you contributed more to your traditional IRAs for 2004 than is allowable or you had an amount on line 17 of your 2003 Form 5329.

9	Enter your excess contributions from line 16 of your 2003 Form 5329 (see instructions). If zero, go to line 15		**9**	
10	If your traditional IRA contributions for 2004 are less than your maximum allowable contribution, see instructions. Otherwise, enter -0-	**10**		
11	2004 traditional IRA distributions included in income (see instructions)	**11**		
12	2004 distributions of prior year excess contributions (see instructions)	**12**		
13	Add lines 10, 11, and 12		**13**	
14	Prior year excess contributions. Subtract line 13 from line 9. If zero or less, enter -0-		**14**	
15	Excess contributions for 2004 (see instructions)		**15**	
16	Total excess contributions. Add lines 14 and 15		**16**	
17	**Additional tax.** Enter 6% (.06) of the **smaller** of line 16 **or** the value of your traditional IRAs on December 31, 2004 (including 2004 contributions made in 2005). Include this amount on Form 1040, line 59 . . .		**17**	

Part IV   **Additional Tax on Excess Contributions to Roth IRAs**

Complete this part if you contributed more to your Roth IRAs for 2004 than is allowable or you had an amount on line 25 of your 2003 Form 5329.

18	Enter your excess contributions from line 24 of your 2003 Form 5329 (see instructions). If zero, go to line 23		**18**	
19	If your Roth IRA contributions for 2004 are less than your maximum allowable contribution, see instructions. Otherwise, enter -0- . . .	**19**		
20	2004 distributions from your Roth IRAs (see instructions)	**20**		
21	Add lines 19 and 20		**21**	
22	Prior year excess contributions. Subtract line 21 from line 18. If zero or less, enter -0-		**22**	
23	Excess contributions for 2004 (see instructions)		**23**	
24	Total excess contributions. Add lines 22 and 23		**24**	
25	**Additional tax.** Enter 6% (.06) of the **smaller** of line 24 **or** the value of your Roth IRAs on December 31, 2004 (including 2004 contributions made in 2005). Include this amount on Form 1040, line 59		**25**	

For Paperwork Reduction Act Notice, see page 5 of the instructions.   Cat. No. 13329Q   Form **5329** (2004)

$24,000 from your IRA. Box 7 incorrectly shows a Code 1. Consequently, you must complete Part I of Form 5329 and file it with the rest of your tax return. Lines 1-4 of Form 5329 should look like the sample form on the previous page.

C. Modifying the Payments

In general, the substantially equal periodic payment exception will save you from the early distribution tax only if you do not discontinue your payments or alter your computation method (other than in the approved ways, such as recalculation based on annual changes in life expectancy or account balance under the required minimum distribution method) once payments have begun. If you change your computation method, the early distribution tax can be applied retroactively to all distributions.

Fortunately, Congress didn't intend that your payments remain fixed until your death—just for a well-defined period of time. And, of course, there are exceptions to the no-modification rule that allow you to change the payments under certain circumstances, even if you don't satisfy the time-period requirement.

1. What Constitutes a Modification?

Once you establish a schedule and begin receiving substantially equal periodic payments, you may not modify them or discontinue them for five years or until you attain age 59½, whichever period is longer. For example, if you are age 49 when you begin receiving payments, you will be only 54 after five years. Therefore, you must continue the payments until you reach 59½. On the other hand, if you begin payments when you are 58, you must continue them for five full years, even though you will have passed the age 59½ milestone in the meantime.

The time-period requirement is quite literal. If you begin monthly payments at 49 and wish to stop at age 59½, you must take your last payment on or after the day you reach age 59½. You may not simply stop payments on January 1 of the year you turn 59½. Similarly, if you begin monthly payments on your 58th birthday, you must continue them at least until your 63rd birthday, when five full years will have passed.

As mentioned above, you may not prematurely discontinue or alter the size of the payments. Furthermore, if you transfer any additional amounts into the account or transfer any amounts to another retirement account, the IRS will consider those actions a modification of your payment. And of course, you may not withdraw additional amounts in excess of the periodic payment because the IRS sees that as a simple (and disallowed) increase in the amount of the annual payment.

2. Exceptions

There are several exceptions to the rule that payments cannot be modified.

a. Death

If you die before the required period has passed, your beneficiary may discontinue the payments.

b. Disability

If you become disabled, you are no longer tied to your periodic payment schedule, and subsequent distributions will not be subject to the early distribution tax. For this exception to apply, you must satisfy the IRS's definition of disabled. (See Chapter 3 for more information on the disability exception.)

c. Complete Depletion of Assets

If your account balance goes to zero while you are taking substantially equal periodic payments, the IRS will not penalize you for failing to continue the payments. Even the IRS recognizes that your investment losses should be penalty enough.

d. One-Time Change to Required Minimum Distribution Method

In the early years of the new millennium, taxpayers watched their retirement funds shrink in lockstep with the tumbling stock market. The IRS sought to offer some relief to those who had started periodic payments at the market peak and now faced a rapidly depleting retirement nest egg because of high periodic payments.

Had taxpayers chosen to use the required minimum distribution method at the outset, their payments would have fluctuated with their retirement plan account balance. If you now think you would be better off with that method, the IRS will allow anyone currently using either the amortization or the annuitization method to make a one-time permanent switch to the required minimum distribution method.

If you choose to switch, you may not switch back to either of the other methods. Furthermore, if you are currently using the required minimum distribution method, you may not switch to the amortization or the annuitization methods. Once you choose the required minimum distribution method, you are stuck with it.

Bear in mind that if you switch to the required minimum distribution method, you will almost certainly be reducing your payments, so make some calculations first to be sure you can get by on the smaller amounts.

3. Penalties for Modification

If you modify your payments in any but the approved ways before the required period has expired, then all distributions you have received since you initiated periodic payments will be subject to the early distribution tax. Because a modification invalidates the substantially equal periodic payment exception, all of the payments are treated (retroactively) as though they were normal discretionary distributions. Therefore, funds that were distributed before you turned 59½ are subject to an early distribution tax, but amounts received after age 59½ are not.

The cumulative payments for all years must be reported on your tax return for the year in which you first modify the payments. You must pay the taxes with that return. You must also pay interest on any early distribution taxes that would have been due from and after the year of the first periodic payment.

> **EXAMPLE 1:** You began taking substantially equal periodic payments of $6,000 per year on July 1 of the year you turned 49. You took the last one on July 1 of the year you turned 54. Then you stopped the payments altogether. Because you were required to continue payments until you reached age 59½, the substantially equal periodic payment exception became invalid in the year you turned 55

when you failed to take a payment. When you file the tax return for that year, you must report all distributions received and pay the early distribution tax with your tax return. The tax is 10% of all distributions that would have been subject to the early distribution tax if you had not been using the substantially equal periodic payment exception. The total of all distributions is $36,000 (six payments multiplied by $6,000). The early distribution tax is $3,600 ($36,000 x .10).

In addition, you will owe interest retroactively on the early distribution tax itself, as if the tax had been imposed on the due date of the tax return for the year in which you received the early distribution. In this example, your early distribution tax for each year was $600. You didn't pay any of it until the year you turned 55. For the distribution you took during the year you were 49, you owe six years of interest on the $600. For the distribution you took during the year you were 50, you owe five years of interest on $600. You get the idea. The rate used to compute the interest you owe is the IRS's standard rate on underpayment of tax. The rate is based on the applicable federal short-term rate and therefore changes from time to time. As of the second quarter of 2005, the rate for underpayment of tax was 6%.

EXAMPLE 2: Your birthday is August 1. You began taking substantially equal periodic payments of $6,000 per year on December 31 of the year you turned 58. You took an identical payment every December 31 through the year you turned 61 and then stopped. Because you were required to continue payments for five full years, you will be subject to an early distribution tax of 10% on distributions that would have been subject to the tax if you had never invoked the substantially equal periodic payment exception. You took four payments of $6,000, the last one in December of the year you turned 61. However, if you had not been using the substantially equal period payment exception, only the distributions you took in the years you turned 58 and 59 would have been subject to an early distribution tax. All other distributions occurred after age 59½ and thus would not have been subject to penalty. (Note that because your birthday is August 1, you didn't turn 59½ until the same year you turned 60, so the distribution you took in December of the year you turned 59 was an early distribution, because you weren't yet 59½.)

Your early distribution tax will be $1,200 ($6,000 x 2 years x .10), plus interest.

Key Tax Code Sections, Regulations, and Notices

§ 72(t)(2)(A)(iv)
Substantially Equal Period Payment Exception

§ 72(t)(3)(B)
Separation From Service Requirement for Age 55 Exception

§ 1.72-9
IRS Life Expectancy Tables

§ 402(c)(4)
Prohibition Against Rollover of Periodic Payment

§ 1.401(a)(9)
Regulations for Minimum Distribution Calculation

Revenue Ruling 2002-62
IRS Guidelines for Computing Substantially Equal Payments

Chapter 5

Required Distributions:
Taking Money Out When You Have To

Who Should Read Chapter 5

➡️ This chapter gives an overview of situations in which you are required to take money out of your retirement plan or IRA. Chapter 6 provides the details you will need to compute required distributions during your lifetime. Chapters 7 and 8 provide the information your heirs will need to compute distributions after your death.

*S*omeone once said that the government's strategy for encouraging people to use their retirement money is a lot like herding cattle through a gate. If a cow heads off to the left of the gate, a cattle prod nudges her back on track. Similarly, if you wander off the retirement trail and withdraw your funds too early, you're brought up short with an early distribution tax. If our proverbial cow meanders too far to the right, she receives another painful poke, just as you are hit with another penalty if you wait too long to withdraw your retirement money. That penalty—for waiting too long—is the focus of this chapter.

To avoid being penalized for delaying distributions, you must comply with what are called the required distribution rules. Those rules mandate that you take a minimum amount from your retirement plan each year, beginning in the year you turn 70½ or, under certain circumstances, in the year you retire if you work past age

70½. The minimum amount is calculated according to a formula in the income tax regulations. You may take more than the minimum, but you may not take less. If you do take less, you will be fined 50% of the amount that should have come out of your plan but didn't—the shortfall, in penalty parlance.

The required distribution rules evolved from Congress's desire that you use up your retirement funds during your own retirement, instead of passing the assets on to your heirs. The law presents you with a date by which you must start withdrawing money from your retirement plan. It also answers questions such as the following: What happens if you die before the date you are supposed to begin distributions? Does the law provide income tax relief to your heirs? Is your beneficiary allowed to defer distributions from your plan even though the funds were never intended for his or her retirement? Does your spouse have special privileges?

As if those issues didn't complicate matters enough, there is a flip side to the premature death issue: What happens if you die after you have started receiving required distributions but before you have used up all your retirement money? Does this change anything? Are your heirs given relief in this situation? And, again, does your spouse have special privileges?

The required distribution rules attempt to address all of these questions and more. In this chapter we offer a summary of these rules.

Helpful Terms

Beneficiary. The person or entity entitled to receive the benefits from insurance or from trust property, such as a retirement plan or IRA, usually after the insured or the owner of the property dies.

Deferral period. The number of years over which distributions from a retirement plan or IRA can be spread.

Distribution. A payout of property (such as shares of stock) or cash from a retirement plan or IRA to the participant or a beneficiary.

Grandfather provision. A part of a new law that exempts an individual or entity from the new law and allows the individual or entity to use the old law or special transitional laws.

TDA or Tax-deferred annuity. Many university professors and public school employees are covered by a TDA, which is a retirement annuity plan for public charities or public schools. These retirement plans are usually funded with individual annuity contracts purchased from an insurance company. Retirement benefits are frequently paid as a monthly annuity for life.

Waiver. Intentional dismissal, as of a penalty.

A. Required Distributions During Your Lifetime

You don't have to worry about taking required distributions from your own retirement plan until the year in which you turn 70½. At that time, however, you must start taking distributions under one of the following two scenarios:

- You may withdraw everything by your required beginning date, or RBD, which for most people is April 1 of the year after turning 70½, but for some people will be April 1 of the year after they retire. (See Chapter 6, Section A, for more information about determining your RBD.)

- Alternatively, you may distribute your retirement plan money over a period of years. Most people will use the Uniform Lifetime Table (see Table III in Appendix B) to determine the number of years over which they may spread distributions. If your spouse is your beneficiary and is more than ten years younger than you are, however, you will use a different and more favorable table called the Joint Life and Last Survivor Table. (See Table II in Appendix B.)

When faced with those two distribution options, few people would choose the first—to distribute the entire amount of their retirement plan at once—because of the income tax implications. A whopping distribution all in one year could put you in the top tax bracket for that year, allowing the government to take a huge tax bite out of your nest egg.

In contrast, the second option allows people to spread distributions over a period of years, thereby keeping their tax burden lower. As an added bonus, the second option is flexible: If people want to take only the minimum required amount, they can, but they also have the option of taking more money out when they need it.

Chapter 6 describes the steps involved in determining your required distributions during your lifetime.

B. Death Before Required Beginning Date

If you die before your RBD, your beneficiary generally may spread distributions from your retirement plan over his or her life expectancy.

If your retirement plan requires or permits it, your beneficiary might also take distributions according to the five-year rule. This is almost always a less favorable method, so if your beneficiary has a choice, he or she should probably choose another method.

Under the five-year rule, your retirement plan assets must be completely distributed by December 31 of the year containing the fifth anniversary of your death. The law does not prescribe a distribution method.

In order to mitigate the tax impact, your beneficiary might choose to take money out of the plan in annual installments over that five-year period. This strategy is perfectly acceptable as long as the plan administrator will allow it. But the plan has the authority to determine the distribution method during the five-year period. Some plans will permit installment payments; others will require a lump sum payment.

If you have no beneficiary, the five-year rule is mandatory.

If your beneficiary is your spouse, he or she has some additional privileges. After your death, your spouse may defer distributions from your retirement plan until you would have been 70½. At that point, the distributions will be spread over your spouse's own life expectancy. Alternatively, your spouse can roll over your retirement plan (whether a qualified plan or an IRA) into an IRA or plan of his or her own. Your spouse would then name new beneficiaries and begin distributions in the year he or she turns 70½.

If there are other beneficiaries. If your spouse is not the sole beneficiary but is instead one of several, then he or she might lose some of these special privileges.

Chapter 7 describes the effect of premature death on your retirement distributions, and it includes a detailed explanation of the life expectancy rule, the five-year rule, and the special privileges accorded a surviving spouse.

C. Death After Required Beginning Date

If you survive to your RBD, you must begin taking required distributions as described in Section A, above. If there is still some money in your retirement plan when you die, your beneficiary must continue to take distributions every year—generally based on his or her life expectancy. Your beneficiary can elect to receive more than the prescribed amount, but not less.

If you did not name a beneficiary, the assets will generally be distributed to your estate over your own remaining life expectancy as of the year of your death.

Some special rules apply if your spouse is your sole beneficiary. For example, your spouse may take distributions as though he or she were a nonspouse beneficiary. Alternatively, your spouse can roll over your retirement plan into an IRA or plan of his or her own. After the rollover, the retirement assets belong to the spouse, and the required distribution rules apply as though the spouse had been the original owner.

Chapter 8 explains your beneficiary's options if you die after you begin receiving required distributions.

D. Special Rules for Tax-Deferred Annuities

If you were a participant in a tax-deferred annuity (also known as a TDA or 403(b) plan) established before 1987, some special required distribution rules apply. Specifically, all contributions and earnings added to your account after 1986 are subject to the same required distribution rules described in Sections A, B, and C, above.

But the amount in your account on December 31, 1986 was grandfathered under an older set of rules and is not subject to the current required distribution rules.

Because of this grandfathering, when it comes time for you to start required distributions from your TDA, you may subtract your pre-1987 balance and compute your required distribution on the difference. You may continue to subtract the pre-1987 balance when computing required distributions every year until you reach age 75, at which time your entire account, including the pre-1987 balance, will be subject to current required distribution rules.

Grandfathering rules are strict. Although you may exclude the pre-1987 balance when computing required distributions, you may not exclude any subsequent earnings attributable to the grandfathered amount. The grandfathered portion is a fixed dollar amount—the precise balance of your account on December 31, 1986.

EXAMPLE: On December 31, 1986 the balance in your TDA was $130,000. You are now retired and will turn 70½ this year. The total value of your account is $220,000. Because you are not yet 75, you may exclude $130,000 (your pre-1987 balance) when you compute your first required distribution, which means the required distribution will be based on an account balance of $90,000 ($220,000 – $130,000). You may use this approach until the year you turn 75. From that year forward, you must use the total value of your account when computing your required distribution.

All required distributions you take before age 75 are deemed to come from your post-1986 accumulation. Any amount you withdraw in excess of the required amount, however, is deemed to come from the pre-1987 portion.

EXAMPLE: As in the previous example, your pre-1987 account balance is $130,000, and your post-1986 accumulation is $90,000. You compute your first required distribution to be $5,625, but decide to take an extra $5,000 to pay some unexpected medical expenses. Your total distribution for the year is $10,625. The minimum required amount of $5,625 is deemed to come from your post-1986 account (the $90,000 portion). The remaining $5,000 is deemed to come from your pre-1987 accumulation. Therefore, next year when you subtract your pre-1987 balance before computing your required distribution, you will subtract $125,000 (which is $130,000 – $5,000), instead of $130,000.

 Be careful not to forfeit your option to defer. If at any time before you reach age 75 you roll over your entire TDA into an IRA, then you forfeit the option to defer until age 75 distributions on your pre-1987 accumulation. Similarly, if you roll over your TDA assets to another TDA (that is, you, yourself, take the money from one TDA and move it to another), you lose the deferral option. To avoid this, simply transfer the funds (trustee to trustee) from the first TDA to the second. Transfers to an IRA don't work, though.

In addition, if the trustee or custodian of your TDA at any time ceases to keep accurate records of the year-end balances of your grandfathered and nongrandfathered portions, the entire balance of your TDA will be subject to current required distribution rules and you will no longer have the option of deferring distributions on your pre-1987 accumulation.

E. Special Rules for Roth IRAs

Roth IRAs conform to some of the required distribution rules described in Sections A, B, and C, above, but not others. Specifically, you are not required to take lifetime distributions. But if you die leaving a balance in your Roth IRA, the post-death rules introduced in Section B, above, and described fully in Chapter 7, will apply whether you die before or after your RBD. Chapter 9 contains a detailed discussion of the Roth IRA rules.

⚠️ **Roth 401(k) plans are hybrids.** A Roth 401(k) plan is treated like a traditional 401(k) plan for purposes of lifetime required distributions. In other words, Roth 401(k) plans are not exempt from lifetime required distributions. However, if you roll over your Roth 401(k) plan into a Roth IRA, either at retirement or when you leave your job, then once the assets are in the Roth IRA (and no longer in the Roth 401(k) plan), the Roth IRA rules would apply and no distributions would be required during your lifetime. Because Roth 401(k) plans are new, it is not clear whether this strategy will survive when the final regulations are written, but currently it's available.

F. Penalty

The penalty for failing to take a required distribution is one of the worst in all the Tax Code: 50% of the shortfall. Some call it onerous, others call it Draconian, but everyone calls it punitive. If you were required to take a $10,000 distribution but took only $4,000, you would owe the IRS $3,000 for your mistake—50% of the $6,000 you didn't take.

And don't think your failure to take a distribution will go unnoticed. The IRS requires trustees and custodians of IRAs to identify on IRS Form 5498 those IRAs for which a minimum distribution is required.

1. Failure to Distribute

When meting out punishment for failure to comply with a rule or regulation, enforcers of the law sometimes attempt to discern your intent so that the punishment better fits the crime. For example, in the case of a required distribution violation, did you make an inadvertent error? A once-in-a-blue-moon blunder? Or are your failures chronic? Perhaps you attempted to cash in on a perceived loophole? The more egregious the violation, the more severe the penalty is likely to be.

a. Innocent Blunders

If you simply forget to take your required distribution one year, the 50% penalty is probably the worst you'll face. And as painful as it is, at least it hits only once. So even if you don't correct the shortfall the next year, the excise tax will not be assessed again with respect to the first transgression.

> EXAMPLE: You forgot to take your required distribution of $6,000 for the year 2004. In 2005 you computed your required distribution for 2005 and withdrew it, but you still hadn't discovered your error for the year 2004. Your mind cleared sometime in the year 2006 and you withdrew the $6,000 for 2004 along with your distribution for the year 2006. You must pay a penalty of $3,000 (50% of $6,000) plus interest

for the year 2004 mistake. However, you only have to pay it once, even though the mistake remained uncorrected through 2005. (See Section 2, below, for information on how to report the distribution and penalty.)

Once you stumble and are faced with an unavoidable penalty, you might think there is nothing to be gained by distributing the required amount. But here are two good reasons to withdraw it:

- Only if you correct your mistake can you hope to obtain an official waiver of the penalty. (See Section G, below, for more information about waivers.)
- If you don't correct the shortfall, you risk disqualifying the plan, which would force a total distribution of the account and loss of all future tax-deferred growth. The Tax Code states that a plan will not be a qualified plan unless it complies with the required distribution rules. Arguably you will not be in compliance for as long as a shortfall remains uncorrected.

b.   Chronic Errors

Make no mistake, the IRS will look askance at the taxpayer who habitually fails to take proper required distributions, whether those distributions are late, incorrect, or nonexistent. Once a problem becomes chronic, not only will the IRS's sympathy wane, but plan disqualification becomes a serious risk.

c.   Ineligible Rollovers

There is one more way for you or the trustee of your retirement plan to mess up your required distribution. You might roll it over. Required distributions from plans and IRAs are not eligible for rollover. (See Chapter 2 for more information about rollovers.) If they were, you would be able to withdraw your required distribution each year and roll what you don't need into another plan or IRA. That strategy might fit in with your financial and estate planning goals, but it flies in the face of Congressional intent, which is to encourage you to deplete your retirement account during your retirement, instead of preserving the assets for your heirs.

When Congress enacted the no-rollover rule, lawmakers recognized the rule would be difficult to enforce without help. Consequently, income tax regulations were fashioned to push the rule a step further, tacking on penalties for ineligible rollovers and requiring trustees of qualified plans to lend a hand in enforcement. The regulations for IRAs and TDAs are slightly different from those for qualified plans and qualified annuities.

i.   Qualified Plans and Qualified Annuities

If you decide to roll over an amount from one qualified plan to another qualified plan or to an IRA during a year you are required to take a distribution, then only the amount that exceeds the required distribution is eligible for rollover. The amount of the required distribution itself must be distributed to you, and if it is not, it must be included in your taxable income for the year anyway.

> EXAMPLE: When you retired, you left your 401(k) assets with your employer. When you turned 70½ several years ago, your employer began distributing your minimum required distributions to you. On January 1 of this year, you decide to roll over your remaining 401(k) account balance into an IRA so that you can manage your own investments. The balance of your 401(k) is $500,000. Your minimum distribution for the current year is $40,000. When you receive your 401(k) distribution, you are permitted to roll over only $460,000, because your required distribution for the current year is not eligible for rollover. If you roll over the entire $500,000 anyway, you must still report $40,000 of income on your tax return as though you had not rolled over the required distribution. And there could be other penalties, as well.

If you roll over an ineligible amount into an IRA, the consequences extend beyond including the ineligible portion in your income for the year. The ineligible amount is considered an excess contribution to the IRA. If it is not promptly withdrawn, it will be subject to excess contribution penalties

in the year of the contribution (rollover) and again each year the excess remains uncorrected. (See Subsection d, below, for more about excess contributions.)

To help ensure that the required distribution is not rolled over, the regulations require trustees of retirement plans to compute required distributions for all participants. There is good reason for placing this burden on a trustee: The portion of any distribution that exceeds the participant's required distribution is eligible for rollover. When a trustee distributes any amount that is eligible for rollover, the trustee must comply with a host of procedural rules and regulations related to withholding, disclosure, and participant notification of tax options. In order to comply with these administrative rules, the trustee must determine whether or not some or all of a distribution is eligible for rollover. That in turn requires computation of the required distribution.

 Required distributions are not only ineligible for rollover, they are also ineligible for transfer. This means that a trustee must compute the minimum required distribution not only during a rollover, but also when benefits are being transferred by the trustee directly to a new plan. Consequently, the trustee must distribute the required amount to the participant either at the time of transfer or segregate the amount and distribute it before the required distribution deadline for the year.

ii. IRAs and TDAs

Required distributions from IRAs and TDAs also are ineligible for rollover, but compliance can be a little tricky. If you have more than one IRA (whether traditional, SEP or SIMPLE IRA), you must compute the required distribution for each one. You are then permitted to withdraw the total required amount from one or more of the IRAs. This aggregation rule applies to TDAs as well. So if you have more than one TDA, you may calculate the required distribution for each and withdraw the total from only one. Note, however, that you may not mix and match. You may not calculate a required distribution from your IRA and withdraw it from your TDA, or vice versa.

> **EXAMPLE:** You have two IRAs and a TDA. Your required distribution from IRA #1 is $3,000 and from IRA #2 is $2,500. Your required distribution from your TDA is $4,000. You may total the required distributions from your two IRAs and withdraw the entire $5,500 from either IRA #1 or IRA #2 (or part from both). But the $4,000 required distribution from the TDA must be distributed from the TDA, not from one of the IRAs.

Inherited IRAs and inherited TDAs. You are not permitted to aggregate inherited IRAs and inherited TDAs with your own IRAs and TDAs for required distribution purposes. For example, assume you have an IRA to which you have made contributions over the years. You also have an IRA that you inherited from your father. When the time comes to take required distributions, you must compute the distribution for each IRA separately and withdraw the required amount from the respective IRA.

Aggregation does not apply to qualified plans or qualified annuities. For example, if you have more than one 401(k) plan, you must compute the distribution for each and withdraw the required amount from the respective plan.

Because of this aggregation option for IRAs, the IRS cannot really require IRA custodians to distribute to you the required amount before moving the funds. After all, what if you had already computed and withdrawn the requisite amount from another IRA—or you intend to do so? Because of this potential problem, the IRS relaxed the IRA transfer rules a little. But just a little. If you transfer your funds from one IRA to another in a direct custodian-to-custodian transfer, then the IRS will not require the custodian to withhold (and distribute to you) a required distribution from that IRA. The entire IRA can be transferred.

But if you roll over the funds instead (that is, you, yourself, take the funds out of one IRA and deposit them in another IRA), it is a different story. The law says required amounts cannot be rolled over. Therefore, the custodian would have to withhold a computed required distribution from the IRA funds you want to roll over, even though you intend to take—or already did take—the required amount from another IRA.

d. Excess Contributions

One of the most intimidating characteristics of the tax law is that penalties sometimes seem to come out of nowhere. One small mistake can turn a manageable tax liability into a financial albatross.

A rollover into a plan or IRA of an amount that is not permitted to be rolled over can lead to catastrophe. Unless the mistake is corrected promptly, usually by the filing deadline for the tax return, the IRS will consider the rollover an excess contribution to the plan or IRA. Excess contributions are subject to a penalty—6% for excess contributions to an IRA or 10% for excess contributions to a qualified plan. This penalty is assessed in addition to any other penalties or taxes that might apply, and it will be imposed every year until the excess is removed.

> EXAMPLE: In 2005 you received a required distribution of $6,000 from your 401(k) plan and rolled it over into an IRA. Because required distributions are ineligible for rollover, the $6,000 is an excess contribution. You were unaware of the problem until the IRS audited your 2005 tax return

in late 2007. You removed the $6,000 in December 2007. The $6,000 must be reported as income on your tax return for the year 2007. In addition, you will owe an excess contribution penalty of $360 (6% of $6,000) for each of the years 2005 and 2006. Because you distributed the excess before filing your 2007 tax return, you will owe no penalty for the year 2007.

2. Reporting the Penalty

If you owe a penalty for failing to take your required distribution, you must complete IRS Form 5329 (you can find a copy of this form in Appendix A) and include it when you file your tax return. If you have already filed your tax return for the year, then you must file an amended tax return for the year of the error and pay the penalty plus interest.

> EXAMPLE: You began taking required distributions from your IRA in 2000 and took them regularly until 2003. In 2004, you inherited some money, so you didn't need to draw on the IRA for living expenses as you had in the past. Consequently, you simply forgot to take your required distribution of $6,000. In fact, you forgot to take your 2003 distribution, too, which would have been $6,500. Finally, in February of 2005, you realized your error.

For 2004, you must file an amended tax return and include a completed Form 5329. You must also pay a penalty of $3,000 (50% of $6,000), plus interest, for which the IRS will bill you.

For 2005, because you have not yet passed the filing deadline for your tax return, you may simply file as usual by April 15, 2006 and include a completed Form 5329. Along with any regular income tax you owe, you will owe a penalty of $3,250 (50% of $6,500). You will not have to pay interest, though, as long as the tax return and payment are filed on time.

Finally, you should correct the distribution errors by withdrawing the required amounts for both 2004 and 2005. If you correct the problem in 2006, you must report the distributions of $6,000 (for 2003) and $6,500 (for 2005) on your 2006 tax return. In addition, you will have to take a required distribution for 2006 and include it as income on your tax return.

In general, you have until December 31 to take your required distribution for any given year. If you miss the deadline, you must pay the penalty when you file your tax return (or pay the penalty with an amended return). The one exception to the December 31 deadline is the first year of required distributions. A grace period gives you until April 1 of the following year to withdraw your first required distribution. (See Chapter 6, Section A, for more information about when distributions must begin.) Thus, if you don't take a distribution by December 31 of the first year of required distributions, you won't owe a penalty unless you miss the April 1 deadline as well. If you happen to miss that one, too, you must pay the penalty, but you would pay it when you file your tax return for the year containing the April 1 distribution deadline.

EXAMPLE: You turned 70½ in 2005, so your required beginning date (with the grace period) was April 1, 2006, although your first distribution year is officially 2005. This means that you were supposed to take your first required distribution by April 1, 2006, and your second distribution by December 31, 2006. Unfortunately, you forgot to take any distribution at all until January 2007. You will owe penalties for 2005 and 2006, because you missed the deadline for both required distributions. But because both distribution deadlines were in 2006, you can simply complete a Form 5329 and attach it to your tax return for the 2006 tax year (which is due by April 15, 2007). At that time, you must pay the 50% penalty on the required distribution shortfalls for both 2005 and 2006. You do not have to file an amended return for 2007, because the distribution for 2005 did not have to be made until April 1, 2006.

G. Waiver

Mistakes happen. Even Congress knows it. That's why a waiver has been written into the penalty provisions of the required distribution law.

1. Terms of the Waiver

There are four short paragraphs in the Tax Code section that assesses a penalty for delaying distributions from your retirement plan. But the entire fourth paragraph is devoted to a waiver of the penalty. It says that if you demonstrate that your failure to withdraw the proper amount was due to reasonable error and you are taking steps to correct the shortfall, the penalty may be waived. "May" is the operative word, though. The IRS is not required to waive the penalty; it simply has the authority to do so.

 Sometimes, the penalty will be waived automatically. Remember: The required distribution rules apply to inherited plans and IRAs, too. If a beneficiary inherits a retirement plan, he or she must generally take distributions over his or her life expectancy beginning in the year after the original participant's death (the life expectancy rule). But if the beneficiary fails to take the first distribution on time, he or she can fall back on the five-year rule to avoid a penalty. The five-year rule requires that all assets be distributed by December 31 of the year containing the fifth anniversary of the participant's death. To fall back on the five-year rule, the plan must permit the five-year rule as an option. If it does and if the beneficiary chooses to use it, the penalty for failing to take a distribution under the life expectancy rule will be waived automatically. (See Chapter 7 for more information about the life expectancy rule and the five-year rule.)

2. Requesting a Waiver

To request a waiver, you must first explain how the mistake came about. Perhaps you didn't understand the computation formula. Or maybe you wrote a letter to the custodian of your plan requesting a distribution, but you broke your leg on the way to the post office to mail the letter and forgot to drop the letter in a mail box after you were released from the hospital.

Your excuse must accompany a description of the steps you have taken to correct the mistake. For example, you might report that as soon as you discovered you didn't take the appropriate amount from your IRA, you asked the custodian to distribute the funds, which the custodian did the following week.

These explanations must be attached to a completed Form 5329 and filed along with the rest of your return at tax time. If you are submitting an amended return, send it in right away. There is one catch: Even though you intend to request a waiver, you must still pay the 50% penalty and mail it with your tax return. If the IRS accepts your explanation and approves the waiver, you will receive a refund.

The IRS has been generous with these waivers, so don't assume your excuse is too lame to pass muster. For example, taxpayers have argued that they didn't understand the formula for computing the required distribution or that they made an arithmetic error. One taxpayer claimed that he signed the request for a distribution but forgot to mail it to his custodian. In all of those cases, the taxpayers had corrected their mistakes by the time they reported the error to the IRS, and they were all granted waivers.

If you have a plausible explanation for your error and you have taken steps to correct it, you stand a good chance of obtaining a waiver. Even the IRS is aware that 50% is a stiff penalty and is more interested in curbing abuse than punishing the computationally challenged. But if you consistently fail to take appropriate distributions, or if the IRS discovers your mistake during an audit, the IRS is likely to be less forgiving.

Key Tax Code Sections
§ 401(a)(9)
Required Distributions From Qualified Plans
§ 402(e)(4)
Eligible Rollover From Qualified Plan
§ 408(d)(3)(E)
Ineligible Rollover From IRA
§ 4974
50% Excise Tax on Required Distributions
§ 1.403(b)-2
Treatment of Pre-1987 Accumulation in TDA

Chapter 6

Required Distributions During Your Lifetime

Who Should Read Chapter 6

➡ Everyone will need to read this chapter. It tells you precisely when you are required to begin taking money out of your own retirement plan or IRA, how you compute the amount to withdraw, and what other decisions you must make at that time.

*C*omedians and accountants have long pondered the origin of the numbers that appear in the Tax Code—the ones that don't seem to make any sense. Why must we start taking money out of our retirement plans at age 70½? Why not 70? Or even 71? Some of us like to think Congress has a sense of humor, although cynics believe there's a conspiracy to keep the Tax Code complex. More likely, it's the result of a compromise.

Whatever its history, 70½ has become an important milestone; it's the age when most people must crack open their retirement nest eggs, even if they don't want to. Before age 59½, you have to worry about penalties for tapping your retirement money too early. (See Chapter 3 for information on the early distribution penalty.) Age 59½ to 70½ is the penalty-free zone. You can take distributions any time you want—or not—without penalty. But once you reach 70½, you are required to begin taking distributions.

Some or all of your retirement plan nest egg might be paid to you as an annuity after you retire, which means you will receive your money in installments—usually in the form of monthly payments. The payments might continue for a fixed number of years (a term certain) but more often will be spread over your lifetime. Annuities are a common form of payment if you were covered by your employer's defined benefit plan while you were working.

Annuity payments must also satisfy the required distribution rules described in this chapter. Annuity plan administrators are aware of the distribution rules, and the plans are generally structured to ensure that your payments satisfy the requirements; however, ultimately the responsibility is yours.

If, instead of an annuity, some or all of your nest egg is in an IRA or another type of retirement plan account, then when it is time for you to begin required distributions it is your responsibility to compute and withdraw the appropriate amount each year.

In this chapter, we discuss in detail the rules governing required distributions that you must take during your lifetime.

Helpful Terms

Annuity. A contract, sold by an insurance company, that promises to make monthly, quarterly, semiannual, or annual payments for life or for a specified period of time.

Contingent beneficiary. A person or entity who is entitled to receive the benefits of a retirement plan or IRA only if and when a specific event occurs, such as the death of a primary beneficiary.

Distribution. A payout of property (such as shares of stock) or cash from a retirement plan or IRA to the participant or a beneficiary.

Irrevocable trust. A trust that cannot be changed or terminated by the person who created it. Once assets are transferred to an irrevocable trust, the assets are subject to the terms of trust for as long as the trust exists.

Applicable distribution period (ADP). The divisor used for determining a required distribution. An account balance is divided by an ADP to arrive at the required distribution for a given year.

Primary beneficiary. A person or entity entitled to receive benefits from a retirement plan or IRA upon the death of the original participant.

Revocable trust. A trust whose terms allow the creator of the trust to alter its provisions, cancel it, or remove some or all of the property from the trust and return the property to the creator.

Term certain or period certain. A fixed, identifiable period, such as a specific number of years. For example, a retirement plan that is distributable over a term certain of 20 years must be completely liquidated (distributed) after 20 years.

A. Required Beginning Date

The absolute deadline for taking your first required distribution (withdrawal) from your retirement plan is called your "required beginning date," or RBD. If you are the original owner of your retirement plan (as opposed to the beneficiary of someone else's plan), then your RBD is April 1 of the year after you turn 70½.

EXAMPLE: You were born January 1, 1934. You will turn 70½ on July 1, 2004. Your RBD is April 1, 2005.

Your RBD marks the deadline for taking the required distribution for your first distribution year only. For all subsequent years, the deadline is December 31.

You can defer your RBD for an employer plan if you work past age 70½. In that case, your RBD for that particular plan is April 1 of the year after you retire, no matter what age you are.

⚠ Self-employed people beware.
This special deferral option is not available if you own 5% or more of the business that sponsors the retirement plan, which of course includes virtually all self-employed individuals.

You generally cannot defer your RBD for any IRAs you have. There are exceptions for people who are covered by a federal or state government plan or by a church plan. (A church plan is one maintained by a church for church employees. This would include any type of religious organization or house of worship, as long as the organization qualifies as a tax-exempt organization.) If neither of those situations applies, the RBD for an IRA is April 1 of the year after you turn 70½, even if you continue to work.

As you can see, it's possible to have more than one RDB if you work beyond age 70½—one for an employer plan and one for an IRA.

📖 If you inherit a retirement plan.
You must use a different set of rules to determine your RBD for plans that you inherit. We discuss those rules in Chapters 7 and 8.

Because April 1 of the year after age 70½ is the RBD for most people, that is the date we will use for discussion purposes in this chapter.

1. First Year

You must withdraw at least the required minimum amount from your retirement plan account by your RBD or you will face a stiff penalty. To satisfy this requirement, you may count all distributions that take place between January 1 of the year you turn 70½ and April 1 of the following year (which is your RBD). In other words, you have 15 months to complete your first distribution.

Although you are permitted to take the required distribution in one big chunk, you don't have to. You can take it out as you need it, for example in monthly installments, as long as you have removed the minimum required amount for the first year by your RBD.

It is important to remember that amounts distributed before January 1 of the year you turn 70½ do not count toward your first required distribution, nor do amounts distributed after your RBD.

> **EXAMPLE 1:** You turn 70½ in 2006, and 2006 is your first distribution year. Although you were not required to take money out of your IRA in 2005, you took $20,000 on October 1, 2005, to buy a car. In 2006, your required minimum distribution is $10,000. You may not count the $20,000 you took in 2005 toward your 2006 required distribution.

EXAMPLE 2: You turn 70½ in 2006, and your RBD is April 1, 2007. Your required distribution for 2006 is $10,000. You decide to wait until 2007 to take the distribution for your first year. You take $9,000 on March 1, 2007, and another $1,000 on May 1, 2007. Because the $1,000 that you took on May 1 is after your RBD, you cannot use it as part of your required distributions. Because you are $1,000 short of the amount required to be distributed, you will owe the IRS penalties on the $1,000 shortfall.

2. Second Year and Beyond

For the second and all future distribution years, you must take at least the required amount out of your retirement account between January 1 and December 31. There are no more three-month grace periods.

⚠ Waiting can be costly. If you decide to wait until your RBD (which is April 1 of your second distribution year) to take your first required distribution, you must still take the full required distribution for the second year by December 31. That means you would have to take two required distributions in the same year, which could push you into a higher income tax bracket. For example, let's say you turn 70½ in 2006, which is your first distribution year, and your RBD is April 1, 2007. Your required distribution for your first distribution year is $20,000

and for the second year is $22,000. You are single and have no other taxable income. You also use the standard deduction. If you take your first distribution in 2006 and the second in 2007, the tax rate for both distributions is 15%. If you take both distributions in the same year, however, your gross income will be $42,000. At that level, some of your distributions will be taxed at a 28% rate.

Again, you may take the distribution in bits and pieces during the 12-month period, or you may take the entire amount on December 31. If you happen to take more than the required amount in one year, which is permissible, you may not count the excess toward your required distributions for the next year (or beyond).

EXAMPLE: Your required distribution for your second distribution year is $10,000 and for your third distribution year is $12,000. If you take $16,000 in your second distribution year, you may not apply the extra $6,000 to your third distribution year and withdraw only $6,000. Instead you must withdraw the full $12,000 during the third year.

B. Computing the Required Amount

To compute your required distribution for a given year, simply divide your account balance by what the IRS calls the "applicable distribution period," or ADP (see Section 2, below). The resulting number is the minimum amount you must withdraw from the account for that year.

You must compute this required minimum distribution separately for each retirement plan that you have. When it comes to actually withdrawing the computed amounts, however, you have some flexibility. For example, you may be able to withdraw the total amount from only one account. (See Section 4, below, for more information about this strategy.)

1. Determining the Account Balance

According to tax regulations, the account balance for computing your required distribution each year is determined as of "the last valuation date in the calendar year before the distribution calendar year." For the vast majority of people who are computing their own required distributions, this would be December 31 of the year before the distribution year.

If your retirement assets are in a qualified plan when you begin required distributions instead of in an IRA, however, it is possible that the plan itself specifies a date other than December 31 for valuing the plan assets and computing require distributions. Nevertheless, we will use December 31 for discussion purposes in this book.

EXAMPLE: You turn 70½ in 2006. To compute the required distribution for your first distribution year (2006), you use your account balance as of Decem-

ber 31, 2005. To compute the required distribution for the year 2007, you look at your account balance as of December 31, 2006, and so on.

Recall that you are permitted to take your first required distribution in the year after you turn 70½, as long as you take it on or before your RBD (which is April 1 of the year after you turn 70½). Deferring your first distribution, however, does not alter the date for determining the appropriate account balance. For example, if you turn 70½ in 2006 and decide to take your first distribution in March of 2007, you must still use your account balance as of December 31, 2005, to compute the amount of your first distribution.

2. Determining the Applicable Distribution Period

Once you have determined the appropriate account balance to use for a particular distribution year, you must divide it by the applicable distribution period, or ADP, to arrive at your required distribution.

a. First Year

To find your ADP for your first distribution year, you must use one of two tables provided by the IRS. Most people will use what the IRS calls the Uniform Lifetime Table (Table III in Appendix B), but some people will be able to use the Joint Life and Last Survivor Table (Table II in Appendix B). The table you use depends on whom you designate as your beneficiary.

(See Section C, below, for more information about designating a beneficiary.)

i. General Rule

The vast majority of people will use the Uniform Lifetime Table to find their ADP. The only time you would not do so is when your spouse is the sole beneficiary of your retirement account and is more than ten years younger than you are. (See Subsection ii, below.)

In all other cases, you will use the Uniform Lifetime Table. Thus, if your beneficiary is a child, grandchild, friend, charity, your estate, or a spouse who is not more than ten years younger than you are, you will use the Uniform Lifetime Table. And if you haven't yet named a beneficiary, you will still use the Uniform Lifetime Table.

To find the ADP for your first distribution year, you determine your age as of your birthday in the year you turn 70½. If that age is 70, then find the ADP next to age 70 in the Uniform Lifetime Table (Table III in Appendix B). That number is 27.4.

If your age is 71 on your birthday in the year you turn 70½, the ADP from the table is 26.5.

⚠ It depends on when your birthday is. You are not always age 70 in your first distribution year. If your birthday falls after June 30, you will turn 70½ in the same year in which you.turn 71. In that case, you must use age 71 when looking up the ADP for your first distribution year.

ii. Spouse More Than Ten Years Younger

If your beneficiary is your spouse and he or she is more than ten years younger than you are, the rules are slightly more favorable. You do not use the Uniform Lifetime Table. Instead, you use the Joint Life and Last Survivor Table (Table II in Appendix B) to find your ADP—the actual joint life expectancy of you and your spouse.

To determine your ADP, look up the number that corresponds to your age and your spouse's age on your respective birthdays in your first distribution year. For example, if you are age 70 on your birthday in your first distribution year (the year you turn 70½) and your spouse is age 55 in that year, your ADP from Table II is 31.1.

Be careful, though. In order to use Table II for your ADP, you must satisfy both of the following requirements:

- your spouse must be more than ten years younger than you are, and
- your spouse must have been the sole designated beneficiary of your retirement account for the entire year. (See Section C, below, for more information about designating a beneficiary.)

For purposes of this last requirement, your marital status is determined as of January 1 of the distribution year. For example, if you would have been eligible to use Table II except for the fact that your spouse died during the year—or that you and your spouse divorced during the year—you would still be able to use Table II in the year of the death or divorce.

Chart B-21
Yes — Can transfer stock from IRA
to Regular acct. — RMD amount

However, in the following year, you would use the Uniform Lifetime Table (assuming you were still single on January 1 of that following year).

b. Second Year and Beyond

Determining the ADP for the second and future distribution years is done in precisely the same way you determined the ADP for the first year.

i. General Rule

In your second distribution year, you will again use the Uniform Lifetime Table, or Table III, to find your ADP—unless your spouse-beneficiary is more than ten years younger than you are. (In that case, see Subsection ii, below.) For the second year calculation, use your age as of your birthday in the second year. If your age in that year is 71, find the ADP next to age 71 in Table III. That number is 26.5. For the third year, assuming you are age 72 on your birthday, your ADP is 25.6, and so on.

ii. Spouse More Than Ten Years Younger

If your spouse is more than ten years younger than you are, and if he or she was the sole designated beneficiary of your retirement plan or IRA for the entire year, then you use Table II to find the ADP for your second distribution year. Look up the number that corresponds to your age and your spouse's age on your respective birthdays in your second distribution year. For example, if you are age 71 on your birthday in your second distribution year and your spouse is age 56 in that year, Table II

indicates that your joint life expectancy—your ADP—for the second year is 30.1.

EXAMPLE: You turned 70½ in 2006. At that time, your brother was the beneficiary of your IRA. In November of 2006, you married someone 20 years younger than you and changed the beneficiary designation of your IRA to your new spouse. For 2006 you must use the Uniform Lifetime Table—Table III—to compute your first required distribution. For 2007, you may use Table II to find your ADP, as long as your new spouse remains the beneficiary for all of 2007.

3. Computing the Required Distribution

Once you have determined the appropriate account balance and ADP, you simply divide the account balance by the ADP to arrive at your required minimum distribution. You can withdraw more than the required amount each year, but you may not withdraw less without incurring a penalty. (See Chapter 5, Section F, to learn more about the penalty.)

EXAMPLE: You turn 70 on March 1, 2006 and your IRA account balance on December 31, 2005 is $50,000. Your niece is the beneficiary of your IRA. Your ADP for your first distribution year is 27.4 (from Table III). Therefore, your first required distribution is $1,824 ($50,000 divided by 27.4).

$$\frac{170,000}{27.4} = 6204.40 \quad 1^{st} yr.$$

yr 2

$$\frac{170,000 - 6204 = 163,796}{26.5} = 6181$$

Special opportunity for after-tax contributions. If you retire and receive a lump sum distribution from your employer's plan, your distribution might include after-tax contributions that you made to the plan. Because these amounts are not taxable, you have an interesting planning opportunity if your retirement date is in the year you turn 70½ or later. Specifically, you may count the distribution of after-tax amounts as part of your required distribution from the plan for that particular year. By doing so you can reduce your income tax while leaving additional pretax amounts in the account to grow for another year.

EXAMPLE: You retire in 2006, which is also the year you turn 70½. Over the years, you created quite a nest egg of pretax dollars inside your employer's qualified retirement plan. You have also made $10,000 in after-tax contributions. Your required distribution for your first distribution year is $19,000. When you retire in 2006, your employer distributes your retirement benefits to you as a lump sum. You decide to take your first required distribution by December 31, 2006. Your intention is to roll over into an IRA all but your required distribution for 2006. You keep out your after-tax contributions of $10,000 and an additional $9,000. You then roll over the remainder of the lump sum into an IRA. Thus, you have distributed from your retirement plan the entire amount of your first required distribution ($19,000), but only $9,000 of it is taxable.

4. Special Aggregation Rule for IRAs and TDAs

If you have more than one IRA, you must compute the required distribution for each IRA separately, but then you may add up all the computed amounts and take the total from only one or several IRAs, as long as the aggregate or total amount is distributed before the deadline.

This strategy also works if you have more than one TDA (tax deferred annuity) plan. You may compute the required distribution for each plan, and then distribute the total from just one or more of the plans. You may not mix and match IRAs and TDAs, however. If you have one IRA and one TDA, you must calculate and distribute the required amount from each separately.

You are not permitted to aggregate either inherited IRAs or inherited TDAs with your own IRAs or TDAs for required distribution purposes. For example, let's assume you have an IRA to which you have made contributions over the years. You also have an IRA that you inherited from your father. Your required distribution must be computed separately for each IRA and withdrawn from the respective account.

⚠️ **No aggregation for other types of plans.** You are allowed to use the aggregation rule only for IRAs and TDAs. If you have another type of plan (such as an employer plan or Keogh), you must compute the required amount separately for each plan and take the computed amount from the respective plan account.

5. Reporting Distributions From IRAs

It's up to you to compute the correct required distribution and report it on your tax return. However, in the case of an IRA, help is available. The law requires IRA custodians to tell IRA owners who have reached age 70½ either the amount of the required distribution or the fact that a distribution is required. If the custodian simply gives notice of the required distribution, the custodian must offer to calculate the amount for the IRA owner.

Custodians also must identify those IRAs for which a minimum distribution must be made. They must do this each year. They do not, however, have to report the amount of the required distribution.

C. Designating a Beneficiary

In the old days, if you did not name a person as beneficiary of your IRA or retirement plan, you would feel the impact of that decision as soon as you reached age 70½. That was because, without a designated beneficiary, you would have been required to distribute your retirement plan a lot faster than you would have if you had named a designated beneficiary.

In 2001, however, the IRS relaxed that requirement. Now it doesn't matter who your beneficiary is when you start taking required distributions. You are permitted to use the Uniform Lifetime Table, even if you fail to name any beneficiary at all.

But even though the IRS won't punish you for not naming a beneficiary by your RBD, naming a designated beneficiary is still important. First, if your spouse is more than ten years younger than you are and you want to use Table II to compute required distributions, you can do so only if your spouse is your designated beneficiary.

Second, if you die without a designated beneficiary of your retirement plan or IRA, the distribution of the plan or IRA assets could be accelerated after your death, possibly leaving your heirs with significant tax problems. (See Chapters 7 and 8 for more information about what happens if you die without a designated beneficiary.)

Bear in mind that you may name any person or entity as the beneficiary of your retirement plan. But not all beneficiaries are "designated" beneficiaries. If you choose a beneficiary who does not fall within the definition of designated beneficiary, you are deemed to have no beneficiary at all for required distribution purposes. (To find out who is, and who is not, a designated beneficiary, see immediately below.)

1. Definition of Designated Beneficiary

A designated beneficiary must be a natural person, as opposed to an entity such as a charity or a corporation. There is one exception to this natural person rule: a trust that has certain qualifications (known as a qualified trust—see Subsection c, below) can be a designated beneficiary.

If you fail to name a natural person or a qualified trust as your beneficiary and instead name your estate, a charity, a corporation, or a nonqualified trust, then you are deemed to have no designated beneficiary for required distribution purposes.

⚠ Just because you do not complete a beneficiary designation form and record the name of a beneficiary does not necessarily mean that you have no designated beneficiary. Some plans provide for a default beneficiary, usually a spouse, when the owner does not name a beneficiary. Be sure to find out if your plan has such a default provision. If it does not, then you are deemed to have no designated beneficiary even if the laws of your state dictate who should receive your assets.

Designated beneficiaries fall into the following three categories:
- spouse
- nonspouse natural person, and
- qualified trust.

We look at each category in the following sections.

a. Spouse

If your spouse is your designated beneficiary, your spouse will have certain privileges after your death—such as a rollover option—that other beneficiaries will not have. (See Chapters 7 and 8.)

b. Nonspouse Natural Person

Any human being—what the Tax Code calls a "natural person"—qualifies as a designated beneficiary. For example, your designated beneficiary could be a friend, relative, or a nonmarital partner.

c. Qualified Trust

A trust can be a designated beneficiary if it meets all of the following requirements:
- The trust must be valid under state law, meaning the terms must be enforceable.
- The trust must be either irrevocable while you are alive (meaning you cannot change its terms or cancel it) or irrevocable upon your death.
- The beneficiaries of the trust must be natural persons (humans) and must be identifiable. They don't have to be identified by name, however. For example, you may use the terms "spouse" or "children."
- You must provide a copy of the trust to the trustee or custodian of your retirement plan or IRA. If the trust is revocable (meaning you can change or amend it), you must give the trustee or custodian a copy of any subsequent amendments. As an alternative

to submitting the entire trust agreement, you may also provide a list of beneficiaries with a description of the amount each is to receive and the conditions, if any, under which they will receive benefits.

If the trust meets all of the above qualifications, then the beneficiary of the trust is treated as the designated beneficiary for purposes of computing your required distributions. If your spouse is sole beneficiary of the trust and is more than ten years younger than you are, you can use Table II to find your ADP each year when computing required distributions. If there is more than one beneficiary of the trust, however, the multiple beneficiary rules of Section 2, below, will apply.

The trust must satisfy all of the above for any period during which the trust is named beneficiary and during which the beneficiary of the trust is being used to determine required distributions.

So, for example, if you want to use the joint life expectancy of you and your spouse to compute required distributions when you turn 70½, then in order to satisfy the fourth requirement (the fourth bullet point, above), you must provide the custodian with a copy of the trust document by your RBD.

2. Multiple Beneficiaries

If you want to name more than one person as the beneficiary of your retirement plan, you should be aware of the consequences.

a. Primary Beneficiaries

You can name several primary beneficiaries of your retirement plan who may or may not share equally in the plan assets after your death. If any one of the primary beneficiaries fails to qualify as a designated beneficiary, then you are deemed to have no designated beneficiary at all. This is true even if all other beneficiaries would qualify as designated beneficiaries. For example, if you name your sister to receive 50% of your IRA and a charity to receive the rest, you are deemed to have no designated beneficiary (because the charity is not a natural person).

You can avoid this problem by setting up a separate IRA for each beneficiary. For example, you can direct the custodian of the IRA, in writing, to set up a second IRA and transfer half of your existing IRA assets into the new IRA. You would name the charity as sole beneficiary of the new IRA and your sister as sole beneficiary of the old IRA.

Sometimes, your heirs can cure the problem. If you die having named multiple beneficiaries of your retirement plan and if one of those beneficiaries is not a designated beneficiary, all is not lost. Your heirs might be able to cure the problem by splitting the account or by distributing assets to one or more beneficiaries by December 31 of the year after your death. For more information about these strategies, see the "Multiple Beneficiaries, One Account" sections of Chapters 7 and 8.

b. Contingent Beneficiaries

A contingent beneficiary is a beneficiary you name to receive your retirement plan assets in the event your primary beneficiary does not qualify to receive the benefits. Usually a primary beneficiary fails to qualify because he or she has already died. If you name a primary beneficiary and then name a contingent beneficiary who will receive the retirement benefits only if the primary beneficiary predeceases you, then the contingent beneficiary has no effect on required distributions.

If the contingent beneficiary could become the primary beneficiary for any reason other than the death of the original primary beneficiary, then the contingent beneficiary is treated as one of multiple beneficiaries (along with the primary beneficiary) when determining required distributions.

> EXAMPLE: You have instructed the custodian of your IRA in writing that you name your spouse, who is 15 years younger than you, as primary beneficiary of your IRA, but only if you are married at the time of your death. In the event you and your spouse divorce, your father will become the primary beneficiary of your IRA. Because your father's interest is not contingent solely on the death of your spouse, both your spouse and your father are considered beneficiaries of your retirement plan. Consequently, because your spouse is not the sole designated

beneficiary, you may not use Table II to compute required distributions. Instead you must use the Uniform Lifetime Table—Table III.

D. Special Rules for Annuities

If you are taking some or all of your retirement plan benefits in the form of an annuity, those annuity payments must also satisfy the required distribution rules described in this chapter.

Although the required distribution rules for annuities are essentially the same as those for IRAs and other retirement plans, there are some differences worth noting.

1. Form of Payment

To satisfy the required distribution rules, annuity payments must come at regular intervals of at least once a year. For example, you can receive payments monthly, quarterly, semiannually, or annually, but not every 18 months.

The payments may be in the form of either a life annuity or a term certain.

If you choose a life annuity, the payments must last for your lifetime or the joint lifetime of you and your beneficiary.

If you choose a term certain, the term must satisfy one of the following:

- it must be no longer than the ADP for your age (from Table III), or
- it must be no longer than the joint life expectancy of you and your spouse beneficiary (from Table II), if

your spouse beneficiary is more than ten years younger than you are.

Once payments begin, the term certain may not be lengthened and payments generally must be level, although they might be increased to reflect changes in cost of living or benefit increases under the plan.

2. Required Beginning Date

When you receive your retirement benefits as an annuity, the first payment must be made on or before your RBD to satisfy the required distribution rules. The amount of the first required payment is simply your regular annuity payment for that period. For example, if the terms of your annuity

---

Types of Annuities

In order to understand how the required distribution rules apply to your annuity, you must first know what type of annuity you have:

Life annuity: A life annuity makes payments to you or to you and your beneficiary for your entire life. You might have a single life annuity or a joint and survivor annuity. Payments from a single life annuity continue throughout your lifetime and stop when you die, regardless of how much has been paid. No further payments are made to any heirs or to your estate. In the case of a joint and survivor annuity, payments continue until your death or the death of your beneficiary—whichever occurs later—and then the payments stop. No additional payments are made to any other heirs or to your estate.

Term certain annuity: A term certain annuity makes payments for a fixed number of years regardless of when you die or when your beneficiary dies. If you die before the term is over, payments will be made to your beneficiary, your estate, or your heirs for the remainder of the term.

Life annuity with term certain: A life annuity with a term certain will make payments for your lifetime or for a term certain if you die before the term is up. For example, assume you are taking a single life annuity with a term certain of ten years. If you live more than ten years, the annuity payments will continue throughout your life and stop when you die. If you die after five years, the annuity will continue payments for five more years. Similarly, if you have a joint and survivor annuity with a term certain, and both you and your beneficiary die before the term is up, the annuity will continue to be paid to your heirs for the remainder of the term.

require that you be paid $2,000 per month for life, then you must receive your first $2,000 payment on or before your RBD. You are not required to receive any payments before that date.

3. Starting Early

If you elect to start receiving your annuity before your RBD, and if you comply with the form of payment rules described in Section 1, above, then the start date of your annuity becomes your RBD for all purposes. For example, the designated beneficiary is determined as of your annuity start date. And distributions must continue according to the established schedule even if you die before turning 70½.

4. Young Beneficiaries

If the beneficiary of your annuity is more than ten years younger than you are (and is not your spouse), then you must use special tables to determine whether or not your annuity satisfies the required distribution rules. You will need to know what type of annuity you have in order to determine which table to use.

a. If You Have a Term Certain Annuity

If you have elected to take your annuity over a term certain and have named a nonspouse beneficiary who is more than ten years younger than you are, you may still use Table II to find your joint life expectancy, but only until your RBD. Once you reach your RBD, you must satisfy the

required distribution rules, which means the term certain may not exceed the period found in Table III (see Appendix B) beginning in the year you turn 70½ and for all subsequent years.

EXAMPLE: You retire and begin taking your annuity when you are age 65. You name your grandson as beneficiary. He is 35 years old and your joint life expectancy, according to Table II, was 48.9 years. You elected to begin taking distributions over a term certain of 48.9 years. Five years later, when you turn 70½, the remaining term certain is 43.9 years (48.9 − 5). According to Table III, however, which you must use when you reach age 70½, the remaining term certain may not exceed 27.4 years. In order to satisfy required distribution rules, your annuity plan must automatically adjust your payments beginning in the year you turn 70½ so that the annuity is paid out over 27.4 years (instead of 43.9 years).

b. Joint and Survivor Annuity

If you elect to receive a life annuity (without a term certain) over the joint life of you and a nonspouse beneficiary who is more than ten years younger than you are, then at all times from and after your first distribution year (the year you turn 70½), the projected payment to your beneficiary cannot exceed a certain percentage of the payment you are currently receiving. The percentage is based on the difference in your ages and is determined from Table IV (see Appendix B).

As in the case of a term certain annuity, if you begin receiving payments before your RBD and they do not satisfy the required distribution rules, the payments must be adjusted beginning in the year you turn 70½.

> EXAMPLE: You are taking your retirement benefits as a joint and survivor annuity over the joint life of you and your daughter. The year you turn 70½, your monthly payment is $3,000. The age difference between you and your daughter is 21 years. From Table IV, you see that your daughter's projected benefit when you die cannot exceed 72% of your current benefit—that is, it cannot exceed $2,160 per month ($3,000 x .72). So when you die, the payment to your daughter must drop from $3,000 per month to no more than $2,160 per month.

If you name more than one beneficiary of your annuity, then you must use the youngest beneficiary to determine the percentage from Table IV. And similarly, if you change your beneficiary to a younger beneficiary (for any reason other than the death of a primary beneficiary), your payments may need to be adjusted so that projected payments to the beneficiary satisfy the percentage requirements from Table IV.

c. Joint and Survivor Annuity With Term Certain

If you have a life annuity with a term certain, you must satisfy both the term certain requirements described in Subsection a, above, and the survivor benefit limitations described in Subsection b, above. In other words, the term of your annuity may not exceed the number corresponding to your age in Table III, and the projected payments to your beneficiary after your death may not exceed the percentage in Table IV.

It's not always this difficult. Although the annuity rules seem (and can be) complex, most people's annuities take the form of a single life annuity or a joint life annuity with a spouse. If you have selected either of these forms of payment, then you should not have to make new computations every year. It is only when you use a much younger nonspouse beneficiary or when you change beneficiaries that your situation could become more complicated.

E. Divorce or Separation

If you are divorced or separated, part of your qualified plan, qualified annuity, or TDA might be payable to an "alternate payee" (such as a spouse, former spouse, or child) under the terms of a QDRO—a court-approved divorce or maintenance agreement. (See Chapter 2, Section C4, for more information about QDROs.)

When you reach your RBD, the required distribution rules will apply to the alternate payee's portion, as well as to your own. And because you are the plan participant, it is your RBD that determines when distributions must begin. Furthermore, if the required amount is not withdrawn in timely fashion, you, not the alternate payee, must pay the penalty. As for other required distribution rules, the way in which they are applied will depend on whether or not the alternate payee's portion is in a separate account.

⚠️ **Alternate payee must wait.** The terms of your QDRO might provide that the alternate payee is to receive immediate and total distribution of his or her share of the plan. Unless the plan itself permits such a distribution, however, the alternate payee must wait to receive his or her share until the time when you distribute assets from the plan, either at your retirement or when you begin required distributions or at some other time specified by the plan.

1. Separate Account

A QDRO might require that an alternate payee's portion be divided and separately accounted for. If so, the following variations in the required distribution rules apply:

- The alternate payee's separate share is not to be combined, or aggregated, with the rest of your plan benefits when you compute required distributions. In other words, you would separately compute the required distribution amount for your portion and the alternate payee's portion. You would then distribute the alternate payee's portion from his or her share.

- In computing the required distribution from the alternate payee's portion, you may use one of the following to determine the ADP:
  - the Uniform Lifetime Table (Table III) based on your age
  - the joint life of you and the alternate payee, if the alternate payee is your ex-spouse and is more than ten years younger than you are, or
  - the alternate payee's single life expectancy.

The decision about which ADP to use belongs to you—not to the alternate payee—even though the distribution will come from the alternate payee's portion and will be distributed to the alternate payee. (See Section B2, above, for more information about ADP.)

⚠️ **If the alternate payee dies.** Although you have several options for selecting a distribution period to compute required distributions from the alternate payee's portion, one option that you do not have is to use the joint life expectancy of the alternate payee and his or her beneficiary. If the alternate payee dies before your RBD, however, the alternate payee's beneficiary will be treated as the beneficiary for required distribution purposes.

> EXAMPLE: Your ex-husband is entitled to half of your pension plan under the terms of your QDRO. The pension plan administrator separated your ex-husband's share into a separate account, and your ex-husband named his sister as beneficiary of his separate share of the pension. The plan provides that no distributions can be made until you retire or reach your RBD. If your ex-husband dies before your RBD, then your ex-husband's sister becomes the designated beneficiary when computing distributions from your ex-husband's portion of the pension.

Even if a QDRO mandates dividing the retirement benefit between you and the alternate payee, the terms of the plan might not permit physically separating the shares. The plan administrator can get around this using a reasonable method to separately account for the alternate payee's portion. For example, a reasonable method would be to allocate on a pro rata basis all investment gains and losses, as well as contributions and forfeitures (if applicable).

2. No Separate Account

In some instances, you will not physically separate your share from the alternate payee's share. Some QDROs do not require an actual separation of the alternate payee's share, and some plans don't permit actual separation.

In either case, the retirement plan remains undivided, and a portion of each distribution goes to the alternate payee. Under this scenario, the alternate payee's portion does not have to separately satisfy the minimum distribution requirement. Instead, it is combined, or aggregated, with your other plan assets for purposes of determining the account balance and calculating your required distribution for the year.

Thus, aggregation means that the required distribution rules work as though there was no alternate payee. When calculating required distributions, you may use either the uniform table or Table II (if your spouse-beneficiary is more than ten years younger than you are). But you may not use the alternate payee's single life expectancy.

3. Income Taxes and Penalties

Generally speaking, the rules governing the payment of taxes and penalties on QDRO distributions are essentially the same whether the alternate payee is a spouse, former spouse, or child.

There are, however, two exceptions to that general rule. We explain those in the following sections.

a. Spouse or Former Spouse Alternate Payee

If the alternate payee named in the QDRO is your spouse or former spouse, the alternate payee must pay all income taxes on distributions he or she receives. But you are responsible for penalties on any shortfall in required distributions, even though the alternate payee is receiving a portion.

b. Nonspouse Alternate Payee

If the alternate payee is someone other than your spouse or former spouse (for example, your child), you must pay all income taxes, as well as any penalties that might apply. This is true even though the distribution actually goes to the alternate payee.

4. Rollovers

The option to roll over a distribution from a qualified plan into an IRA or another qualified plan is a big tax benefit. Traditionally, the benefit has been reserved for plan participants, and occasionally the participant's spouse. Under the QDRO rules, the privilege is extended to a former spouse.

a. Spouse or Former Spouse Alternate Payee

A spouse or former spouse may roll over any distributed portion of his or her interest in your plan if there is a QDRO in place. This is the case whether or not the spouse or former spouse's portion was held in a separate account. Once the spouse or former spouse completes the rollover to an account in his or her name, the account belongs to the spouse or former spouse in every way, and the required distribution rules apply to that account as though the alternate payee were the original owner.

The plan has the final word. Although the QDRO rules permit your spouse or former spouse to roll over an interest in your retirement plan, some plans will not permit it. Furthermore, some plans will not make any distribution at all until you have reached a certain retirement age—one that is specified in the plan. Because the plan rules ultimately govern distributions, spouses and former spouses often have little control over how they receive QDRO payments.

b. Nonspouse Alternate Payee

Nonspouse alternate payees may not roll over their interest in your retirement plan under any circumstances. The law does not allow it.

When the rules don't apply.

Remember: The special rules described in this section apply only to qualified plans, qualified annuities, and TDAs, and they apply only if there is a QDRO in place. If there is no QDRO, your retirement plan is treated as though it is entirely yours for required distribution purposes. If your divorce agreement states that your former spouse is to share in your plan, you must generally give your former spouse his or her share as it is distributed from the plan. In other words, a portion of each distribution would go to your former spouse and you would keep your share. As for IRAs, there are no corresponding QDRO rules. As long as the IRA remains in your name, the required distribution rules apply as though your former spouse had no interest in the IRA. But if some or all of your IRA is transferred into your former spouse's name as a result of a written divorce or separation agreement, then from the time the transfer is complete, the transferred portion belongs to your former spouse in every respect. That means the required distribution rules apply as though your former spouse were the original owner. (See Chapter 2, Section E4, for more information about IRAs and divorce.)

Key Tax Code and Regulation Sections
§ 401(a)(9)   Required Distributions From Qualified Plans
§ 1.401(a)(9)   Required Distribution Regulations
§ 1.408-8   Required Distribution Rules for IRAs

Chapter 7

Distributions to Your Beneficiary If You Die Before Age 70½

he law says you must start taking money out of your retirement plan by a certain date—your "required beginning date" (RBD). But what if you never make it to that date? What would your premature death mean for your beneficiaries (other than the obvious sadness), and how can you prepare for it?

In this chapter, we look at the answers to those questions, paying particular attention to the ways you can help your beneficiaries avoid onerous taxes and penalties.

A. Determining the Designated Beneficiary

If you die before your RBD, which for most people is April 1 of the year after they turn 70½ (see Chapter 6, Section A, for information about determining your RBD), your designated beneficiary (if you have one) generally must begin taking distributions from your retirement plan in the year after your death, with some exceptions. Just how rapidly the assets must be distributed and according to what schedule depends primarily on who the designated beneficiary is. So before we look at distribution methods, let's see how the IRS will determine who your designated beneficiary is.

Recall that you can name any person or organization you want as the beneficiary of your retirement plan or IRA. However, when determining how your retirement plan assets should be distributed after your death, only designated beneficiaries are taken into account. (See Chapter 6, Section C, for more information about designated beneficiaries.) If one or more of your named beneficiaries is not a designated beneficiary, you are deemed to have no designated beneficiary and distributions must be accelerated.

1. Deadline for Determining Designated Beneficiary

The designated beneficiary of your retirement plan is determined as of September 30 of the year after your death. Although the determination date occurs after you die, this doesn't mean that someone can come along and name beneficiaries of your retirement plan after your death. If you fail to name any beneficiary of your retirement

Helpful Terms

Annuity. A contract, sold by an insurance company, that promises to make monthly, quarterly, semiannual, or annual payments for life or for a specified period of time.

Contingent beneficiary. A person or entity who is entitled to receive the benefits of a retirement plan or IRA only if and when a specific event occurs, such as the death of a primary beneficiary.

Deferral period. The number of years over which distributions from a retirement plan or IRA can be spread.

Disclaimer. A renunciation of or a refusal to accept property to which a person is entitled by gift, by law, or under the terms of a will or a trust.

Distribution. A payout of property (such as shares of stock) or cash from a retirement plan or IRA to the participant or a beneficiary.

Estate. All property that a person owns.

Irrevocable trust. A trust that cannot be changed or terminated by the person who created it. Once assets are transferred to an irrevocable trust, the assets are subject to the terms of the trust for as long as the trust exists.

Primary beneficiary. A person or entity entitled to receive benefits from a retirement plan or IRA upon the death of the original participant.

Revocable trust. A trust whose terms allow the creator of the trust to alter its provisions, cancel it, or remove some or all of the property from the trust and return the property to the creator.

Term certain. A fixed, identifiable period, such as a specific number of years. For example, a retirement plan that is distributable over a term certain of 20 years must be completely liquidated after 20 years.

plan, you generally will be deemed to have no designated beneficiary.

But if nobody can add a beneficiary after your death, why, you might ask, is the deadline for determining the beneficiary so long after your death? That's the issue that we address in the following section.

2. Changing Beneficiaries Before the Deadline

Even though no one can add beneficiaries to your retirement plan after you die, your beneficiary could change after your death. For example, suppose you name your spouse as primary beneficiary and your children as contingent beneficiaries. After your death, your spouse decides she has enough money to live on for the rest of her life without using any of your retirement plan assets. She might disclaim (renounce) her interest in your retirement plan. In that case, the plan assets would go to your children as contingent beneficiaries.

The IRS inserted this extended deadline into the regulations as a relief provision. It gives beneficiaries an opportunity to do some postmortem planning, whether to make administration of distributions easier or to clean up a disadvantageous situation you left behind.

For example, suppose you named your wife and your favorite charity as equal beneficiaries of your retirement account. When you die, if the charity and your spouse are still equal beneficiaries on September 30 of the year after your death, you are deemed to have no designated beneficiary (because the charity isn't a designated beneficiary) and distributions to all beneficiaries must be accelerated. (See Section B2, below.) This could have disastrous tax consequences for your spouse.

As a cleanup measure, however, the charity can receive its entire distribution before September 30 of the year after death, leaving only your spouse as beneficiary. Then the post-death rules apply as though your spouse were sole beneficiary of the account. This would produce a much more favorable result. (See Section C, below.)

B. Distribution Methods

If you die before your RBD, your retirement plan benefits will be distributed using one of three methods: the life expectancy rule (see Section 1, below), the five-year rule (see Section 2, below), or a spousal rollover (see Section 3, below).

1. Life Expectancy Rule

The life expectancy rule allows your beneficiary to spread distributions over his or her life expectancy after your death, if both of the following conditions are met:

- the beneficiary of your plan or IRA as of September 30 of the year after your death is a designated beneficiary; and
- the plan itself either permits the life expectancy rule or is silent (meaning it doesn't indicate one way or another which rule should be used).

Distributions under the life expectancy rule generally must begin in the year after your death and continue until the entire account has been depleted. (Some unusual twists apply if your spouse is your beneficiary. See Section C, below.)

Sections C through I, below, provide detailed information about calculating distributions for each type of designated beneficiary.

2. Five-Year Rule

The five-year rule is mandatory in cases where both of the following are true:

- you die before your RBD, and
- your retirement plan or IRA is deemed to have no designated beneficiary as of September 30 of the year after your death. (See Chapter 6, Section C, for more information about

which beneficiaries qualify as designated beneficiaries.)

If the five-year rule applies, all of your retirement plan assets must be distributed within five years after your death.

Actually, it's five years plus.
Practically speaking, your beneficiary has a little more than five years to withdraw the assets when the five-year rule applies. This is because the official distribution deadline is December 31 of the year containing the fifth anniversary of your death. For example, if you die on March 3 in the year 2006, your retirement plan need not be completely distributed until December 31, 2011—five years and almost ten months later.

a. Required Beginning Date

The five-year rule applies only if you die before your RBD. If you live past that milestone, a different set of rules will apply when you die without a designated beneficiary. If you have passed your RBD, you can forget about the five-year rule (and you should be reading Chapter 8). But be careful: It is your RBD that counts—not the year you turn 70½. For example, if your RBD is April 1, 2006, but you die on March 15, 2006, the five-year rule will apply even though you have already passed age 70½ and even if you have already taken a distribution for your first distribution year. Technically, you have not begun required distributions until you pass your RBD.

> **EXAMPLE:** You turned 70½ in June 2005, which makes your RBD April 1, 2006. On December 30, 2005 you withdrew $6,000 from your IRA, which was the amount of your first required distribution. But then you died on March 15, 2006, before reaching your RBD. Because you died before your RBD, the five-year rule will apply even though you had already withdrawn an amount that would have satisfied your first required distribution.

b. Distributing the Account

The five-year rule mandates that all assets be distributed from your retirement plan by December 31 of the year containing the fifth anniversary of your death, but it places no restriction on the form of payment. This means, for example, that your beneficiary could receive the entire amount as a lump sum in the month after your death, monthly installments spread over the five-year period, or perhaps nothing at all until the December 31 deadline in the fifth year.

Although the IRS would accept any of those approaches, the retirement plan itself might have more stringent distribution requirements—and the plan controls how payments will be made. (See Section 4, below, for more about plan rules.) Some plans allow beneficiaries to receive install-ment payments or to leave the funds in the plan until the five-year period is up. If the plan requires immediate distribution of the entire account, however, then that's what your beneficiary will be stuck with.

3. Spousal Rollover

If your beneficiary is your spouse and if he or she is the beneficiary of your retirement plan, your spouse will generally have an alternative to the life expectancy rule or the five-year rule. That alternative is to roll over your retirement plan into an IRA in the spouse's own name. (See Section C, below, for more information about spousal rollovers.)

4. Effect of the Retirement Plan's Rules

Although the law provides a framework for required distributions within which retirement plans may operate, the plan's own rules can be—and usually are—more restrictive. In that case, the plan's rules govern. For example, even though the law allows a designated beneficiary to use the life expectancy rule and take distributions over his or her life expectancy, the plan itself might require that even designated beneficiaries use the five-year rule. Or sometimes the plan will allow the designated beneficiary to choose a method of distribution.

a. Optional Provisions

Sometimes, plans give beneficiaries a choice of which rule to use. For example, in the best of all worlds (from the tax-payer's perspective), plans would allow beneficiaries to choose between the five-year rule and the life expectancy rule. And if a beneficiary didn't have a choice and was saddled with the five-year rule, the beneficiary would certainly like to be able to choose how the assets were distributed over that five-year period.

If you do get to choose. Generally, a beneficiary who has the option to use the life expectancy rule would choose it and not the five-year rule. However, if a beneficiary failed to take a timely distribution under the life expectancy rule, he or she might want to fall back on the five-year rule to avoid the hefty penalty for failing to take a required distribution.

But this isn't the best of worlds, and plan administrators don't always put taxpayers' needs first. In fact, some plans offer no options at all to beneficiaries, instead mandating distribution of the entire plan in the year of death. At the other extreme, some plans might distribute nothing at all until the end of the fifth year.

Furthermore, many plans have different policies for different beneficiaries. For example, the terms of a plan might require that nonspouse beneficiaries receive a distribution of the entire plan immediately following the participant's death (without the five-year grace period), but allow a spouse beneficiary to use the life expectancy rule.

b. Default Provisions

If the plan is resolutely silent on how distributions will occur after the death of the plan participant, certain default provisions kick in by law. Specifically, if the plan has a designated beneficiary, the life expectancy rule applies by default.

C. Spouse Beneficiary

If your spouse is the beneficiary of your retirement plan, he or she has two options for taking distributions from your retirement plan after your death. Your spouse can:

- leave the account in your name and use the life expectancy rule to take distributions over his or her own life expectancy beginning in the year you would have been 70½—or the year after your death if that is later (see Section 1, below), or
- roll over the plan or IRA into a plan or an IRA in his or her own name (see Section 2, below).

For purposes of this Section C, we assume that the spouse was the sole beneficiary of the retirement plan. The rules change if a spouse is one of several beneficiaries. (See Section G, below, for the multiple beneficiary rules.)

1. Life Expectancy Rule

If your spouse is the beneficiary of your retirement account, your spouse can wait until the year you would have turned 70½ to begin receiving required distributions. This additional deferral—until the deceased participant would have turned 70½—is available only to a spouse. Your spouse can choose this option even if he or she has already turned 70½ as long as he or she leaves the account in your name.

If your spouse chooses the life expectancy rule, he or she would use the following steps to compute the first required distribution from your account:

Step 1: Determine the account balance.

Your spouse must use your retirement account balance as of December 31 of the year before you would have turned 70½ to compute the first required distribution.

Step 2: Determine the ADP.

Using his or her age in the year you would have turned 70½, your spouse must look up the appropriate life expectancy factor in Table I (see Appendix B). That factor is the applicable distribution period—or ADP—for the first year.

Step 3: Calculate the required distribution.

To determine the first required distribution, your spouse divides the account balance by the ADP—which is Step 1 divided by Step 2. The resulting amount must be distributed by December 31 of the year you would have turned 70½.

> EXAMPLE: Ed was born March 15, 1936 and died on June 1, 2003, at age 67— before reaching his RBD. His wife, Bertha, is the beneficiary of his retirement plan. Bertha intends to use the life expectancy rule to determine required distributions from the plan. She wants to defer distributions until 2006—the year Ed would have turned 70½. To calculate the first required distribution, she must do the following:
>
> Step 1: **Determine account balance.**
> To compute the required distribution, Bertha must use the account balance as of December 31, 2005—the year before Ed would have turned 70½. That amount is $100,000.
>
> Step 2: **Determine ADP.**
> Bertha will be age 68 on her birthday in 2006—the year Ed would have turned 70½. Her single life expectancy at age 68 (from Table I in Appendix B) is 18.6 years.

Step 3: Calculate the required distribution.

Bertha's first required distribution is $100,000 divided by 18.6 (Step 1 divided by Step 2), or $5,376. Bertha must withdraw at least that amount by December 31, 2006.

For the second and future years, your spouse would find the ADP from Table I each year, using his or her age for the current year. Your spouse would then divide the account balance as of December 31 of the previous year by the new ADP.

> **EXAMPLE:** Continuing the example, above, for the year 2007, Bertha will use the December 31, 2006 balance of Ed's retirement account and divide it by her ADP. The ADP for age 69 (from Table I) is 17.8.

If you turned 70½ in the year of your death. Remember, if you turned 70½ (or would have turned 70½) in the same year that you died, your spouse does not have to begin distributions that same year. Instead, she can delay the start of distributions until the year after your death. In that case, she would use the account balance as of December 31 of the year of your death and her age in the year after your death to compute the first required distribution.

2. Rollover

If a spouse is the beneficiary of a retirement plan or IRA, the spouse has another quite valuable deferral option. The spouse can roll over the plan assets into a plan or IRA of his or her own. (Note: This option is available only to a spouse.)

If your plan is not an IRA, the only way your spouse can make the plan her own is by rolling the plan assets over into an IRA or plan in the spouse's own name.

But if your retirement plan is an IRA, your spouse has several ways to make your IRA her own. She can do so by:

- rolling over the assets into a new or preexisting IRA or plan in her own name (see Subsection a, below)
- failing to take one of your post-death required distributions at the proper time (see Subsection b, below), or
- contributing additional amounts of her own to your IRA.

a. Convert to Spouse's Plan or IRA by Rollover

A spouse can roll over a deceased participant's IRA into a plan or IRA in the spouse's own name. This method is the cleanest because there is a clear record of what happened and when.

Once the account becomes the spouse's own, it belongs to the spouse in every way—as though he or she were the original owner. Required distributions will begin when the spouse reaches his or her own RBD and will be based on the ADP for the spouse's age at that time.

> EXAMPLE: Grace died in 2003 at the age of 69. Her husband, George, was the beneficiary of her IRA, and he turned 64 on February 14, 2003. At the end of 2003, George rolled over Grace's IRA into an IRA in his own name. George will not need to begin required distributions until his own RBD, which is April 1 of the year after he turns 70½, or April 1, 2010.

If a surviving spouse rolls over a deceased participant's IRA into a new IRA in the spouse's name, the spouse may name a new beneficiary of his or her own choosing.

> EXAMPLE: Your husband is the primary beneficiary of your IRA, and your brother will inherit the plan if your husband dies before you do. But let's say you predecease your husband and he decides to roll over your IRA into an IRA in his own name. He completes the rollover and names his sister as primary beneficiary. His action is completely legal under the rollover rules. Once he rolls over your IRA, the assets are his. His sister will receive the IRA assets; your brother will not.

Your spouse may roll over your retirement plan and name a new beneficiary after you die, even if your spouse has

passed his or her RBD at the time of the rollover. In that case, your spouse's RBD for purposes of the new IRA is December 31 of the year of the rollover, and required distributions must begin at that time.

> EXAMPLE: You died in 2005 at the age of 69. Your wife turned 72 in 2005. In March 2006, she rolled over your retirement plan into an IRA in her name and designated your children as beneficiaries. Your wife must take her first required distribution by December 31, 2006.

b. Convert to Spouse's IRA by Failing to Take Required Distribution

If you die before your RBD, and your spouse fails to take a required distribution under the life expectancy rule—either by December 31 of the year after your death or by December 31 of the year you would have been 70½—your spouse is deemed to have made an election to treat your IRA as his or her own. The IRA becomes your spouse's own on December 31 of the year of the failure, and your spouse will not be required to take a distribution until his or her own RBD.

> EXAMPLE: Your wife died in the year 2004 at age 63. You were the beneficiary of her IRA. You did not take any distributions in 2005, nor had you taken any distributions by December 31, 2011—the year your wife would have

been 70½. Therefore, by missing all of the deadlines for taking a distribution from your wife's retirement account, the account is deemed to be your own as of December 31, 2011.

c. Timing

The IRS imposes no deadline for a spouse to roll over a deceased participant's retirement plan into the spouse's own plan or IRA. That means a spouse can begin taking distributions as a beneficiary under the life expectancy rule and then some years later roll over the assets into a plan or IRA of the spouse's own.

As a practical matter, if a spouse is past age 59½ and intends to roll over a participant's retirement plan, there is nothing to be gained from waiting. If the spouse needs money, the spouse can take it freely from the IRA even after rolling it over, because there is no penalty for taking distributions after age 59½.

If the spouse is younger than 59½, however, free use of the IRA funds could be dicey. Recall that one of the exceptions to the early distribution tax is a distribution to a beneficiary after the death of the original participant. (See Chapter 3 for more information on the early distribution tax.) But that particular exception is not available to a spouse after the spouse rolls over the deceased person's plan into a plan or IRA in the spouse's name. Once it is rolled over, it is the spouse's, and because the spouse is still alive, the after-

death exception does not apply. Thus, the spouse must generally postpone distributions until age 59½ to avoid the early distribution tax.

Consequently, if the spouse is younger than 59½ and needs to use the retirement plan money to live on, the spouse might be better off leaving the plan or IRA in the name of the deceased so that the after-death exception can be used. The one disadvantage of this approach is that, according to at least one IRS private letter ruling, once a spouse invokes the after-death exception to the early distribution tax, the spouse forever forfeits the right to roll over the account into a plan or IRA of the spouse's own.

3. Death of Spouse Beneficiary

If a spouse beneficiary inherits a retirement plan or IRA and begins taking required distributions on December 31 of the year after the participant's death (or December 31 of the year the deceased participant would have turned 70½) but dies before all assets of the retirement account are distributed, the spouse's beneficiary must take distributions in the following way:

- In the year of the spouse's death, the spouse's beneficiary will divide the account balance as of December 31 of the year before the spouse's death by the ADP for the spouse in the year of the spouse's death (using the spouse's age on his or her birthday in the year of death and looking up the respective ADP in Table I in Appendix B).

- In the second year and beyond, the spouse's beneficiary will reduce the ADP determined in the previous paragraph by one and divide it into the account balance as of the previous December 31. The computation continues in this way each year until the entire account is depleted.

EXAMPLE: You died in 2004 at age 69. Your wife was the beneficiary of your IRA and began taking required distributions from your IRA in 2005. She died in 2007. She would have been 64 on her birthday. Her sister is the sole beneficiary of her estate. On December 31, 2006 the balance in the IRA was $60,000. Your wife's ADP in 2007 (for age 64) is 21.8 (from Table I). The required distribution for 2007 is $2,752 ($60,000 divided by 21.8).

In the second year—2008—the ADP will be reduced by one. On December 31, 2007 the balance in the IRA was $63,000. The ADP for 2008 is 20.8 (which is 21.8 − 1). Therefore, the sister's required distribution for 2008 is $3,029 ($63,000 divided by 20.8).

If a spouse beneficiary dies after the participant, but before beginning required distributions under the life expectancy rule (and before rolling over the account into an IRA in the spouse's own name), then the following rules apply:

- In general, the life expectancy rule or the five-year rule will apply to the spouse's beneficiary as though the spouse had been the original participant. Specifically, the age of the spouse's beneficiary will determine how required distributions are computed under the life expectancy rule. (If the spouse remarries and names his or her new spouse as beneficiary, however, the new spouse will be treated as a nonspouse beneficiary. See the next bullet point.)

EXAMPLE: You die in 2002 at age 65. Your wife is the beneficiary of your retirement plan account and therefore is not required to begin distributions until you would have been age 70½ (in the year 2007). Her sister is the sole beneficiary of your wife's estate. Your wife died in 2005 before beginning required distributions from your retirement account. The life expectancy rule will apply to distributions to her sister, the beneficiary. Under the life expectancy rule, your wife's sister must begin distributions by December 31, 2006, and take them over her life expectancy. For her first distribution, she would use her age in 2006 and find the ADP in Table I. For subsequent years, she would reduce the ADP by one.

- If your spouse remarried and named his or her new spouse as beneficiary, the special additional deferral option, described in Section 1, above, is not available to the new spouse beneficiary. Specifically, the spouse's new wife or husband is not permitted to wait until the spouse would have been 70½ to begin required distributions. The spouse's beneficiary is simply treated as a nonspouse and is subject to the rules in the previous bullet point.

EXAMPLE: You die in 2002 at age 65. Your wife is the beneficiary of your retirement plan account and therefore is not required to begin distributions until you would have been age 70½ (in 2007). Your wife remarried in 2004 and named her new husband as beneficiary of her entire estate. She died in 2005 before beginning required distributions from your retirement account. The life expectancy rule applies and your wife's new husband must begin distributions by December 31, 2006, and take them over his life expectancy. He is not entitled to use the special deferral option of a spouse, however. He may not wait until his spouse (your wife) would have been 70½ to begin distributions.

D. Nonspouse Beneficiary

As a participant in a retirement plan, or as the spouse of a participant, it is easy to take for granted the special privileges, exceptions, and additional distribution op-

tions the Tax Code offers. But when the beneficiary is a nonspouse beneficiary, that person typically has only one option—the life expectancy rule.

If there is more than one beneficiary. The rules in this section apply if there is only one beneficiary named on the account. If there is more than one beneficiary, a different set of rules applies. See Sections F and G, below, for more about the multiple beneficiary rules.

1. Life Expectancy Rule

The law allows a nonspouse beneficiary to use the life expectancy rule to calculate required distributions after the plan participant's death. Those distributions must begin no later than December 31 of the year after the participant's death. No additional deferral is permitted.

Don't forget, however, to check the plan to see what it says. Remember: When the plan rules are more restrictive than the law, the plan controls. For example, the plan can require that benefits be paid out according to the five-year rule, in which case the beneficiary is stuck with it. On the other hand, if the plan is silent on post-death distributions, the life expectancy rule applies by default.

EXAMPLE: You died on March 15, 2005, before reaching your RBD. Your son is the beneficiary of your retirement plan, and he turns 48 in 2006. Your account was valued at $100,000 on December 31, 2005. Your son will use the life expectancy rule to compute required distributions.

Step 1: Determine the account balance.

To compute the first payment, your son must use the account balance as of December 31, 2005, the year of your death. That amount is $100,000.

Step 2: Determine the ADP.

Your son will be age 48 on his birthday in the year after your death (2006). His single life expectancy—or ADP—at age 48 (from Table I in Appendix B) is 36.0 years.

Step 3: Calculate the required distribution.

Your son's first required distribution is $100,000 divided by 36.0 (Step 1 divided by Step 2) or $2,778. Your son must withdraw at least that amount by December 31, 2006.

For distributions in years after the first year, a nonspouse beneficiary must reduce the previous ADP by one. A nonspouse beneficiary is not permitted to use Table I for any year but the first year of required distributions.

EXAMPLE: Continuing the above example, for the year 2007, your son will use the December 31, 2006 balance of your retirement account and divide it by the new ADP, which is 35.0 (36.0 – 1).

Remember, too, that a beneficiary can always take more than the minimum amount each year, but not less.

2. No Rollover

A nonspouse beneficiary is never permitted to roll over a deceased person's retirement plan. If the beneficiary attempts to do so, the entire rollover could be considered a taxable distribution and an excess contribution to an IRA—and it would be subject to penalties. Even if the excess contribution is corrected, the retirement plan assets cannot be redeposited into the deceased participant's account. Consequently, the beneficiary will owe income tax on the entire amount, whether or not penalties are assessed as well.

A nonspouse beneficiary really has only one option: to leave the retirement account in the name of the deceased participant until the account is completely distributed under the life expectancy rule (or more rapidly). (See Section G3b, below, for more information about titling accounts.)

3. Death of Nonspouse Beneficiary

If a nonspouse beneficiary dies after the participant has died, but before the retirement plan has been completely distributed, the distribution method remains the same. For example, if distributions were made under the life expectancy rule, distributions will still be made over the life expectancy of the deceased beneficiary, using the beneficiary's age on his or her birthday in the year after the participant's death, reduced by one in each subsequent year.

EXAMPLE: Sara named her brother, Archie, as beneficiary of her retirement plan. She died in 2005 at the age of 68. Archie intended to begin taking distributions over his life expectancy beginning in 2006. He would have turned 55 on March 1, 2006, but he died on February 15, 2006. Nonetheless, distributions will be made to his beneficiary as though he were still alive. Archie's ADP at age 55 would have been 29.6 years (from Table I). The ADP will be reduced by one each year until the entire account is distributed.

If the plan had required the beneficiary to use the five-year rule, the entire account must still be distributed by December 31 of the year containing the fifth anniversary of the original participant's death, even though the beneficiary has since died.

 Who is the beneficiary's beneficiary? When a primary beneficiary dies after the original participant has died but before all the retirement plan assets have been distributed, where does the remainder go? The answer depends on the laws of your state. If the primary beneficiary had designated a beneficiary, the path is clear. If not, typically, the retirement plan will be distributed according to the terms of the primary beneficiary's will. In the absence of a will, the assets would be distributed to the heirs of the primary beneficiary according to state law.

E. No Designated Beneficiary

If you have no designated beneficiary for your retirement account, then payout options at your death are restricted. Recall that a designated beneficiary must usually be a natural person, although it may also be a special type of trust. (See Chapter 6, Section C, for more information about designated beneficiaries.) And although you are permitted to name any beneficiary you choose, whether a person or an entity, some privileges are reserved for beneficiaries that qualify as designated beneficiaries.

1. Five-Year Rule

If the beneficiary of your retirement plan is not a designated beneficiary and if you die before your RBD, the five-year rule applies and the entire account must be distributed by December 31 of the year containing the fifth anniversary of your death.

2. No Life Expectancy Rule

If your beneficiary is not a designated beneficiary, the life expectancy rule is never an option under any circumstances. The five-year rule is mandatory, and all of the assets in the plan must be distributed by December 31 of the year containing the fifth anniversary of your death.

The law allows installments. Even if the life expectancy rule is not an option, it is still permissible for the beneficiary to take distributions in installments over the five-year period, if the plan will allow it.

F. Multiple Beneficiaries, Separate Accounts

If you have several IRAs or retirement plans, each with a different beneficiary, then each plan is treated separately for purposes of the required distribution rules. You are not considered to have multiple beneficiaries.

Even if you do name multiple beneficiaries of a single retirement plan, your beneficiaries might still be deemed to have separate accounts. If the plan administrator or custodian agrees to do so, he or she can segregate each beneficiary's share and treat each as a separate account payable to one beneficiary. And even if the administrator does not segregate the shares, the shares may be treated as separate accounts if the administrator or custodian sets up separate accounting procedures (under which, for example, investment gains and losses are allocated to beneficiaries on a pro rata basis). Under either of these scenarios, each beneficiary could take distributions over his or her own life expectancy after your death without being subject to the multiple beneficiary rules. (See Section G3, below, for more information about multiple beneficiaries with one account.)

Don't count on administrators allowing separate accounting. As a practical matter, many qualified plan administrators are reluctant to shoulder the burden of separate accounting or even to physically split the account. Consequently, the beneficiaries may be stuck with the multiple beneficiary/one account rules described in the next section. IRA custodians, too, are often unwilling to provide a separate accounting for each beneficiary when multiple beneficiaries are named on one account. In the case of an IRA, however, there is nothing to prevent you from splitting the account during your lifetime into separate IRAs, one for each beneficiary. And in most cases, the account can be split after your death, as well.

G. Multiple Beneficiaries, One Account

The rules change significantly if there is more than one beneficiary of a single retirement account. Bear in mind, the date for determining the beneficiaries is September 30 of the year following your death. If on that date all beneficiaries are designated beneficiaries, then they have until December 31 to split the account so that each beneficiary gets his or her separate share. (See Section 3, below, for more about splitting accounts.) If the accounts are split in timely fashion, the required distribution rules apply separately to each share or account. Then, for example, each beneficiary could use his or her own life expectancy to compute required distributions.

 This won't work if one or more beneficiaries is not a designated beneficiary. Splitting accounts in this manner will work only if all beneficiaries are designated beneficiaries as of September 30 of the year after your death. If on that date there are multiple beneficiaries named on the account and even one of them fails to qualify as a designated beneficiary, then you are deemed to have no designated beneficiary and the five-year rule will apply. (See Section G5, below.)

But let's assume that multiple designated beneficiaries remain on the account through December 31 of the year after your death. What are the consequences?

First of all, the beneficiaries are not free to use their own life expectancies to take distribution of their respective shares. Also, a spouse might lose some special privileges if both your spouse and child are beneficiaries of a single account.

When you have multiple beneficiaries, for purposes of the life expectancy rule and the five-year rule, all beneficiaries are treated as nonspouse beneficiaries, even if one of them is your spouse. As a result, the most restrictive rules—those that produce the worst result—will apply to all beneficiaries. For example, if you name your spouse and your children, the beneficiaries must choose from the options available to your children because children have fewer options than spouses.

1. Life Expectancy Rule

The life expectancy rule still applies when there are multiple beneficiaries on a single account (as long as the plan does not require accelerated payments). But the least favorable distribution period is the one your beneficiaries must use: The account must be distributed over the single life expectancy of the oldest beneficiary. This will yield the largest distribution and deplete the account most rapidly—exactly what Congress wants. The oldest beneficiary's life expectancy is determined (from Table I) as of his or her age in the first distribution year—the year after your death. Once the distribution amount is calculated and withdrawn, it is divided among the beneficiaries in proportion to their interest in the account.

EXAMPLE: You name your mother and your three children as equal beneficiaries of your retirement plan. You die in 2006. Under the terms of the plan, your beneficiaries are permitted to use the life expectancy rule when distributing your retirement account. Because your mother is the oldest beneficiary, the account must be distributed over her life expectancy. She will turn 85 in 2007, the first distribution year. Her life expectancy—or ADP—at that time will be 7.6 years (from Table I). To compute the first distribution, your beneficiaries must divide the December 31, 2006 account balance by 7.6. That amount will then be distributed and divided equally among your mother and your three children. Each will get a fourth. The ADP will drop by one each subsequent year, and the account will be completely distributed in just eight years.

2. Five-Year Rule

Again, it's important to remember that the plan can require that distributions be made according to the five-year rule. If the plan provides that the five-year rule applies to nonspouse beneficiaries, but the life expectancy rule is available for a spouse, the spouse is nonetheless prohibited from using the life expectancy rule if the spouse is one of multiple beneficiaries.

3. Splitting Accounts After Death

If you die before your required beginning date having named multiple beneficiaries of your single retirement account, and as of September 30 of the year after your death all beneficiaries are designated beneficiaries, your beneficiaries have until December 31 of the year after your death to separate their respective shares. If they complete the separation in time, the distribution rules will apply separately to each beneficiary and his or her respective share.

As we explained in Section F, above, the biggest benefit will be that each beneficiary will be able to use his or her own life expectancy to calculate distributions from his or her share. Furthermore, the separation will give each beneficiary autonomy over investment decisions and will also simplify accounting and other record keeping. As long as the plan itself permits the separation, the law won't prevent it.

One cautionary note: Beneficiaries may use their own life expectancies beginning in the year after the accounts are separated. So if the accounts are separated in the year after death, the required distribution for that year must be based on the life expectancy of the oldest beneficiary (presumably because there were, in fact, multiple beneficiaries named on the account for part of the year). Confused? Here's an example.

EXAMPLE: You named your mother, Josephine, and your three children, Holly, Herman, and Hank, as equal beneficiaries of your retirement plan. You died in 2005. In March 2006, your mother and the three children instructed the custodian to split your IRA into four separate but equal IRAs. All of the new IRAs remain in your name, but one names your mother as beneficiary, one names Holly, one names Herman, and one names Hank. For the year 2006 (the year of the split), the beneficiaries must use your mother's life expectancy to compute required distributions. But then beginning in 2007 (the year after the split), each beneficiary can take required distributions from his or her share of the IRA over his or her own life expectancy.

Splitting the account in the year of death. If, in the above example, the account were split in 2005 (the year of death), each beneficiary could use his or her own life expectancy to compute the 2006 required distribution (as well as future distributions) from his or her share.

If you name a trust as beneficiary. Splitting the account will not work when a trust is named beneficiary of your retirement account and the trust itself has multiple beneficiaries. (See Section H3, below, for more information.)

a. Transfer

When separating each beneficiary's share into a separate account after your death, assets must be transferred directly from the trustee or custodian of the original single plan account to the trustee or custodian of each separate account. The beneficiary must not have control of the funds at any time. If the beneficiary is deemed to have control, the IRS will consider the assets fully distributed and fully taxable in the current year.

Furthermore, in the case of nonspouse beneficiaries, the account must remain in the name of the deceased (see Section b, below), so it cannot be transferred to one or more of the beneficiaries' existing retirement plans or even into a new retirement account in a beneficiary's name. If a spouse is one of the beneficiaries, however, the spouse could presumably separate his or her share and roll it over to either an existing or a new IRA in the spouse's name.

b. Name on Account

When transferring a portion of the plan assets to a new account, the IRS requires that the new account also be in the original participant's name. But financial institutions generally do not like to maintain accounts, let alone set up new ones, in the name of a deceased person. To accommodate both the IRS requirements and their own internal accounting procedures, many custodians construct account titles that identify both the original participant (now deceased) and the beneficiary who is to receive distributions.

> **EXAMPLE:** Joe Corpus died leaving a substantial IRA equally to his three children, Dan, Irwin, and Bruce. The children want to split the IRA into three separate IRAs so that each can manage his own investments. The IRA custodian set up three new IRA accounts in Joe's name and transferred a third of Joe's original IRA into each one. The title on Dan's account reads: "Joe Corpus, Deceased, for the benefit of (or FBO) Dan Corpus." The other two accounts are titled "Joe Corpus, Deceased, FBO Irwin Corpus" and "Joe Corpus, Deceased, FBO Bruce Corpus."

Reporting Requirements

The IRS has issued what is called a "revenue procedure" outlining a set of reporting requirements that IRA custodians must adhere to after an IRA participant dies. The custodian must file IRS Form 5498 (you can find a sample of one in Appendix A) for each beneficiary. The form reports the name of the original owner, the name of the beneficiary, the beneficiary's tax ID or Social Security number, and the value of the beneficiary's share of the IRA as of the end of the year.

With this information, the IRS can trace the source of the IRA for income tax purposes and determine who is liable for the deferred tax. The form must be filed every year until the account is depleted.

No rollover allowed. Some non-spouse beneficiaries and, unfortunately, even some custodians are under the mistaken impression that a beneficiary may roll over a deceased participant's retirement plan into an IRA in the beneficiary's own name. This option, however, is available only to a spouse beneficiary. (See Section B3, above, for more information about spousal rollovers.) Nonspouse beneficiaries are never permitted to roll over retirement plan assets into a new or existing IRA in their own names.

c. Choosing a Distribution Option

As we explained above, the effect of naming multiple beneficiaries of one retirement plan account (assuming the account is not split by December 31 of the year after death) is to limit the deferral period to the life expectancy of the oldest beneficiary. As long as the plan permits, however, there is nothing to prevent one beneficiary from accelerating distributions of his or her share while the remaining beneficiaries use the life expectancy rule. The remaining beneficiaries' deferral period would be limited to the life expectancy of the oldest, even if the oldest had already withdrawn some or all of his or her share.

EXAMPLE: Mary, Paul, and Peter inherited an IRA from their father, Jake. The children had not split the account by December 31 of the year after Jake's death. Now, Mary, the oldest child, wants to take her share and use it to buy a house. The boys don't need the money right now and want to take their portions out slowly, spreading distributions over as many years as possible. Mary may take her share outright, and the boys may continue to spread distribution of their shares over Mary's life expectancy.

4. When a Spouse Is One of the Beneficiaries

If your spouse is one of multiple beneficiaries of your retirement account, your spouse loses the option to defer distributions until you would have been 70½. Also, even if your spouse is the oldest beneficiary, your spouse would not be permitted to look up her ADP in the Single Life Table (Table I) each year. Instead, she would look up his or her ADP in the year after death (using Table I), but in subsequent years, she would reduce the ADP by one each year.

If the account is an IRA, your spouse also would lose the option to make the IRA her own by failing to take a required distribution or by making a contribution of her own. (See Section C2, above.) However, she can still roll over any distribution she receives into an IRA in her own name, whether or not she is the sole beneficiary of your retirement account.

A spouse is the sole beneficiary of your retirement account if he or she is the sole beneficiary on September 30 of the year after your death. If your spouse is one of several designated beneficiaries (see Section 5, below) as of September 30, all is not lost. If your spouse's share is then separated on or before December 31 of the year after death, making your spouse the sole beneficiary of his or her share, then your spouse is deemed to be the sole beneficiary of her share, and all the special privileges accorded a spouse-beneficiary would apply to that separate share.

5. Designated and Nondesignated Beneficiaries

If as of September 30 of the year after your death, any one of the beneficiaries of your retirement account is not a designated beneficiary, the account is deemed to have no designated beneficiary, even if one or more of the other beneficiaries on the account would otherwise be a designated beneficiary. If the account is deemed to have no designated beneficiary, the life expectancy rule is not available. Instead, the assets must be distributed under the five-year rule. Many a charitably inclined taxpayer, wanting to leave a portion of his or her retirement plan to charity and a portion to a spouse or child, has been blindsided by this unfavorable application of the rules.

EXAMPLE: Paul named his son and the American Cancer Society as equal beneficiaries of his IRA. Paul died in 2005. The beneficiaries did not get around to splitting the account or paying out the charity's portion by September 30, 2006. Because the American Cancer Society is not a natural person or a qualified trust, it is not considered a designated beneficiary. Therefore, the IRA is deemed to have no designated beneficiary, even though Paul's son would have qualified had he been the sole beneficiary. As a result, the entire account must be distributed by December 31, 2009, with half going to Paul's son and half to the American Cancer Society.

Remember, though, this problem can be cured by separating the account or by distributing the charity's share before September 30 of the year after death.

 All beneficiaries must be designated beneficiaries. The December 31 deadline for splitting accounts applies only if all beneficiaries are designated beneficiaries as of September 30 of the year after death.

H. Trust Beneficiary

Generally, a beneficiary must be a natural person to qualify as a designated beneficiary and be eligible for the life expectancy rule. The exception to this general rule applies when the beneficiary is a trust that meets certain stringent requirements. As explained in Chapter 6, Section C, if the trust satisfies all of those requirements, then the beneficiaries of the trust will be treated as designated beneficiaries for purposes of the life expectancy rule. In other words, the trustee or custodian of the retirement plan may look through the trust to find the designated beneficiary whose life expectancy can be used to compute required distributions.

One of those requirements is to provide a copy of the trust to the trustee or custodian of your retirement plan. For purposes of post-death distributions, the trust document must be in the hands of the trustee or custodian by October 31 of the year after death.

1. Nonspouse Beneficiary of Trust

If you do name a trust as beneficiary and if it meets the requirements of a designated beneficiary (see Chapter 6, Section C), distributions under the life expectancy rule or the five-year rule will be computed as though there were no trust in place—as though the beneficiary of the trust had been named beneficiary of the retirement plan. Therefore, if the beneficiary of the trust is not your spouse, the life expectancy rule would apply and the beneficiary may spread required distributions over the beneficiary's life expectancy beginning in the year after your death. In any case, all distributions would go into the trust and become subject to the terms of the trust, which may or may not call for an immediate distribution to the beneficiary.

Bypass Trusts and Estate Planning

You must jump through a raft of hoops to name a trust as beneficiary of a retirement plan and feel confident that you have accomplished what you intended. Sometimes, you never do achieve a high level of confidence. So with all the risk and uncertainty, why would anyone bother?

People name trusts as beneficiaries for all kinds of reasons, and one of the most significant of those is to fund what is called a bypass trust to minimize estate taxes.

The use of trusts in estate planning to minimize estate taxes and other costs is complex, but here's a brief summary of what it means to use a retirement plan to fund a bypass trust.

The law allows each individual to leave a certain amount, called an "exclusion amount," to his or her heirs free of estate taxes. (The exclusion amount is scheduled to increase incrementally from $1.5 million in 2005 to $3.5 million by the year 2009.) In addition, an individual may leave an unlimited amount to a spouse. If an individual leaves everything outright to a spouse, however, some or all of the individual's exclusion amount could be wasted.

For example, assume a husband and wife have a combined net worth of $3 million. The husband dies in January 2005 and leaves everything to his wife, never using his $1.5 million exclusion amount. Although there will be no estate taxes when the husband dies, when the wife dies, she can leave only her own exclusion amount tax free to the children. The remainder will be subject to estate taxes. If the wife dies in December 2005 and the estate is still worth $3 million, she leaves $1.5 million tax free to the children, but the remaining $1.5 million is subject to estate taxes. If the husband had given his $1.5 million to the children when he died, instead of to his spouse, the entire estate could have passed to the children tax-free.

Many people choose not to give large amounts to their children outright because they don't want to risk leaving a spouse strapped for cash. That's where the bypass trust concept comes in. When the husband dies, he can direct his exclusion amount to a trust which is accessible to the wife during her lifetime and which flows to the children upon her death. Technically, the assets in the trust do not belong to the wife, so when she dies, she can give additional amounts equal to the exclusion to the children—all of it tax free.

Now, what role does the IRA or retirement plan play in all of this? For many people, a retirement plan is their most substantial asset, and a bypass trust couldn't be fully funded unless the plan assets were used. In other words, many people don't have enough assets outside the plan to put the exclusion amount into a bypass trust. But the law won't allow a trust to "own" a retirement plan, which means it is not possible to simply transfer the plan into the trust. To fund the trust, a person would have to name the trust as beneficiary so that after-death distributions from the plan would be directed into the trust every year until the trust is fully funded. The spouse could then have access to the funds once they have been distributed from the retirement plan to the trust.

2. Spouse Beneficiary of Trust

If your spouse is sole beneficiary of the trust, your spouse will be treated as the designated beneficiary for purposes of the life expectancy rule. That means your spouse could take distributions over his or her life expectancy either beginning on December 31 of the year you would have been 70½ or beginning the year after your death if that is later. In either case, your spouse would use his or her age each year to find the corresponding ADP in Table I.

Your spouse cannot make your IRA her own. If you name a trust as beneficiary of your IRA, IRS regulations state that even if your spouse is the sole beneficiary of your trust, she cannot make the IRA her own, either by failing to take a required distribution or by making additional contributions. However, she might be able to receive a distribution of IRA assets from the trust and then roll them over into her own IRA. See Section 4, below.

3. Multiple Beneficiaries of Trust

If a trust has multiple beneficiaries and meets the criteria for looking through the trust for a designated beneficiary, then for purposes of applying the life expectancy rule, the multiple beneficiary rules described in Section G, above, will apply as though the individuals themselves were named beneficiaries of the retirement plan.

Splitting the account won't work if a trust is the beneficiary. If you have named a trust as beneficiary of your retirement plan and there are multiple beneficiaries of the trust, splitting the retirement plan into separate accounts for each beneficiary of the trust—whether it is done before or after your death—won't allow beneficiaries to use their own life expectancies to compute required distributions. The multiple beneficiary rules would still apply, and distributions would have to be taken over the life expectancy of the oldest beneficiary of the trust.

4. Trust Beneficiary and Spousal Rollovers

Recall that a trust is often named the beneficiary of a retirement plan in order to fund a bypass trust. Assuming the spouse is the beneficiary of the trust, distributions from the plan go into the trust when the participant dies, and then the trust makes distributions to the spouse.

But sometimes the surviving spouse discovers after the participant dies that the retirement plan assets are not needed to fund the bypass trust after all. In that case, the surviving spouse might prefer to simply roll over the retirement plan assets into his or her own IRA, name his or her own beneficiary, and begin a new schedule of required distributions.

Unfortunately, the law says that only a spouse beneficiary (and not a trust) may roll over retirement plan assets—and then only if the spouse acquires the assets directly from and by reason of the participant's death.

But taxpayers have argued that if the spouse is the sole beneficiary of the trust and can distribute all of the assets without interference from any third party, then the assets essentially pass directly from the deceased to the spouse—making the rollover within the spirit of the law.

Between 1987 and 2001, the IRS established a pattern of approving such actions in private letter rulings—despite the lack of explicit legal approval.

In final regulations issued in April 2002, however, the IRS stated specifically that a spouse cannot make a deceased participant's IRA her own if a trust is named primary beneficiary of the IRA—even if the spouse is the sole beneficiary of the trust.

Nonetheless, some practitioners believe that if the spouse has the power to distribute all assets of the trust, he or she could distribute the IRA assets to the trust and then distribute the assets from the trust to the spouse. Having done so, the spouse could then roll over the assets into an IRA of his or her own. Although this strategy is not specifically sanctioned by the IRS, some practitioners believe it will pass muster, even under the new regulations.

We think you should proceed with caution. If you name a trust as beneficiary of your retirement plan with the expectation that the spouse can fall back on a roll-over, you are taking a risk.

As an alternative to taking this risk, consider naming your spouse as primary beneficiary (thus preserving the rollover opportunity) and your trust as contingent beneficiary. After your death, your spouse would have the option of disclaiming some or all of his or her interest in your retirement plan, allowing it to flow to the bypass trust. Ultimately, however, no strategy involving a trust is completely simple or safe.

I. Estate as Beneficiary

In cases in which an estate was named beneficiary of a retirement plan, private letter rulings issued before 2001 closely paralleled those in which a trust was named beneficiary. If the participant's spouse was the sole beneficiary of the estate, and no one had the authority to restrict the spouse's access to the estate, several IRS private letter rulings permitted the spouse to take a distribution of the plan assets and roll them over into an IRA in the spouse's name.

It is still unclear, however, how much weight these old private letter rulings will carry under the new regulations. We believe it is safest to avoid using this strategy.

 Think twice before naming your estate as beneficiary. Although many people name their estate as beneficiary of their retirement plan or IRA, there is little advantage to doing so and some significant disadvantages. For example, because your estate is not a designated beneficiary, you are deemed to have no designated beneficiary for required distribution purposes. As a result, distributions could be accelerated after your death unless your spouse is the sole beneficiary of your estate and is permitted to roll over the plan assets. Relying on such an option for your spouse is risky business, however, given that the strategy has thin support from only a few IRS private letter rulings. Whatever it is you want to accomplish by naming your estate as beneficiary of your retirement plan can almost certainly be achieved through another strategy.

J. Annuities

If your retirement plan benefits are to be paid in the form of an annuity, whether to you or to your beneficiary, the required distribution rules must still be satisfied.

1. Start Date

If you die before your RBD, the date by which payments to your beneficiary must begin (the start date) depends on whether or not your beneficiary is your spouse.

If you have named a nonspouse beneficiary, the start date is December 31 of the year after your death.

If your beneficiary is your spouse, however, the start date is the later of December 31 of the year after your death or December 31 of the year you would have turned 70½.

If you had already started receiving your annuity payments and died before your RBD, payments still must satisfy the required distribution rules described below as of the start date. (If payments had begun under an irrevocable annuity, see Section 3, below.)

2. Form of Payment

In order to satisfy required distribution rules, payments must be in a particular form, although the form varies with the type and terms of the annuity. (See Chapter 6, Section D, for more information about types of annuities.) After your death, your beneficiary must take his or her first payment by one of the start dates described in Section 1, above. That payment, however, can be a normal payment. For example, if your beneficiary intends to take monthly payments over his or her life expectancy, the first monthly payment can be paid in December of the year after your death and monthly thereafter. Your beneficiary need not take the full annual amount in December of that first year.

3. Irrevocable Annuity

If you had already begun receiving payments under an irrevocable annuity at the time of your death, your beneficiary must continue to receive payments with no break in the distribution schedule.

K. Divorce or Separation

If you were divorced or separated at some time during your life, part of your qualified plan, qualified annuity, or TDA may be payable to an alternate payee (such as a spouse, former spouse, or child) under the terms of a QDRO—a court-approved divorce or maintenance agreement. (See Chapter 2, Section C4, for more information about QDROs.)

If the alternate payee's entire share has not yet been paid at the time of your death, then the alternate payee's distribution options are determined by whether or not the alternate payee's interest was held in a separate account or aggregated with the rest of your benefit.

1. Separate Account

If an alternate payee's share is segregated or separately accounted for (see Chapter 6 for more information about separate accounts), then the life expectancy rule applies to that share, and the alternate payee may take distributions over his or her own life expectancy, beginning no later than December 31 of the year after your death. Remember, though, the plan itself could require application of the five-year rule, in which case the alternate payee's share must be distributed by December 31 of the year containing the fifth anniversary of your death.

a. Spouse or Former Spouse Alternate Payee

A spouse or former spouse alternate payee has all the rights and privileges of a surviving spouse beneficiary as long as the alternate payee's share is in a separate account. The life expectancy rule would apply unless it is prohibited under the plan. Distributions may be made over the ex-spouse's life expectancy, and must begin by the later of December 31 of the year following the death of the participant or December 31 of the year the participant would have turned 70½.

And if the plan permits, the spouse or former spouse alternate payee may roll over his or her share distribution into a retirement plan or IRA in his or her own name.

b. Death of Alternate Payee

If the alternate payee dies before his or her interest has been completely distributed, the alternate payee's beneficiary will be treated as the designated beneficiary of the alternate payee's portion for purposes of the life expectancy rule and the five-year rule.

> EXAMPLE: Your former wife is entitled to one-half of your retirement plan benefits under the terms of a QDRO. Your former wife has named her brother as beneficiary of her share of the retirement plan. Your wife died when you were age 60, before she had received any portion of your retirement plan. You die a year later at the age of

62. Your beneficiary may take distribution of his or her share of the account over his or her own life expectancy. At the same time, your wife's brother can receive your wife's portion over his own life expectancy.

2. No Separate Account

If the plan administrator has not maintained a separate account for the alternate payee of your retirement plan, the beneficiary designation will determine how distributions will be made after your death. Specifically, the multiple beneficiary rules, described in Section G, above, will apply. The distribution would then be divided among the alternate payee and the beneficiaries in proportion to their interests.

EXAMPLE: Your former husband is entitled to one-half of your retirement plan benefits under the terms of a QDRO. You have named your father as beneficiary of the other half. Your former husband's share has not been segregated or separately accounted for. You die an untimely death at the age of 56. Under the terms of the plan, your beneficiary will use the life expectancy rule. Because the interests of your father and your former husband are aggregated in one account, your father, as beneficiary, is the one whose life expectancy must be used to determine required distributions. Each distribution will be split equally between your former husband and your father.

L. Reporting Distributions From IRAs

If you are the beneficiary of an IRA, it is up to you to compute the required distribution each year and report it on your tax return. If you were the original owner of the IRA, the custodian would be required to help you compute the proper amount. However, the law does not currently extend this benefit to beneficiaries. As a beneficiary, you will still receive a Form 5498, reporting the value of the IRA each year, but when it comes to calculating the required distribution, you're on your own.

Key Tax Code and Regulation Sections
§ 401(a)(9) Required Distributions From Qualified Plans
§ 1.401(a)(9) Required Distribution Regulations
§ 402(c) Rollovers From Qualified Plans
§ 408 Individual Retirement Accounts
§ 1.408-8, A-5 Election by Spouse to Treat Decedent's IRA as Own
Rev. Proc. 89-52 After-Death IRA Reporting Requirements

Chapter 8

Distributions to Your Beneficiary If You Die After Age 70½

<table>
<tr><td>

Who Should Read Chapter 8

➡ Read this chapter if you want to know what happens to your own retirement plan after you die or if you inherit a retirement plan or IRA from someone who died after reaching age 70½ and who had already begun mandatory distributions from the plan or IRA. This chapter describes how the remainder of the account must be distributed.

</td></tr>
</table>

*E*ven though you are required to start taking money out of your retirement account on your required beginning date (which, for most people, is April 1 of the year after they turn 70½), the account might not be empty when you die. It might even be quite large, especially if you had been withdrawing only the minimum required amount each year—or if you die soon after your RBD. So what happens to the leftovers? The answer to that question is the subject of this chapter.

A. Administrative Details

Although the rules for computing required distributions after your death might vary depending on who your beneficiary is, the following administrative procedures apply almost across the board.

1. Name on the Account

Unless your beneficiary is your spouse, your retirement account must remain in your name until the account is entirely depleted. If a beneficiary other than your spouse attempts to change the name on the retirement plan account to his or her own name, the action could be a deemed distribution of the entire account. Worse, if the beneficiary attempts to roll over your account into the beneficiary's own IRA, not only will it be a deemed distribution, but penalties for contributing more to an IRA than is allowed may be assessed as well.

Despite the above rule, the trustee or custodian might want to retitle the account to show that you have died. This is permissible as long as the custodian complies with certain procedures for titling the account and reporting distributions. (See Chapter 7, Section G, for more information about titling accounts.)

A special rule allows your spouse to treat your retirement plan account as his or her own. See Section B3, below, to learn how this can be done.

2. Timing of Distributions

Once you pass your RBD, distributions from your account must continue, even after your death. There can be no hiatus in distributions. If you failed to take some or all of your required distribution in the

Helpful Terms

Annuity. A contract, sold by an insurance company, that promises to make monthly, quarterly, semiannual, or annual payments for life or for a specified period of time.

Beneficiary. The person or entity entitled to receive the benefits from insurance or from trust property, such as a retirement plan or IRA.

Deferral period. The number of years over which distributions from a retirement plan or IRA can be spread.

Distribution. A payout of property (such as shares of stock) or cash from a retirement plan or IRA to the participant or a beneficiary.

Estate. All property that a person owns.

Primary beneficiary. A person or entity entitled to receive benefits from a retirement plan or IRA upon the death of the original participant.

Term certain. A fixed, identifiable period, such as a specific number of years. For example, a retirement plan that is distributable over a term certain of 20 years must be completely liquidated after 20 years.

---

year of your death, your beneficiary must take the remainder before the end of the year. Then your beneficiary must continue to take distributions in all subsequent years until the account is depleted.

The only exception to this rule occurs if your spouse elects to treat the account as his or her own. In that case, required distributions from the account (after the spouse makes it his or her own) will be determined as if the spouse had been the original owner of the account. (See Section B, below, for more about this strategy.)

3. Designated Beneficiary

Recall that you can name any person or organization you choose as the beneficiary of your retirement plan or IRA. When determining how your retirement assets should be distributed after your death, however, only designated beneficiaries are taken into account. (See Chapter 6, Section C, for more information about designated beneficiaries.) If one or more of your beneficiaries is not a designated beneficiary, you are deemed to have no designated beneficiary.

a. Deadline for Determining Designated Beneficiary

For purposes of computing post-death required distributions, your designated beneficiary is determined as of September 30 of the year after your death. That doesn't mean someone else can name a new beneficiary of your retirement plan after you die. In fact, no new beneficiaries can be added. Therefore, it is important that you carefully consider and then formally select a beneficiary before you die (using the plan's Designation of Beneficiary form). Not only will that beneficiary receive the assets of your plan, but his or her life expectancy will determine how quickly assets must be distributed after your death.

b. Changing Beneficiaries Before the Deadline

The IRS allows this extended deadline for determining beneficiaries specifically to give those beneficiaries an opportunity to do some postmortem planning—to make administration of the retirement plan easier or to clean up a disadvantageous situation you left behind. For example, suppose you name your spouse as primary beneficiary and your daughter as contingent beneficiary. After your death, your spouse might decide she has no need for the assets in your retirement plan. She might disclaim (renounce) her interest in those assets. If she does, the plan assets would go to your daughter, and your daughter's life expectancy would determine how your retirement plan assets are ultimately distributed.

4. Reporting Distributions

If you are the beneficiary of an IRA or other retirement plan, it is up to you to compute the required distribution each year and report it on your tax return. In the case of an IRA, the custodian will send you a Form 5498, reporting the value of the IRA each year, but you are responsible for the calculation. If you had been the original owner of the IRA, the law would require the custodian to help you compute the proper amount. (See Chapter 6, Section B5.) However, the law does not extend this benefit to beneficiaries.

B. Spouse Beneficiary

If your spouse is the beneficiary of your retirement account, he or she may take distributions under the rules described in this section.

For sole beneficiaries only. For purposes of this Section B, we assume that the spouse was the sole beneficiary of the retirement plan. The rules change if a spouse is one of several beneficiaries. (See Section F, below, for the multiple beneficiary rules.)

1. Year of Death

The minimum required distribution for the year of your death will be computed in exactly the same way you would have computed it if you had lived to the end of the year. If you did not take a distribution of the required amount before your death, your spouse beneficiary must do so on your behalf by December 31 of the year of your death. In other words, your spouse would use the Uniform Lifetime Table and find the ADP for your age on your birthday in the year of your death. Then your spouse would divide the account balance as of December 31 of the previous year by the ADP.

If your spouse is more than ten years younger than you are, and if you had been using Table II (Joint and Last Survivor Table) to compute lifetime distributions, your spouse would use Table II to find the ADP in the year of your death, as well.

⚠ Spouse must take required distribution for year of death. A spouse beneficiary has the option to treat a deceased participant's retirement plan as the spouse's own. Nonetheless, if you die after your RBD, your spouse must take your required distribution for the year of your death (if you had not already done so) before your spouse can make the account his or her own. Once the account is in the spouse's name, all the required distribution rules apply as though the spouse were the original owner. (See Section 3, below, to learn what happens when the account is rolled over or placed in the name of a surviving spouse.)

2. Second Year and Beyond

If your spouse is younger than you are, beginning in the second year (and assuming your spouse does not roll over the account into a retirement account in his or her own name), your spouse will use his or her own age and Table I (Single Life Table) to look up the ADP each year.

EXAMPLE: Richard died on October 14, 2004, at the age of 75. Richard's wife, Pat, was the sole beneficiary of his IRA. She was 74 in 2004. Richard had been computing required distributions using the Uniform Lifetime Table (Table III). Richard withdrew his required distribution for 2004 before he died.

To compute the required distribution for 2005, Pat uses Table I to find her ADP for her age in 2005. Pat turned 75 in 2005, so her ADP from Table I is 13.4. Pat will divide the December 31, 2004 balance of Richard's IRA by 13.4 to determine the required distribution for 2005.

In 2006, Pat turns 76. Her ADP (from Table I) is 12.7. Pat will divide the December 31, 2005 balance of Richard's IRA by 12.7 to determine the required distribution for 2006.

If your spouse is older than you, your spouse will use your remaining life expectancy to compute required distributions for the year after your death and beyond.

EXAMPLE: You died in 2006 at age 73, after having taken your required distribution from your IRA for the year. Your spouse, who was the sole beneficiary of your IRA, turned 76 in 2006. Your spouse elects not to roll over your IRA into an IRA of her own. Because your spouse was older than you, your spouse must take a distribution in 2007 based on your single life expectancy.

The ADP for 2007 is your single life expectancy in 2006 (the year of your death) reduced by one. The single life expectancy for age 73, your age in 2006, is 14.8. Therefore, for 2007, your spouse must use an ADP of 13.8 (14.8 − 1). To compute the 2007 required distribution, your spouse will divide the December 31, 2006 IRA balance by 13.8.

To compute the 2008 required distribution, your spouse will divide the December 31, 2007 IRA balance by one less than the previous ADP, which is 12.8 (13.8 − 1). In future years, the ADP will be reduced by one until the entire account is depleted.

3. Rollover

When you die, your spouse may choose to leave your retirement plan or IRA in your name, applying all the distribution rules described above until the account has been completely liquidated.

Fortunately for your spouse, however, she has another, usually more favorable, option. She can roll over the plan assets into a plan or IRA of her own. (Note that this option is available only to a spouse beneficiary.)

If your plan is not an IRA, a rollover to a plan in the spouse's name is the only way to make the plan or IRA the spouse's own.

But if the retirement plan is an IRA, your spouse has several ways to make the IRA her own. She can do so by:

- rolling over the assets into a new or preexisting IRA or plan in the spouse's own name (see Subsection a, below)
- failing to take your post-death required distribution at the proper time (see Subsection b, below), or
- contributing additional amounts of the spouse's own to your IRA.

a. Convert to Spouse's Plan or IRA by Rollover

Most spouses choose the rollover method because it is convenient and because it leaves a clear trail. Once the rollover is complete, the account belongs to your spouse in every way. Not only can your spouse name a new beneficiary, but your spouse's RBD will determine when future required distributions must begin.

If your surviving spouse is not 70½ or older when he or she rolls over your retirement plan or IRA, required distributions may be discontinued until your spouse reaches his or her RBD. Then on your spouse's RBD, your spouse must begin required distributions anew, using the Uniform Lifetime Table to determine the ADP—or using Table II if your spouse has since married someone else and if the new spouse is more than ten years younger.

![warning icon] **Spouse must take a distribution in the year of death.** As mentioned in Section 1, above, if you had not withdrawn your required distribution before your death and if your spouse wants to roll over the account into his or her own name, your spouse must withdraw the required amount for the year of your death before he or she can complete the rollover.

After you die, your spouse may roll over your retirement plan or IRA even if your spouse has passed his or her own RBD. In this case, however, there can be no hiatus in required distributions. If your spouse rolls over your IRA in the year of your death, she must take a distribution on your behalf (if you had not done so). The following year, she must take a distribution on her own behalf (because it is now her IRA and she is past her RBD).

> **EXAMPLE:** Richard died on October 14, 2005 at the age of 75. Richard's wife, Pat, was the sole beneficiary of his IRA. She was 74 in 2005. Richard had already withdrawn the required distribution for 2005.
> On January 19, 2006 Pat opened an IRA in her own name and rolled over Richard's IRA into her new account. She named her daughter Tash

as beneficiary of the new account. To determine her required distribution for 2006, Pat will use the December 31, 2005 IRA balance. She will divide that balance by the ADP for her age in 2006, which is 75. Her ADP (from the Uniform Lifetime Table—Table III), is 22.9.

b. Convert to Spouse's IRA by Failing to Take a Required Distribution

If you die after your RBD, and if your spouse fails to take a required distribution on your behalf in any year after the year of your death, your spouse is deemed to have made an election to treat your IRA as his or her own. (Remember that because you are past your required beginning date, your spouse must take your required distribution for the year of your death if you had not already done so.) The IRA becomes the spouse's own on December 31 of the year of the failure, and the spouse will not be required to take a distribution until his or her own RBD.

If your spouse has passed his or her own RBD, then your spouse must take a distribution in the year your spouse makes the IRA his or her own. The distribution will be based on your spouse's age in that year, and the ADP will be determined from the Uniform Lifetime Table. If your spouse has remarried by that time to someone who is more than ten years younger, the ADP will be determined from Table II, using the surviving spouse's and his or her new spouse's ages.

c. Timing of Rollover

The income tax regulations give your spouse no deadline for converting or rolling over your retirement account to his or her own IRA after your death. Your spouse should be able to make the election at any time—even years after your death—as long as he or she continues to take timely required distributions on your behalf for as long as the account remains in your name.

As a practical matter, if a spouse is past age 59½ and intends to roll over a participant's retirement plan into the spouse's own IRA, there is nothing to be gained from waiting. If the spouse needs money, the spouse can take it freely from his or her own IRA even after rolling it over, because there is no penalty for taking distributions after age 59½.

If the spouse is younger than age 59½, however, free use of the IRA funds could be dicey. Recall that one of the exceptions to the early distribution tax is a distribution to a beneficiary after the death of the original participant. (See Chapter 3 for more information on the early distribution tax.) But that particular exception is not available to a spouse after the spouse rolls over the deceased person's plan into the spouse's own plan or IRA. Once it is rolled over, it is the spouse's IRA. Because the spouse is still alive, the after-death exception does not apply. Thus, the spouse must generally postpone distributions until age 59½ to avoid the early distribution tax.

Consequently, if the spouse is younger than age 59½ and needs to use the retirement plan money to live on, the spouse might be better off leaving the plan in the name of the deceased so that the after-death exception can be used. The one disadvantage of this approach is that, according to at least one IRS private letter ruling, once a spouse invokes the after-death exception to the early distribution tax, the spouse forever forfeits the right to roll over the account into an IRA in the spouse's own name.

4. Death of Spouse Beneficiary

When your spouse dies, assuming your spouse did not roll over your retirement plan into a plan or IRA of his or her own, the spouse's beneficiary must continue to take distributions according to the rules discussed in this section.

a. Year of Spouse's Death

The spouse's beneficiary must take a distribution in the year of the spouse's death. The beneficiary will use Table I to find the ADP that corresponds to the spouse's age on his or her birthday in the year of death, and then the beneficiary will divide the account balance as of December 31 of the year before the spouse's death by the ADP for the year of death.

b. Second Year and Beyond

For subsequent years, the ADP is reduced by one each year. The account balance for the previous December 31 is divided by the ADP for the current year to determine the required distribution. This calculation method continues until the account is completely distributed, regardless of whether or not the spouse's beneficiary survives until the account is empty.

EXAMPLE: Pierre was born on January 10, 1934 and turned 70½ in 2004. Pierre's wife, Zoe, was his designated beneficiary. She turned 68 in 2004. To compute his required distribution for 2004, Pierre used an ADP of 27.4, which he found in the Uniform Lifetime Table next to his age of 70.

2004 Distribution:

Pierre's December 31, 2003, IRA account balance was $100,000. Thus, Pierre's first required distribution (for 2004) was $3,650 ($100,000 divided by 27.4.).

2005 Distribution:

Pierre died in 2005 before taking his required distribution. Zoe found Pierre's ADP of 26.5 (for age 71) from the Uniform Lifetime Table (Table III in Appendix B). The IRA account balance on December 31, 2004 was $106,000. The required distribution for 2005, the year of Pierre's death, was $4,030 ($106,000 divided by 26.3).

2006 Distribution:

Zoe decides not to roll over Pierre's IRA into an IRA in her own name. The required distribution for 2006 is based on Zoe's single life expectancy. Therefore, she will use Table I. Zoe turned 70 in 2006. The ADP for age 70 is 16. The December 31, 2005 IRA balance was $111,000. Therefore, the 2006 required distribution is $6,938 ($111,000 divided by 16).

2007 Distribution:

Zoe died in 2007 before taking her required distribution. Her beneficiaries will again use Table I to find Zoe's ADP for 2007, the year of her death. The ADP for Zoe's age that year, which was 71, is 16.3. The December 31, 2006 balance of the IRA was $115,000. The required distribution is $7,055 ($115,000 divided by 16.3).

2008 Distribution:

For the year after Zoe's death and each subsequent year, Zoe's beneficiaries must reduce the ADP for the previous year by one. Therefore, the ADP for 2008 is 15.3 (16.3 – 1). The December 31, 2007 balance of the IRA was $120,000. The required distribution is $7,843 ($120,000 divided by 15.3).

C. Nonspouse Beneficiary

If the beneficiary of your retirement plan or IRA is not your spouse, distributions after your death are computed according to the rules described in this section.

If there is more than one beneficiary. The rules in this section apply if there is only one beneficiary named on the account. If there is more than one beneficiary, a different set of rules applies. See Sections E and F, below, for more about the multiple beneficiary rules.

1. Year of Death

In the year of your death, if you had not yet taken your required distribution for the year, your beneficiary must do so before the end of the year. Your beneficiary will use the Uniform Lifetime Table (Table III in Appendix B) one last time, looking up the ADP for your age on your birthday in the year of your death. If you had already taken your required distribution, your beneficiary need not take another distribution in the year of your death.

2. Second Year and Beyond

Beginning in the year after your death, required distributions are calculated differently depending on whether you were younger or older than your beneficiary. First, let's assume that your beneficiary was younger than you. In that case, your beneficiary would compute required distributions for the second year and beyond using the beneficiary's single life expectancy in the year after your death (from Table I). In subsequent years, the beneficiary will reduce the ADP by one each year.

EXAMPLE: You turned 70½ in 2002 and began taking required distributions from your IRA at that time. Your designated beneficiary was your daughter, Prudence, who turned 45 in 2002. You

had been using the Uniform Lifetime Table (Table III, Appendix B).

You died in the year 2006 after having taken your required distribution for the year. In 2007, the year after your death, Prudence must take a distribution based on her own single life expectancy, determined as of her birthday in 2007. Prudence turned 50 in 2007, and her single life expectancy, or ADP (from Table I), was 34.2. To determine the required distribution for 2007, Prudence divides the December 31, 2006 IRA balance by 34.2.

In 2008, Prudence will reduce the ADP by 1 and divide the December 31, 2007 balance by 33.2 (34.2 – 1). In future years, the ADP will be reduced by one until the entire IRA is depleted.

Second, let's assume you were younger than your beneficiary. In that case, your beneficiary would calculate the required distribution for the year after your death using your single life expectancy (from Table I) in the year of your death, reduced by one (that is, the ADP for the year after your death). In subsequent years, your beneficiary will reduce the ADP by one each year.

EXAMPLE: You turned 70½ in 1996 and began taking required distributions from your IRA at that time. Your designated beneficiary was your brother Ernest, who turned 73 in 1996. You had been using the Uniform Lifetime

Table (Table III, Appendix B).

You died in 2006 after taking your required distribution for the year. In 2007, the year after your death, Ernest must take a distribution based on your single life expectancy. He must determine your life expectancy in 2006 (the year of death) and reduce it by one. In 2006, you would have been 80 on your birthday. Your single life expectancy in that year (from Table I) was 10.2. Therefore, Ernest must use an ADP of 9.2 (10.2 – 1) to compute the required distribution for the year 2007. He will divide the December 31, 2006 balance by 9.2.

In 2008, Ernest will reduce the ADP by one. Therefore, he must divide the December 31, 2007 balance by 8.2 (9.2 – 1). In future years, he will reduce the ADP by one until the entire account is depleted.

3. Death of Nonspouse Beneficiary

If your nonspouse beneficiary dies after you do but before the account is completely empty, the computation method for required distributions will not change at the beneficiary's death. Distributions will be made to the beneficiary's beneficiary according to the schedule established at your death, using the original beneficiary's life expectancy (or yours if you were younger) as the ADP in the year after your death and reducing the ADP by one each subsequent year. Bear in mind, however,

that beneficiaries are always permitted to take more than the minimum required distribution.

4. Rollover

A nonspouse beneficiary is never permitted to roll over a deceased participant's retirement plan or IRA. Furthermore, the consequences are the same whether or not the deceased had passed his or her RBD at the time of death. Any rollover attempt will be deemed a distribution, and if the assets are actually deposited into an IRA in the beneficiary's name, the deposit will be considered an excess contribution to an IRA and will be subject to penalties if not withdrawn in timely fashion.

D. No Designated Beneficiary

If you did not name a beneficiary of your retirement plan or if the beneficiary does not qualify as a designated beneficiary, then distributions are based on your own single life expectancy in the year of your death, reduced by one for each subsequent year until the account is depleted.

> EXAMPLE: You turned 70½ in 2002. You named your estate as beneficiary and never got around to changing the designation before your death.
>
> You died in the year 2006 before taking your required distribution for the year. Your beneficiary (that is, the beneficiary of your estate) must use

the Uniform Lifetime Table (Table III in Appendix B) and your age in 2006 to compute the required distribution for 2006. The ADP for age 74 is 23.8.

For 2007, your beneficiary must find your single life expectancy (from Table I) for your age in 2006 (the year of your death) and reduce it by one. Your single life expectancy for age 74 is 14.1. Therefore, the ADP for the 2007 required distribution is 13.1 (14.1 – 1). In the future, the ADP will be reduced by one each year.

E. Multiple Beneficiaries, Separate Accounts

If you have several IRAs or retirement plans, each with a single beneficiary, then the required distribution rules are applied separately to each plan. You are not considered to have multiple beneficiaries.

Therefore, a spouse beneficiary of an IRA or plan would use the rules described in Section B, above. A nonspouse beneficiary of an IRA or plan would use the rules described in Section C, above.

F. Multiple Beneficiaries, One Account

If you name more than one designated beneficiary of a single retirement account, then you have multiple beneficiaries for that account, and required distributions after your death will be computed as though

the beneficiary with the shortest life expectancy were your sole beneficiary.

For example, if you name your sister and your children as equal beneficiaries of your IRA, and your sister is the oldest beneficiary, then distributions are computed after your death as though your sister were your sole beneficiary. But once calculated and withdrawn, the distribution will be divided equally among the beneficiaries.

Note, however, that if the beneficiary with the shortest life expectancy is older than you are, your beneficiaries will use your remaining single life expectancy to compute required distributions after your death. This is the same exception that applies if you die on or after your RBD having named a person who is older than you as your only beneficiary. See Section C2, above.

1. Determining the Designated Beneficiary

As is the case if you die before your RBD, the date for determining the beneficiaries is September 30 of the year following your death. If you had more than one beneficiary as of your date of death, your beneficiaries would still have time to make some changes. For example, one or more beneficiaries could disclaim an interest. Or perhaps the interests of one or more beneficiaries could be distributed by September 30 of the year after your death. (See Chapter 7, Section A2, for more information about changes that can be made after your death.)

There's one other cure for multiple beneficiaries. If on September 30 all beneficiaries are designated beneficiaries, then they have until December 31 to split the account so that each beneficiary has his or her separate share. (See Section 3, below, for more about splitting accounts.) If the accounts are split in timely fashion, the required distribution rules would apply separately to each share or account. Then, for example, each beneficiary could use his or her own life expectancy to compute required distributions.

⚠ If one or more beneficiaries is not a designated beneficiary. If on September 30 of the year after death there are multiple beneficiaries named on the account and one of them is not a designated beneficiary, then you are deemed to have no designated beneficiary, and the account must be distributed according to the rules of Section D, above. Splitting the account after September 30 will not cure the problem.

2. Computing the Required Distribution

If there are multiple beneficiaries named on your retirement account and they do not cure the problem, as described above, distributions must be spread over the life expectancy of the oldest beneficiary. In other words, the ADP is determined as though the oldest beneficiary were the sole beneficiary. Once the distribution is calcu-

lated, each beneficiary will receive his or her proportionate share.

EXAMPLE: You have only one IRA, and you name your three children, Tanya, Durf, and Trina, as equal beneficiaries. You die in 2005 at age 74 after having taken your required distribution for the year. As of December 31, 2006 your children were all still named equal beneficiaries of the account. In 2006 Tanya was 40, Durf was 30, and Trina was 22. Because Tanya is the oldest, distributions must be spread over her single life expectancy in the year after your death, reduced by one each subsequent year. In 2006, the ADP for Tanya's age 40 (from Table I) is 43.6. Each child receives one-third of the distribution. In the future, the ADP will be reduced by one each year.

3. Splitting Accounts

Accountants and taxpayers alike rejoiced when the IRS simplified matters by allowing accounts to be split among beneficiaries after the original owner died, whether the owner died before or after the required beginning date.

If you die having named multiple beneficiaries of your single retirement account, and if all beneficiaries are designated beneficiaries as of September 30 of the year after death, your beneficiaries have until December 31 of the year after your death to separate their respective shares. If they complete the separation in time, the distribution rules will apply separately to each beneficiary and his or her respective share.

The biggest benefit of timely separation is that each beneficiary can use his or her own life expectancy to calculate distributions from his or her share. Furthermore, the separation gives each beneficiary autonomy over investment decisions and simplifies accounting and other record keeping. As long as the plan itself permits the separation, the law won't prevent it.

A word of caution, however. Beneficiaries may use their own life expectancies to compute required distributions beginning in the year after the accounts were separated. So if the accounts are separated in the year after death, the required distribution for that year must be based on the life expectancy of the oldest beneficiary (presumably because there were, in fact, multiple beneficiaries named on the account for part of the year).

EXAMPLE: You name your brother, Joseph, and your three children, Holly, Herman, and Hank, as equal beneficiaries of your retirement plan. You die in 2005 at the age of 72 after taking your required distribution for the year. In March 2006, your brother and the three children instructed the custodian to split your IRA into four separate but equal IRAs. All of the new IRAs remain in your name, but one names only your brother as beneficiary, one names Holly, one names Herman, and one names Hank. Because your IRA was split into separate IRAs for each beneficiary before December 31, 2006 (the year after your death), each beneficiary can take required distributions from his or her share of the IRA over his or her own life expectancy—beginning in 2007.

However, for the year 2006 (the year the IRA was split), each beneficiary must use your brother's life expectancy to compute his or her required distribution, because your brother is the oldest beneficiary.

Splitting in the year of death. If, in the above example, the account were split in 2005 (the year of death), each beneficiary could use his or her own life expectancy to compute the 2006 required distribution (as well as future distributions) from his or her share.

When a trust is beneficiary. Splitting the account will not work when you name a trust as beneficiary of your retirement account and the trust itself has multiple beneficiaries. (See Section G3, below, for more information.)

a. Transfer

When separating each beneficiary's share into a separate account after your death, assets must be transferred directly from the trustee or custodian of the original single account to the trustee or custodian of each separate account. The beneficiary must not have control of the funds at any time. If the beneficiary is deemed to have control, the IRS will consider the assets fully distributed and fully taxable in the current year.

Furthermore, in the case of nonspouse beneficiaries, the account must remain in the name of the deceased (see Subsection b, below), so it cannot be transferred to one or more of the beneficiaries' existing retirement plans or even into a new retirement account in a beneficiary's name. If a spouse is one of the beneficiaries, however, the spouse can separate his or her share and roll it over to an existing or a new IRA in the spouse's name.

b. Name on Account

When transferring a portion of the plan assets to a new account, the IRS requires that the new account also be in the original participant's name. But financial institutions generally do not like to maintain accounts, let alone set up new ones, in the name of a deceased person. To accommodate both the IRS requirements and their own internal accounting procedures, many custodians construct account titles that identify both the original participant (now deceased) and the beneficiary who is to receive distributions.

c. Choosing a Distribution Option

As we explained above, the effect of naming multiple beneficiaries of one retirement plan account (assuming the account is not split by December 31 of the year after death) is to limit the deferral period to the life expectancy of the oldest beneficiary. As

long as the plan permits, however, there is nothing to prevent one beneficiary from accelerating the distribution of his or her share while the remaining beneficiaries use the life expectancy rule. The remaining beneficiaries' deferral period would be limited to the life expectancy of the oldest, even if the oldest had already withdrawn some or all of his or her share.

4. When a Spouse Is One of the Beneficiaries

If your spouse is one of several beneficiaries of your retirement account, he or she can still roll over future distributions from the account into an IRA in his or her own name, whether or not your spouse was the sole beneficiary of your retirement account. However, even if your spouse is the oldest beneficiary, your spouse would not be permitted to look up the ADP in the Single Life Table (Table I) each year. Instead, your spouse would look up the ADP in the year after death (using Table I) and reduce it by one in each subsequent year.

If your account was an IRA and your spouse was not the sole beneficiary, your spouse loses the option to make the IRA his or her own by failing to take a required distribution or by making a contribution of his or her own. (See Section B3, above.)

A spouse is the sole beneficiary of your retirement account if he or she is the sole beneficiary on September 30 of the year after your death. If your spouse is one of several designated beneficiaries (see Section 1, above) as of September 30 but separates his or her share on or before December 31 of the year after death (making your spouse the sole beneficiary of his or her share), then your spouse is deemed to be the sole beneficiary of his or her share, and your spouse gets all the special privileges accorded a spouse-beneficiary.

G. Trust Beneficiary

If you name a trust as beneficiary of your retirement plan or IRA and if that trust meets certain requirements (see Chapter 6, Section C, for a discussion of those requirements), then you are permitted to look through the trust to find the beneficiary of the trust. The trust beneficiary can then be treated as a designated beneficiary for purposes of computing required distributions.

All of the retirement plan distributions would go into the trust and become subject to the terms of the trust.

1. Nonspouse Beneficiary of Trust

A nonspouse beneficiary of the trust will use the required distribution rules described in Section C, above. This means the beneficiary may spread required distributions over his or her life expectancy. The beneficiary would find the ADP (from Table I) corresponding to his or her age in the year after your death. The ADP would then be reduced by one each subsequent year.

Older nonspouse beneficiary. If your nonspouse beneficiary is older than you, he or she may use your remaining life expectancy to compute required distributions after your death. (See Section C2, above.)

2. Spouse Beneficiary of Trust

If your spouse is sole beneficiary of the trust, your spouse will be treated as the designated beneficiary for purposes of computing post-death distributions. That means your spouse can take distributions over his or her single life expectancy beginning on December 31 of the year after your death and looking up the ADP for his or her age each year in Table I.

Older spouse beneficiary. As is the case when you name your spouse directly as beneficiary of your retirement plan, if your spouse is older than you, he or she would use your remaining life expectancy to compute required distributions after your death. (See Section B2, above.)

Your spouse cannot make your IRA his or her own. If you name a trust as beneficiary of your IRA, IRS regulations state that even if your spouse is the sole beneficiary of your trust, your spouse cannot make the IRA his or her own, either by failing to take a required distribution or by making additional contributions. However, your spouse might be able to receive a distribution of IRA assets from the trust and then roll them over into his or her own IRA. See Section 4, below.

3. Multiple Beneficiaries of Trust

If a trust has multiple beneficiaries, then for purposes of post-death required distributions, the multiple beneficiary rules described in Section F, above, apply as though the individuals themselves were named beneficiaries of the retirement plan.

⚠️ **Splitting the account won't work if a trust is the beneficiary.** If you name a trust as beneficiary of your retirement plan and there are multiple beneficiaries of the trust, splitting the retirement plan into separate accounts for each beneficiary of the trust—whether it is done before or after your death—won't allow beneficiaries to use their own life expectancies to compute required distributions. The multiple beneficiary rules still apply, requiring your beneficiaries to take distributions over the life expectancy of the oldest beneficiary of the trust.

4. Trust Beneficiary and Spousal Rollovers

Recall that a trust is often named the beneficiary of a retirement plan in order to fund a bypass trust. Assuming the spouse is the beneficiary of the trust, distributions from the plan go into the trust and then the trust makes distributions to the spouse.

But sometimes the surviving spouse discovers after the participant dies that the retirement plan assets are not needed to fund the bypass trust after all. In that case, the surviving spouse might prefer to simply roll over the retirement plan assets into his or her own IRA, name his or her own beneficiary, and begin a new schedule of required distributions.

Unfortunately, the law says that only a spouse beneficiary (and not a trust) may roll over retirement plan assets—and then only if the spouse acquires the assets directly from and by reason of the participant's death.

But taxpayers have argued that if the spouse is the sole beneficiary of the trust and can distribute all of the assets without interference from any third party, then the assets essentially pass directly from the deceased to the spouse—making the rollover within the spirit of the law.

Between 1987 and 2001, the IRS established a pattern of approving such actions in private letter rulings—despite the lack of explicit legal approval.

In final regulations issued in April 2002, however, the IRS stated specifically that a spouse cannot make a deceased participant's IRA her own if a trust is named primary beneficiary of the IRA—even if the spouse is the sole beneficiary of the trust.

Nonetheless, some practitioners believe that if the spouse has the power to distribute all assets of the trust, he or she could distribute the IRA assets to the trust and then distribute the assets from the trust to the spouse. Having done so, the spouse could then roll over the assets into an IRA of his or her own. Although this strategy is not specifically sanctioned by the IRS, some practitioners believe it will pass muster, even under the new regulations.

We think you should proceed with caution. If you name a trust as beneficiary of your retirement plan with the expectation that the spouse can fall back on a rollover, you are taking a risk.

As an alternative to taking this risk, consider naming your spouse as primary beneficiary (thus preserving the rollover opportunity) and your trust as contingent beneficiary. After your death, your spouse would have the option of disclaiming some or all of his or her interest in your retirement plan, allowing it to flow to the bypass trust. Ultimately, however, no strategy involving a trust is completely simple or safe.

H. Estate as Beneficiary

Recall that an estate does not qualify as a designated beneficiary. If an estate is named beneficiary, then the plan assets must be distributed over the original participant's life expectancy. The ADP for the year after death is the participant's single life expectancy (from Table I) in the year of death, reduced by one. The ADP is reduced by one for each subsequent year, as well. This is true even if the participant's spouse or child is beneficiary of the estate.

There is no look-through rule for an estate as there is for certain qualified trusts. Consequently, if a participant was elderly at death, the plan might have to be entirely distributed in a short time.

 Rollover risky. The IRS has frequently allowed a spouse to roll over the assets of a retirement plan into an IRA in the spouse's own name when an estate is named beneficiary of the plan and when the spouse is the sole beneficiary of the estate. But the strategy is not sanctioned by the Tax Code or by tax regulations, so it remains risky.

I. Annuities

If you die on or after your RBD and if you had been receiving your retirement benefits as an annuity, the form of the annuity determines how the remaining benefits will be paid to your beneficiary. (See Chapter 6, Section D, for more information about types of annuities.)

For example, the annuity might have been a joint and survivor annuity that must continue to pay your beneficiary the same benefits you were receiving. Or the annuity might have been a term certain annuity; if you survive only part of the term, your beneficiary receives payments for the remainder of the term.

J. Divorce or Separation

If you were divorced or separated during your lifetime, some or all of your retirement plan might be distributable to an alternate payee such as a spouse, former spouse, or child, under the terms of a QDRO—a court-approved divorce or maintenance agreement. (See Chapter 2, Section C4, for more information about QDROs.)

In such cases, some portion of each distribution during your lifetime was payable to the alternate payee (unless, of course, the alternate payee's share was distributed outright). That doesn't change when you die.

If you die after your RBD, payments from your account will continue to be computed using your beneficiary's ADP in the year after death, reduced by one each subsequent year. If an alternate payee has been receiving a portion of each distribution, the alternate payee is entitled to his or her share of post-death distributions, as well.

> EXAMPLE: On September 30 of the year after your death, the designated beneficiary of your retirement plan was your sister. Under the terms of a QDRO, your former spouse is entitled to half of your retirement plan, and you have been giving your former spouse 50% of each distribution. You died in 2004 after taking your required distribution for the year. In 2005, your sister will take a distribution from your retirement plan using the ADP (from Table I) for her age in 2005. Half of the distribution will go to your sister and half to your former spouse.
>
> In 2006 and beyond, your sister will reduce the previous year's ADP by one when computing required distributions. Half of all distributions must go to your former spouse.

If the alternate payee is a nonspouse, he or she may never roll over a distribution from your retirement plan. However, a spouse or former spouse with an interest in your retirement plan under the terms of a QDRO has all the rights of a surviving spouse beneficiary. When you die, your former spouse may roll over any distribution he or she receives from your plan into an IRA or a retirement plan in his or her own name, provided the former spouse first takes a required distribution on your behalf in the year of your death. If your former spouse has not yet reached his or her RBD, future required distributions may be deferred until that time.

Key Tax Code and Regulations Sections, IRS Pronouncements

§ 401(a)(9)

Required Distributions From Qualified Plans

§ 1.401(a)(9)

Required Distribution Regulations

§ 402(c)

Rollovers From Qualified Plans

§ 408

Individual Retirement Accounts

§ 1.408-8, A-5

Election by Spouse to Treat Decedent's IRA as Own

Rev. Proc. 89-52

After-Death IRA Reporting Requirements

Ann. 95-99

Employee Plans Examination Guidelines

Chapter 9

Roth IRAs

In its eternal quest for the most effective way to encourage people to save for retirement, Congress created in 1997 one of the biggest sugarcoated carrots we've ever seen: The Roth IRA.

Congress designed the Roth IRA to be much like a traditional IRA, but with a few attractive modifications. When the modifications began to fill pages rather than paragraphs, the new creature was given its own section in the Tax Code—Section 408A. The section begins with the statement that all the traditional IRA rules apply to Roth IRAs except as noted. This chapter focuses on the exceptions, with special attention to the unusual treatment of distributions.

The lure of the Roth IRA is powerful. Although contributions are not deductible (meaning they are made with after-tax dollars), all distributions, including the earnings on contributions, are potentially tax free—as will be explained in Section A, below.

Unfortunately, Roth IRAs don't work for everyone. Here's a summary of the key differences between traditional IRAs and Roth IRAs:

- You may make a contribution to a traditional IRA no matter how

Calculating Your Modified Adjusted Gross Income

You are not permitted to make a Roth IRA contribution if your modified adjusted gross income (modified AGI) exceeds a certain amount. When calculating your modified AGI, you make the following adjustments to your regular AGI:

- exclude the converted amount from income
- exclude any distributions from traditional IRAs or other retirement plans that you were required to withdraw because of being older than 70½
- add back income from U.S. savings bonds used for higher education expenses
- add back employer-paid adoption expenses
- add back excluded foreign earned income and payments received for foreign housing
- add back any deduction claimed for a traditional IRA contribution, and
- add back the deduction for educational loan interest.

high your income is, as long as you have earned income (income from employment) and are younger than 70½. But in the case of a Roth IRA, you may not make any contribution if your income exceeds a certain level. If you are married filing a joint

Helpful Terms

Adjusted gross income (AGI). Total taxable income reduced by certain expenses such as qualified plan contributions, IRA contributions, and alimony payments.

After-tax dollars. The amount of income left after all income taxes have been withheld or paid.

Beneficiary. The person or entity entitled to receive the benefits from insurance or from trust property, such as a retirement plan or IRA.

Deferral period. The number of years over which distributions from a retirement plan or IRA can be spread.

Distribution. A payout of property (such as shares of stock) or cash from a retirement plan or IRA to the participant or a beneficiary.

Earned income. Income received for providing goods or services. Earned income might be wages or salary or net profit from a business.

Nondeductible Contribution. A contribution to a retirement plan or IRA that may not be used as a business expense or an adjustment to offset taxable income on an income tax return.

Traditional IRA. Any contributory or rollover IRA that is not a Roth IRA or a SIMPLE IRA.

---

return, the amount that you are allowed to contribute to a Roth IRA is gradually reduced when your modified AGI exceeds $150,000. You may not make any contribution at all once your income reaches $160,000. If you are single, the phaseout begins at $95,000 and is complete when your income reaches $110,000. If you are married filing separate returns, the phaseout begins with your first dollar of income and is complete when your income reaches $10,000.

- No contribution to a traditional IRA is permitted after age 70½. However, you may continue to make contributions to a Roth IRA after age 70½, as long as you have earned income and your adjusted gross income doesn't exceed the limits described above.

- A contribution to a traditional IRA is always deductible if neither you nor your spouse is covered by a qualified plan. If even one of you is covered by a plan, the deduction is phased out as your income increases. On the other hand, no contribution to a Roth IRA is ever deductible, whether or not you are covered by another plan.

- Earnings that accumulate inside a traditional IRA are always subject to income tax when withdrawn. But earnings in a Roth IRA can be completely tax free when distributed if certain requirements are satisfied. (See Section A, below.)

- If you have a traditional IRA, you must begin required distributions on or before your required beginning date—your RBD. If you have a Roth IRA, you are not required to withdraw any amount during your lifetime. (See Section D, below.)

⚠️ **Roth 401(k) plans are different from Roth IRAs.** Roth 401(k) plans are not exempt from the lifetime required distribution rules.

The contrast between traditional IRAs and Roth IRAs is most stark in the treatment of distributions. The differences turn up not only in the ordinary income tax rules, but also in the application of the early distribution tax and the required distribution rules.

A. Taxation of Distributions

The income tax rules for traditional IRAs are straightforward. Generally, distributions are taxed as ordinary income unless they are rolled over into another retirement plan or IRA. If you made nondeductible (after-tax) contributions to your traditional IRA over the years, those amounts are not subject to tax when distributed. That's the good news. The bad news is that those after-tax contributions are deemed to come out pro rata—not all at once. In other words, the nondeductible portion of a traditional IRA comes out as only a part of each distribution you ever take from the IRA. Consequently, only a percentage of each distribution is tax free. (See Chapter 2, Section B2, for more information about calculating the nontaxable portion of a distribution from a traditional IRA.)

The basic rule for Roth IRAs is similar: The taxable portion of any distribution must be reported on your income tax return, and it will be taxed as ordinary income unless you roll it over. But that's where the similarity ends.

The key to squeezing the maximum benefit from a Roth IRA is to be aware of which distributions are taxable and which are not. Maintaining that vigilance is not difficult; you must simply view your Roth IRA as the sum of two distinct parts. One part consists of the contributions you have made. The second part consists of the earnings on those contributions, such as interest earned on bond investments or gains from stock sales.

1. Distribution of Nondeductible Contributions

The portion of your Roth IRA that consists of your contributions is never subject to income tax when it comes out. Never. Even if you take it out the day after you put it in. That's because all contributions you made were nondeductible, which means you have already paid tax on the money. You don't have to pay tax a second time when you take it out. Fair is fair.

Furthermore, any distribution you take from a Roth IRA is presumed to be a return of your contributions until you have withdrawn all contributions you made to it over the years (or to all Roth IRAs, if you have more than one). In other words, all contributions are recovered before earnings are recovered. This simple rule gives the Roth IRA an advantage over a traditional IRA. It means you may retrieve your contributions whenever you want without incurring any income tax. In this way, the contributions can serve as an emergency fund.

EXAMPLE: Dain began making contributions to a Roth IRA three years ago. By the beginning of this year, the Roth IRA had grown to $8,000. Of that amount, $6,000 was from Dain's annual contributions and $2,000 was from investment returns. In February of this year, Dain had an auto accident and totaled his car. Dain needed to purchase a new car but didn't have any resources other than his Roth IRA. He decided to withdraw $6,000 from his Roth IRA. The $6,000 is not subject to tax because Dain's distribution is deemed to be a return of his contributions.

2. Distribution of Investment Returns

When you contribute to an IRA, you ordinarily use the contributed funds to purchase investments that will earn money for you. For example, you might invest in bonds or CDs to generate interest. Or you might buy stock, hoping the price will shoot up so you can make a bundle on a later sale. As long as those earnings—the interest and the stock proceeds—stay inside the IRA, they are not taxed. But what happens when they come out? In the case of a traditional IRA, all of the earnings are subject to ordinary income tax. The advantage of the Roth IRA is that when you distribute earnings, they are tax free—even though they have never been taxed before—as long as the distribution is considered a qualified distribution.

a. Qualified Distributions

It will pay you handsomely to nail down the tax free advantage a Roth IRA offers. All you have to do is follow a few simple rules. First, don't take a distribution of your investment returns for five years. A distribution within five calendar years of when you first establish a Roth IRA can never be a qualified distribution.

If you die before the five years are up. If you die before satisfying the five-year holding period, your beneficiary must wait until you would have satisfied it, or the distribution will not be qualified.

So, counting the year of your first contribution as year one, you will satisfy the five-year requirement if you wait until the sixth year before withdrawing any earnings.

EXAMPLE: Jessica opened a Roth IRA in June 2003. At the end of 2006, her account was worth $15,000, of which $8,000 was from contributions and $7,000 was from investment earnings. In June 2007, Jessica withdrew $10,000 to pay for a trip to China. Of that amount, $8,000 is deemed to be from contributions and will not be subject to income tax. The remaining $2,000 is deemed to come from earnings. Because the distribution did not satisfy the five-year holding requirement, the $2,000 will be subject to income tax. (It might also be subject to an early distribution penalty. See Section B, below).

Although you are permitted to make a contribution to a Roth IRA after the end of the year (until April 15), the five-year holding period for a qualified distribution begins on the first day of the calendar year to which your very first contribution relates, which might be an earlier year than the one during which the contribution was actually made.

EXAMPLE: Soren wanted to set up a Roth IRA and make a contribution for 2005. He finally got around to doing so in February 2006 well before the April 15, 2006 deadline. Because the contribution is for 2005, Soren will count 2005 as year one when computing the five-year holding period, even though he didn't actually make the contribution until 2006.

Simply satisfying the five-year requirement will not automatically make a distribution qualified. It must also be at least one of the following:

- a distribution you take after reaching age 59½
- a distribution you take after becoming disabled
- a distribution to your beneficiary or your estate after your death, or
- a distribution you take to purchase a first home (up to a lifetime withdrawal limit of $10,000).

If your distribution satisfies the five-year requirement and falls into one of the above categories, it will be qualified and thus entirely tax free.

Remember, contributions are never subject to income tax when they come out of a Roth IRA. So even if they are part of a nonqualified distribution, they are tax free. Only the earnings will be taxed if they are part of a nonqualified distribution.

EXAMPLE: Lara began making contributions to a Roth IRA in 2004. By June 2006, she had accumulated $7,500. Of that amount, $7,000 was from contributions she made in the years 2004, 2005, and 2006. The remaining $500 was from earnings on her investments. In December 2006, Lara withdrew $7,200 from the IRA. The distribution is a nonqualified distribution because it occurred within five years of her initial contribution. Only $200 is subject to tax, however, because her contributions, which total $7,000, are deemed to come out first—they are never subject to tax.

 Municipal bonds offer another form of tax free investment. Typically, when you purchase municipal bonds, all of the interest you earn on the bonds is tax free. As an investment vehicle, a Roth IRA has two distinct advantages over a municipal bond. First, inside a Roth IRA, money can be invested in stocks and other diverse investments that are likely to yield a greater return over the long term than do municipal bonds. Second, although the interest on municipal bonds is tax free, you must be diligent about reinvesting the interest or you will soon have taxable income. For example, if you invest $10,000 in a municipal bond that pays 5% interest, you receive $500 of tax free interest during the year. But if you place that interest in a regular interest-bearing account or another investment that generates taxable income, the earnings on the $500 will be taxable. To ensure that all future earnings are tax free, you must reinvest in more municipal bonds, which might be difficult with only $500 of cash. Municipal bonds are rarely sold in increments of $500.

In contrast, all distributions from a Roth IRA are potentially tax free, whether you invest in stocks, corporate bonds, or CDs. Thus, not only can you invest in a variety of securities, but also you won't have the same reinvestment concerns you would have if municipal bonds were your only investment option. For example, if you invest in a CD that generates $500 of interest income, you could reinvest in stocks, bonds, or another CD.

b. Nonqualified Distributions

Any distribution from a Roth IRA that does not satisfy the requirements of a qualified distribution is automatically nonqualified. Nonqualified distributions are treated very much like traditional IRA distributions. The contributions you made will come out tax free, but the earnings are taxable. There is one critical difference, however: As mentioned above, the contributions you make to the Roth IRA (which were made with after-tax dollars) are presumed to come out first—before any earnings. This means if you must take a nonqualified distribution, some or all of it will escape income tax, as long as you have not previously withdrawn all of your contributions.

EXAMPLE: JJ has contributed to a Roth IRA in each of the years 2004, 2005, and 2006. By June 2006, he had accumulated $10,000, of which $9,000 was from contributions and $1,000 was from earnings. In December, JJ withdrew $9,000 from his IRA. Although the distribution was nonqualified, the $9,000 was nontaxable because it was all attributable to his contributions. In April 2007, JJ contributed another

$4,000 to his Roth IRA. By December, he had a total of $5,200 in the IRA. Only $4,000 was attributable to contributions because he had already withdrawn all contributions for prior years. The remaining $1,200 represented earnings. JJ decided to withdraw $5,000. The entire distribution is nonqualified, but the $4,000 attributable to contributions would be tax free. Only $1,000 of the distribution is attributable to earnings, and that portion will be subject to income tax.

3. Conversions and Rollovers

When you have a Roth IRA, your rollover opportunities are limited. You can roll over assets from a Roth IRA to another Roth IRA, or if you qualify, you can roll over—or convert—assets from a traditional IRA or a SEP IRA or SIMPLE IRA to a Roth IRA. No other rollovers or conversions involving Roth IRAs are permitted. For example, you may never roll over assets from a Roth IRA to a traditional IRA. (The rollover can go in only one direction—from a traditional IRA to a Roth IRA.) Also, you are not permitted to roll over a Roth IRA to a qualified plan or vice versa.

SEPs and SIMPLEs. This section applies to SEP IRAs in exactly the same way. In other words, a SEP IRA can be converted to a Roth IRA. You can also convert a SIMPLE IRA to a Roth IRA, but

only after two years from the date you first established a SIMPLE IRA. Before the two years have expired, the SIMPLE IRA is ineligible for conversion.

You can also convert your traditional IRA to a Roth IRA without rolling it over. You can simply instruct your custodian to change the title on the account to show that it is now a Roth IRA. Although the funds aren't technically moved from one account to another, you are deemed to have rolled over the assets from a traditional IRA to a Roth IRA. Whether you convert your traditional IRA by changing title or by rolling it over, the law identifies the assets as converted amounts, meaning they were once in a traditional IRA but are now in a Roth IRA. As explained in the paragraphs below, some special rules apply to converted amounts.

a. Rollover From Roth IRA

If you take a distribution from a Roth IRA with the intention of rolling it over, you may roll it over only to another Roth IRA. This is logical when you think about it. Distributions from Roth IRAs are all potentially tax free, whereas most, if not all, distributions from a traditional IRA or a qualified plan are taxable. If you were allowed to mix plans indiscriminately, the IRS would have a hard time tracking the source of the various distributions to determine which funds are taxable.

Except for the fact that you may only roll a Roth IRA to another Roth IRA, all the rules governing rollovers between IRAs apply to rollovers between Roth IRAs. (See Chapter 2, Section E, for more about IRA rollovers.) Among the most important of those rules are the following:

- Once you take a distribution from a Roth IRA, you have only 60 days to complete the rollover to another Roth IRA.
- You are permitted only one Roth-to-Roth rollover per year.
- Rollover distributions between IRAs are not subject to income tax withholding.

b.   Rollover to Roth IRA

There are only two possible sources of a rollover to a Roth IRA. The rollover may come from another Roth IRA, or it may come from a traditional IRA. A Roth IRA may be rolled into another Roth IRA without any restrictions other than those that apply to rollovers between traditional IRAs, as described in the previous section. A rollover from a traditional IRA is called a conversion and is more complex. (See Subsection c, immediately below, for more information.)

c.   Conversion to Roth IRA

If you want to convert assets from a traditional IRA to a Roth IRA, you must be eligible and you must face the consequences. First the consequences.

i.   Consequences

If you determine that you are eligible to convert your traditional IRA to a Roth IRA (see Subsection ii, below), and if you elect to do so, you must pay the piper. Specifically, the entire pretax amount of the conversion will be subject to income tax at ordinary rates. (If you made nondeductible contributions to your traditional IRA, those amounts will not be taxed a second time when you convert to a Roth IRA.) Congress wasn't about to wipe out all of those deferred taxes with one stroke of the pen. Once you've ponied up the money and converted the assets, however, all future distributions of the converted amounts will be free of income tax. Furthermore, distributions of future earnings on converted amounts will be tax free as long as those distributions satisfy the five-year holding period and are qualified. (See Section 2a, above, for information about qualified distributions.)

EXAMPLE: In 2003, you converted your $20,000 traditional IRA to a Roth IRA. On your tax return for 2003, you included the $20,000 and paid tax on it. By 2009, your Roth IRA has grown to $35,000, and you withdraw $30,000 to throw yourself a 65th birthday party. The entire $30,000 distribution is tax free because you are older than 59½ and you have satisfied the five-year holding period.

Can you find non-IRA sources to pay the tax? The conversion of a traditional IRA to a Roth IRA can be a real boon to young investors who can pay the tax from non-IRA funds. These folks have years of tax free compounding ahead of them. However, if the tax is paid out of IRA funds, the advantage of the conversion declines and may even disappear altogether.

As a practical matter, it may be difficult for people with sizable traditional IRAs to convert the entire account to a Roth IRA unless they have large amounts of cash outside the IRA. Imagine paying regular income tax on a $100,000 IRA. One way around this problem would be to convert the traditional IRA to a Roth IRA in bits and pieces over a number of years to keep the tax at a manageable level. Nothing in the law prevents you from converting part of your traditional IRA instead of the whole thing. Furthermore, there is no time limit on conversion. In fact, many people won't be able to qualify at all until retirement, when they no longer have a salary. As long as the law doesn't change, you can simply wait and convert some or all of your traditional IRA when you do qualify.

For older IRA participants, converting a traditional IRA to a Roth IRA is not necessarily the correct decision. If you must include a large IRA in income, some or all of it could easily be taxed at the maximum tax rate, and you might not recover from that financial outlay (through tax free compounded growth) before your death. If your primary concern is passing wealth to your beneficiaries, however, a conversion could save estate taxes and also give your beneficiaries an opportunity for additional tax free growth after your death.

The decision to convert or not to convert a traditional IRA to a Roth IRA can involve some complex calculations. You must factor in age, health, income and estate tax rates, and investment returns. If you are young, healthy, and able to pay the taxes with money outside the IRA, the rollover is likely to pay off for you.

If you are younger than 59½ and you elect to use some of the converted IRA to pay the tax, the portion that goes to taxes could be subject to the early distribution tax. (See Section B2b, below.)

ii. Eligibility

Even if it makes sense for you to convert a traditional IRA to a Roth IRA, you must determine whether you are eligible to do so. You are not eligible if either of the following is true:

- If your modified adjusted gross income (modified AGI) exceeds $100,000, you may not convert a traditional IRA to a Roth IRA. This income cap applies whether you are married or single. (See the introduction to this chapter for a definition of modified AGI.)

Remember, modified AGI is used only to determine if you qualify to convert. It is not used to compute your tax liability.

EXAMPLE: Tyson's modified AGI for the year is $90,000. He has accumulated $25,000 in a traditional IRA and would like to convert it to a Roth IRA before the end of the year. Because Tyson's modified AGI (not including the $25,000 in his IRA) is under $100,000, he qualifies to convert his traditional IRA to a Roth IRA. On his tax return, he will report income of $115,000 (which is $90,000 plus $25,000).

 Note the income threshold for a conversion. To convert a traditional IRA to a Roth IRA, the income threshold is more restrictive than the threshold for making annual contributions to a Roth IRA. You may set up and contribute some amount to a Roth IRA as long as you have earnings from employment and your modified AGI does not exceed $160,000 (if you are filing a joint return) or $110,000 (if you are single). The conversion threshold, however, is only $100,000.

Another part of the Roth IRA law, which took effect in the year 2005, allows you to exclude from your modified AGI the distributions you are required to take from your traditional IRA because you have passed age 70½. (See Chapter 5 for a summary of the required distribution rules.) But the required distribution may be excluded only for purposes of computing whether or not you qualify to convert your traditional IRA to a Roth IRA. You must still pay tax on it. And again, this benefit is not available until the year 2005.

EXAMPLE: Nolan's income for the year 2007 includes $80,000 from interest and dividends and $30,000 in required distributions he must withdraw from his traditional IRA. Nolan plans to convert another $20,000 of his traditional IRA to a Roth IRA. Although the total income he must report on his tax return is $130,000 (which is $80,000 + $30,000 + $20,000), he still qualifies to convert the $20,000 from his traditional IRA because his income is less than $100,000 when he excludes the required distribution and the converted amount.

You are not permitted to roll over or convert a required distribution. Therefore, in the above example, Nolan's $30,000 required distribution must be placed in a regular account, not an IRA account of any kind. The $20,000 conversion amount must be an additional distribution from his traditional IRA—over and above the required amount of $30,000.

- You cannot convert any portion of a traditional IRA to a Roth IRA if you are a married person using the "married filing separate" status on your tax return (instead of "married filing joint"). Any person using the married filing separate status is automatically ineligible to convert a traditional IRA to a Roth IRA.

 Filing separately doesn't quite leave you out of the Roth IRA boon. Although an individual who is married and filing a separate return may not convert a traditional IRA to a Roth IRA, he or she may still establish a Roth IRA—but only if the modified AGI does not exceed $10,000.

iii. Related Rules

If you decide to proceed with the conversion of a traditional IRA to a Roth IRA, you will find that Congress has built in a little tax relief for you.

- If you convert a traditional IRA to a Roth IRA, the conversion is ignored for purposes of the one-rollover-per-year rule. (See Chapter 2, Section E2, for more information about this rule.)
- Even if you are younger than 59½ when you convert a traditional IRA to a Roth IRA, the distribution will not be subject to the early distribution tax, as long as the entire taxable amount is rolled over. (Beware of using part of the rollover to pay income tax, though. See Section B2b, below.)
- For income tax purposes, later distributions of converted amounts from your Roth IRA are treated like distributions of nondeductible contributions. The converted por-

tion will not be subject to income tax when it is distributed in future years, but the earnings will be subject to tax unless they are part of a qualified distribution. (See Section A2a, above, for the definition of a qualified distribution.)

4. Correcting Errors: Recharacterizing

If you convert a traditional IRA to a Roth IRA during the year and discover at the end of the year that your modified AGI was too high, you won't be in serious trouble. The law allows you to transfer the funds back out of the Roth IRA and into the same or even a different traditional IRA before the due date of your tax return (or the extended due date). This is called a recharacterization.

In fact, you can recharacterize after April 15, even if you have already filed your tax return and did not request an extension. You always have until October 15 of the year after the conversion to recharacterize your Roth IRA. However, if you recharacterize after filing your return, you must file an amended return to report the recharacterization.

The proper method for recharacterizing your Roth IRA is to have the custodian of the Roth IRA transfer the errant funds plus any investment earnings on those funds directly to the custodian of the traditional IRA. If this is all done in timely fashion, there will be no income tax or penalties.

If you recharacterize a converted amount—meaning you undo a conversion from a traditional IRA to a Roth IRA by putting the money back into a traditional IRA—you may not reconvert those funds to a Roth IRA until the following tax year or until 30 days have passed, if that period of time is longer. For example, if you recharacterize in June, you must wait until the next January to reconvert. If you recharacterize on December 31, you can reconvert on January 30 of the next year.

Roth IRA waiting periods. The waiting period for reconverting was added to the Roth IRA laws somewhat belatedly to quash a tax-saving maneuver that was spreading like wildfire. Smart taxpayers were converting and recharacterizing several times during a year to take advantage of dips in the market. When the market dips, the value of an IRA drops—and so does the tax cost of conversion.

EXAMPLE: You converted your $100,000 traditional IRA to a Roth IRA in June. By November, the value of the assets had declined to $75,000. So under the old rules, you would be able to recharacterize the Roth IRA to a traditional IRA (transfer the assets back) and then reconvert before the end of the year. You would then pay tax on $75,000 instead of on $100,000.

B. Early Distribution Tax

Understanding how the early distribution tax applies to Roth IRAs is complicated by the fact that there are two types of distributions (qualified and nonqualified) and a special set of rules for converted amounts. (Early distribution tax rules for traditional IRAs and other retirement plans are discussed in Chapter 3.)

1. Qualified Distributions

Qualified distributions from Roth IRAs are not subject to the early distribution tax. It's as simple as that. This rule, too, has some logic to it. The early distribution tax applies only to distributions that are included in income—those that are required to be reported on your tax return. Because all qualified distributions from Roth IRAs are tax free, they are all exempt from the early distribution tax.

2. Nonqualified Distributions

Nonqualified distributions from Roth IRAs are treated in most respects like distributions from traditional IRAs. Any portion of the distribution that is required to be included on your income tax return is subject to the early distribution tax, unless the distribution qualifies for an exception. The exceptions for nonqualified distributions from Roth IRAs are the same as those for traditional IRA distributions. (See Chapter 3 for a detailed description of all the exceptions to the early distribution tax.) The key exceptions to the early distribution tax include distributions:

- after you reach age 59½
- because of your death or disability
- that are substantially equal periodic payments
- for certain medical expenses
- for certain health insurance
- for higher education expenses, or
- for a first home purchase (limited to $10,000).

a.   Distributions of Nondeductible Contributions

Bear in mind that all of your nondeductible contributions to a Roth IRA will come out before any earnings. Because the contributions are nondeductible, they are not subject to tax when distributed, even if they are part of a nonqualified distribution. And because they are tax free and not includable on your income tax return, they automatically escape the early distribution tax. Any earnings that are distributed as part of a nonqualified distribution are subject to the early distribution tax, unless an exception applies.

Again, for planning purposes, this means you can take your contributions out of a Roth IRA at any time, and they will be subject neither to income tax nor to the early distribution tax.

EXAMPLE: In 2003, you established a Roth IRA. You contributed $3,000 in 2003, 2004, and 2005. By November of the year 2006, the account had grown to $9,600. Finding yourself a little strapped for cash, you withdraw $6,000 from the account in late November. Because the distribution is less than your total contributions of $9,000, the $6,000 will not be subject to either income tax or the early distribution tax.

b.   Distribution of Converted Amounts

A special rule exempts converted amounts from the early distribution tax in the year of the conversion, as long as the entire amount of the conversion goes into the Roth IRA. There are two ways to get caught by an early distribution tax when you convert a traditional IRA to a Roth IRA. You might use some of the converted amount to pay the income tax you owe on the conversion, or you might withdraw the converted amount too soon. But remember, the early distribution tax would never apply if you were older than 59½ at the time of the distribution (or if another exception, described in Chapter 3, applies).

i.   Paying Income Tax With Converted Amounts

If you qualify to convert a traditional IRA to a Roth IRA (see Section A3b, above), the amount actually deposited into the Roth IRA will not be subject to an early distribution tax. Even though it is included on your tax return and you pay income tax on the converted amount, you are spared the early distribution tax if you roll over everything. But if you use some of the money from the traditional IRA to pay the income tax liability instead of rolling it over, the portion used for taxes will be subject to the early distribution tax—unless you are older than 59½ or another exception applies. (See Chapter 3 for more information about the early distribution tax and exceptions to the tax.)

ii. Withdrawing Converted Amounts Too Soon

Even though converted amounts in a Roth IRA are after-tax amounts (because you paid tax in the year of conversion), if you withdraw any converted dollars within five years, that portion of the distribution will be treated as though it is taxable—but only for purposes of determining the early distribution tax. (Recall that the early distribution tax generally does not apply to amounts that are excluded from your income for tax purposes. This is an exception to that rule.)

> EXAMPLE: You have a traditional IRA to which you have been making deductible contributions each year. By the time you are 50, the account has grown to $15,000. You convert the IRA to a Roth IRA, paying tax on the entire $15,000. The following year, you withdraw $10,000 from the Roth IRA to bail your son out of jail. Because you are younger than 59½ and you withdrew the $10,000 within five years of converting your traditional IRA to a Roth IRA, you must pay an early distribution

tax of $1,000 ($10,000 x 10%). You will not owe regular income tax on the $10,000.

The portion of a distribution that is subject to the early distribution tax is limited to the amount that you included in your taxable income and reported on your tax return in the year of conversion.

> EXAMPLE: You have a traditional IRA to which you have made deductible contributions of $4,000 and nondeductible (after-tax) contributions of $6,000. By the time you are 51, the account has grown to $17,000. You convert the IRA to a Roth IRA, paying tax on $11,000. (You don't have to pay tax on the $6,000 of nondeductible contributions.) The next year, when you are 52, you withdraw $17,000 to help your daughter start a new business. You must pay an early distribution tax on the $11,000, because that is the amount that was included on your income tax return in the year of conversion. The early distribution tax is $1,100 ($11,000 x 10%).

 How the earnings are treated. The earnings on converted amounts are treated exactly the same as earnings on contributory amounts. Only qualified distributions of earnings escape the early distribution tax, unless another early distribution tax exception applies.

C. Ordering of Distributions

You might think you should be able to pick and choose which amounts come out of your Roth IRA first. For example, if you take a distribution before the five-year holding period is up, you would want to take your contributions first, because they are not subject to tax or penalties. Or if you converted one of your traditional IRAs six years ago and another two years ago, you would want to take a distribution from the one that was converted six years ago, because those converted amounts satisfy the five-year holding period and would not be subject to an early distribution tax.

Sadly, you cannot pick and choose the origin of each distribution you take. But serendipitously, the ordering rules you are required to use are quite favorable. Distributions are deemed to come out in the following order:

- Regular Roth IRA contributions are distributed first.
- Next come converted amounts, starting with the amounts first converted. If you converted a traditional IRA containing both taxable and nontaxable amounts (for example, if you had made deductible and nondeductible contributions), the taxable portion is deemed to come out first.
- Earnings come out last.

The benefits can be dramatic. For example, if you take a distribution before the five-year holding period is up or if you fail to satisfy the other requirements of a qualified distribution, the withdrawal still won't be subject to the early distribution tax as long as you have taken less than the total amount of all contributions you have made to all your Roth IRAs. Note that for purposes of these ordering rules, all Roth IRAs are considered a single Roth IRA.

EXAMPLE: You have two traditional IRAs: IRA #1 and IRA #2. In 1998, you converted IRA #1, then valued at $10,000, to a Roth IRA. In 2002, you converted IRA #2, valued at $20,000, to a Roth IRA. You also have a separate contributory Roth IRA, which you established in 1998 and to which you have been making annual contributions. By 2006, the contributory Roth IRA has grown to $15,000, of which $8,000 is contributions and $7,000 is earnings. In November 2006, on your 40th birthday, you withdraw $25,000 to pay for your trip to India. The source of the distribution is deemed to be:

- $8,000 from Roth IRA contributions
- $10,000 from the oldest converted amount (IRA #1), and
- $7,000 from the next oldest converted amount (IRA #2).

The $8,000 of contributions are not subject to either income tax or the early distribution tax because they are all from nondeductible after-tax contributions. The $10,000 deemed to be from IRA #1 is also not subject to either income tax (which you already paid in the year of conversion) or the early distribution tax (because the conversion occurred more than five years before). The remaining $7,000 will not be subject to income tax, because it was converted from a traditional IRA and you already paid tax on it in 2002. However, it will be subject to an early distribution tax of $700 (10% of $7,000), because it was distributed within five years of the conversion and you are younger than 59½.

D. Required Distributions

The required distribution rules—those that will eventually force you to start taking money out of your retirement plan or your traditional IRA—have a broad reach. (See Chapter 5 for a summary of the required distribution rules.) They apply to IRAs, qualified plans, plans that behave like qualified plans, and even some nonqualified plans. But as broad as that reach is, a significant exception has been carved out for Roth IRAs.

1. During Your Lifetime

During your lifetime, you are not required to take distributions from a Roth IRA. Ever. In fact, you could die without ever having removed a cent. This rule, which allows Roth IRA participants to accumulate a tax-favored nest egg and then simply pass it on to another generation, seems to conflict with the government's long-standing policy

to ensure that tax-favored retirement plans primarily benefit the original participant.

But there is a logical, if cynical, explanation. Because the Roth IRA was structured to allow all qualified distributions to be tax free, the government has no real incentive to force distributions. There are no deferred taxes to collect. So much for public policy.

2. After Your Death, Before Your RBD

Once you die, the distribution rules for Roth IRAs again merge with those for traditional IRAs. All of the post-death required distribution rules apply to Roth IRAs in the same way they apply to traditional IRAs. Thus, if you die before your RBD, the life expectancy rule or the five-year rule will apply. Those rules, as well as other required distribution rules that kick in if you die before your RBD, are explained in Chapter 7.

3. After Your Death, After Your RBD

If you have a traditional IRA, you must begin required distributions when you reach your required beginning date or RBD. If you die after your RBD, a special set of distribution rules applies. (See Chapter 8.) But because you are not required to take distributions from a Roth IRA during your lifetime, you have no RBD for that purpose. In other words, you are always deemed to have died before your RBD.

Roth IRAs can be a boon to your beneficiaries. Although the post-death required distribution rules for traditional IRAs are essentially the same as those for Roth IRAs, the planning implications could be quite different. Because distributions to beneficiaries from a Roth IRA are not subject to income tax, beneficiaries have access to 100% of the funds when the IRA participant dies (unless some of it must be used to pay estate taxes). For this reason, there will undoubtedly be a real temptation for beneficiaries to take distribution of their shares immediately upon the participant's death. Free money. But because assets inside the Roth IRA could continue to grow tax free, it is usually to the beneficiary's advantage to defer distributions for as long as possible.

Key Tax Code and Regulation Sections

§ 72(t)
Early Distribution Tax and Exceptions

§ 72(t)(2)(F)
First Home-Purchase Exception to Early Distribution Tax

§ 401(a)(9)
Required Distributions From Qualified Plans

§ 1.401(a)(9)
Required Distribution Regulations

§ 408A
Roth IRAs

§ 1.408A
Roth IRA Regulations

Appendix A

IRS Forms, Notices, and Schedules

Form **4972**	**Tax on Lump-Sum Distributions**	OMB No. 1545-0193

Tax on Lump-Sum Distributions
(From Qualified Plans of Participants Born Before January 2, 1936)

Department of the Treasury
Internal Revenue Service (99)

▶ **Attach to Form 1040 or Form 1041.**

OMB No. 1545-0193

20**04**

Attachment
Sequence No. **28**

Name of recipient of distribution | Identifying number

Part I   **Complete this part to see if you can use Form 4972**

			Yes	No
1	Was this a distribution of a plan participant's entire balance (excluding deductible voluntary employee contributions and certain forfeited amounts) from all of an employer's qualified plans of one kind (pension, profit-sharing, or stock bonus)? If "No," **do not** use this form	**1**		
2	Did you roll over any part of the distribution? If "Yes," **do not** use this form	**2**		
3	Was this distribution paid to you as a beneficiary of a plan participant who was born before January 2, 1936?	**3**		
4	Were you **(a)** a plan participant who received this distribution, **(b)** born before January 2, 1936, **and (c)** a participant in the plan for at least 5 years before the year of the distribution?.	**4**		
	If you answered "No" to both questions 3 **and** 4, **do not** use this form.			
5a	Did you use Form 4972 after 1986 for a previous distribution from your own plan? If "Yes," **do not** use this form for a 2004 distribution from your own plan	**5a**		
b	If you are receiving this distribution as a beneficiary of a plan participant who died, did you use Form 4972 for a previous distribution received for that participant after 1986? If "Yes," **do not** use the form for this distribution	**5b**		

Part II   **Complete this part to choose the 20% capital gain election** (see instructions)

6	Capital gain part from Form 1099-R, box 3	**6**	
7	Multiply line 6 by 20% (.20) . . . . ▶	**7**	
	If you also choose to use Part III, go to line 8. Otherwise, include the amount from line 7 in the total on Form 1040, line 43, or Form 1041, Schedule G, line 1b, whichever applies.		

Part III   **Complete this part to choose the 10-year tax option** (see instructions)

8	Ordinary income from Form 1099-R, box 2a minus box 3. If you did not complete Part II, enter the taxable amount from Form 1099-R, box 2a.	**8**	
9	Death benefit exclusion for a beneficiary of a plan participant who died before August 21, 1996	**9**	
10	Total taxable amount. Subtract line 9 from line 8	**10**	
11	Current actuarial value of annuity from Form 1099-R, box 8. If none, enter -0-	**11**	
12	Adjusted total taxable amount. Add lines 10 and 11. If this amount is $70,000 or more, **skip** lines 13 through 16, enter this amount on line 17, and go to line 18	**12**	
13	Multiply line 12 by 50% (.50), but **do not** enter more than $10,000 .	**13**	
14	Subtract $20,000 from line 12. If line 12 is $20,000 or less, enter -0-	**14**	
15	Multiply line 14 by 20% (.20)	**15**	
16	Minimum distribution allowance. Subtract line 15 from line 13	**16**	
17	Subtract line 16 from line 12	**17**	
18	Federal estate tax attributable to lump-sum distribution	**18**	
19	Subtract line 18 from line 17. If line 11 is zero, **skip** lines 20 through 22 and go to line 23 . .	**19**	
20	Divide line 11 by line 12 and enter the result as a decimal (rounded to at least three places).	**20**	.
21	Multiply line 16 by the decimal on line 20	**21**	
22	Subtract line 21 from line 11	**22**	
23	Multiply line 19 by 10% (.10)	**23**	
24	Tax on amount on line 23. Use the Tax Rate Schedule in the instructions	**24**	
25	Multiply line 24 by ten (10). If line 11 is zero, **skip** lines 26 through 28, enter this amount on line 29, and go to line 30	**25**	
26	Multiply line 22 by 10% (.10)	**26**	
27	Tax on amount on line 26. Use the Tax Rate Schedule in the instructions	**27**	
28	Multiply line 27 by ten (10)	**28**	
29	Subtract line 28 from line 25. Multiple recipients, see instructions . . . . ▶	**29**	
30	**Tax on lump-sum distribution.** Add lines 7 and 29. Also include this amount in the total on Form 1040, line 43, or Form 1041, Schedule G, line 1b, whichever applies . . . . . . ▶	**30**	

For Paperwork Reduction Act Notice, see instructions.   Cat. No. 13187U   Form **4972** (2004)

General Instructions

Section references are to the Internal Revenue Code.

Purpose of Form

Use Form 4972 to figure the tax on a qualified lump-sum distribution (defined below) you received in 2004 using the 20% capital gain election, the 10-year tax option, or both. These are special formulas used to figure a separate tax on the distribution that may result in a smaller tax than if you reported the taxable amount of the distribution as ordinary income.

You pay the tax only once, for the year you receive the distribution, not over the next 10 years. The separate tax is added to the regular tax figured on your other income.

Related Publications

Pub. 575, Pension and Annuity Income.

Pub. 721, Tax Guide to U.S. Civil Service Retirement Benefits.

Pub. 939, General Rule for Pensions and Annuities.

What Is a Qualified Lump-Sum Distribution?

It is the distribution or payment in 1 tax year of a plan participant's entire balance from all of an employer's qualified plans of one kind (for example, pension, profit-sharing, or stock bonus plans) in which the participant had funds. The participant's entire balance does not include deductible voluntary employee contributions or certain forfeited amounts. The participant must have been born before January 2, 1936.

Distributions upon death of the plan participant. If you received a qualifying distribution as a beneficiary after the participant's death, the participant must have been born before January 2, 1936, for you to use this form for that distribution.

Distributions to alternate payees. If you are the spouse or former spouse of a plan participant who was born before January 2, 1936, and you received a qualified lump-sum distribution as an alternate payee under a qualified domestic relations order, you can use Form 4972 to make the 20% capital gain election and use the 10-year tax option to figure your tax on the distribution.

See *How To Report the Distribution* on this page.

Distributions That Do Not Qualify for the 20% Capital Gain Election or the 10-Year Tax Option

The following distributions are not qualified lump-sum distributions and do not qualify for the 20% capital gain election or the 10-year tax option.

● A distribution that is partially rolled over to another qualified plan or an IRA.

● Any distribution if an earlier election to use either the 5- or 10-year tax option had been made after 1986 for the same plan participant.

● U.S. Retirement Plan Bonds distributed with the lump sum.

● A distribution made during the first 5 tax years that the participant was in the plan, unless it was paid because the participant died.

● The current actuarial value of any annuity contract included in the lump sum (Form 1099-R, box 8, should show this amount, which you use only to figure tax on the ordinary income part of the distribution).

● A distribution to a 5% owner that is subject to penalties under section 72(m)(5)(A).

● A distribution from an IRA.

● A distribution from a tax-sheltered annuity (section 403(b) plan).

● A distribution of the redemption proceeds of bonds rolled over tax free to a qualified pension plan, etc., from a qualified bond purchase plan.

● A distribution from a qualified plan if the participant or his or her surviving spouse previously received an eligible rollover distribution from the same plan (or another plan of the employer that must be combined with that plan for the lump-sum distribution rules) and the previous distribution was rolled over tax free to another qualified plan or an IRA.

● A distribution from a qualified plan that received a rollover after 2001 from an IRA (other than a conduit IRA), a governmental section 457 plan, or a section 403(b) tax-sheltered annuity on behalf of the plan participant.

● A distribution from a qualified plan that received a rollover after 2001 from another qualified plan on behalf of that plan participant's surviving spouse.

● A corrective distribution of excess deferrals, excess contributions, excess aggregate contributions, or excess annual additions.

● A lump-sum credit or payment from the Federal Civil Service Retirement System (or the Federal Employees' Retirement System).

How To Report the Distribution

If you can use Form 4972, attach it to Form 1040 (individuals) or Form 1041 (estates or trusts). The payer should have given you a Form 1099-R or other statement that shows the amounts needed to complete Form 4972. The following choices are available.

20% capital gain election. If there is an amount in Form 1099-R, box 3, you can use Form 4972, Part II, to apply a 20% tax rate to the capital gain portion. See *Capital Gain Election* on page 3.

10-year tax option. You can use Part III to figure your tax on the lump-sum

distribution using the 10-year tax option whether or not you make the 20% capital gain election.

Where to report. Report amounts from your Form 1099-R either directly on your tax return (Form 1040 or 1041) or on Form 4972.

● If you do not use Form 4972, report the entire amount from Form 1099-R, box 1 (Gross distribution), on Form 1040, line 16a, and the taxable amount on line 16b (or on Form 1041, line 8). If your pension or annuity is fully taxable, enter the amount from Form 1099-R, box 2a (Taxable amount), on Form 1040, line 16b; do not make an entry on line 16a.

● If you do not use Part III of Form 4972, but use Part II, report only the ordinary income portion of the distribution on Form 1040, lines 16a and 16b (or on Form 1041, line 8). The ordinary income portion is the amount from Form 1099-R, box 2a, minus the amount from box 3 of that form.

● If you use Part III of Form 4972, do not include any part of the distribution on Form 1040, lines 16a and 16b (or on Form 1041, line 8).

The entries in other boxes on Form 1099-R may also apply in completing Form 4972.

● Box 6 (Net unrealized appreciation in employer's securities). See *Net unrealized appreciation (NUA)* on page 3.

● Box 8 (Other). Current actuarial value of an annuity.

If applicable, get the amount of federal estate tax paid attributable to the taxable part of the lump-sum distribution from the administrator of the deceased's estate.

How Often You May Use Form 4972

After 1986, you may use Form 4972 only once for each plan participant. If you receive more than one lump-sum distribution for the same participant in 1 tax year, you must treat all those distributions the same way. Combine them on a single Form 4972.

If you make an election as a beneficiary of a deceased participant, it does not affect any election you can make for qualified lump-sum distributions from your own plan. You can also make an election as the beneficiary of more than one qualifying person.

Example. Your mother and father died and each was born before January 2, 1936. Each had a qualified plan of which you are the beneficiary. You also received a qualified lump-sum distribution from your own plan and you were born before January 2, 1936. You may make an election for each of the distributions; one for yourself, one as your mother's beneficiary, and one as your father's. It does not matter if the distributions all occur in the same year or in different years. File a separate Form 4972 for each participant's distribution.

TIP An earlier election on Form 4972 or Form 5544 for a distribution before 1987 does not prevent you from making an election for a distribution after 1986 for the same participant, provided the participant was under age 59½ at the time of the pre-1987 distribution.

When You May File Form 4972

You can file Form 4972 with either an original or amended return. Generally, you have 3 years from the later of the due date of your tax return or the date you filed your return to choose to use any part of Form 4972.

Capital Gain Election

If the distribution includes a capital gain, you can (a) make the 20% capital gain election in Part II of Form 4972 or (b) treat the capital gain as ordinary income.

Only the taxable amount of distributions resulting from pre-1974 participation qualifies for capital gain treatment. The capital gain amount should be shown in Form 1099-R, box 3. If there is an amount in Form 1099-R, box 6 (net unrealized appreciation (NUA)), part of it will also qualify for capital gain treatment. Use the NUA Worksheet on this page to figure the capital gain part of NUA if you make the election to include NUA in your taxable income.

You may report the ordinary income portion of the distribution on Form 1040, line 16b (or Form 1041, line 8) or you may figure the tax using the 10-year tax option. The ordinary income portion is the amount from Form 1099-R, box 2a, minus the amount from box 3 of that form.

Net unrealized appreciation (NUA). Normally, NUA in employer securities received as part of a lump-sum distribution is not taxable until the securities are sold. However, you can elect to include NUA in taxable income in the year received.

The total amount to report as NUA should be shown in Form 1099-R, box 6. Part of the amount in box 6 will qualify for capital gain treatment if there is an amount in Form 1099-R, box 3. To figure the total amount subject to capital gain treatment including the NUA, complete the NUA Worksheet on this page.

Specific Instructions

Name of recipient of distribution and identifying number. At the top of Form 4972, fill in the name and identifying number of the recipient of the distribution.

If you received more than one qualified distribution in 2004 for the same plan participant, add them and figure the tax on the total amount. If you received qualified distributions in 2004 for more than one participant, file a separate Form 4972 for the distributions of each participant.

If you and your spouse are filing a joint return and each has received a lump-sum distribution, complete and file a separate

Form 4972 for each spouse's election, combine the tax, and include the combined tax in the total on Form 1040, line 43.

If you are filing for a trust that shared the distribution only with other trusts, figure the tax on the total lump sum first. The trusts then share the tax in the same proportion that they shared the distribution.

Multiple recipients of a lump-sum distribution. If you shared in a lump-sum distribution from a qualified retirement plan when not all recipients were trusts (a percentage will be shown in Form 1099-R, boxes 8 and/or 9a), figure your tax on Form 4972 as follows. (Box numbers used below are from Form 1099-R.)

Step 1. Complete Form 4972, Parts I and II. If you make the 20% capital gain election in Part II and also elect to include NUA in taxable income, complete the NUA Worksheet below to determine the amount of NUA that qualifies for capital gain treatment. Then, skip Step 2 and go to Step 3.

Step 2. Use this step only if you do not elect to include NUA in your taxable income or if you do not have NUA.

● If you are not making the capital gain election, divide the amount in box 2a by your percentage of distribution in box 9a. Enter this amount on Form 4972, line 8.

● If you are making the capital gain election, subtract the amount in box 3 from the amount in box 2a. Divide the result by your percentage of distribution in box 9a. Enter the result on Form 4972, line 8.

● Divide the amount in box 8 by the percentage in box 8. Enter the result on Form 4972, line 11. Then, skip Step 3 and go to Step 4.

Step 3. Use this step only if you elect to include NUA in your taxable income.

● If you are not making the capital gain election, add the amount in box 2a to the amount in box 6. Divide the result by your percentage of distribution in box 9a. Enter the result on Form 4972, line 8.

● If you are making the capital gain election, subtract the amount in box 3 from the amount in box 2a. Add to the result the amount from line F of your NUA Worksheet. Then, divide the total by your percentage of distribution in box 9a. Enter the result on Form 4972, line 8.

● Divide the amount in box 8 by the percentage in box 8. Enter the result on Form 4972, line 11.

Step 4. Complete Form 4972 through line 28.

Step 5. Complete the following worksheet to figure the entry for Form 4972, line 29:

A. Subtract line 28 from line 25 . _____

B. Enter your percentage of the distribution from box 9a . _____

C. Multiply line A by line B. Enter here and on Form 4972, line 29. Also, write "MRD" on the dotted line next to line 29 . _____

NUA Worksheet (keep for your records)

A. Enter the amount from Form 1099-R, box 3 . . . .   **A.** _____

B. Enter the amount from Form 1099-R, box 2a . . . .   **B.** _____

C. Divide line A by line B and enter the result as a decimal (rounded to at least three places) . . . .   **C.** _____._____

D. Enter the amount from Form 1099-R, box 6 . . . .   **D.** _____

E. Capital gain portion of NUA. Multiply line C by line D . . .   **E.** _____

F. Ordinary income portion of NUA. Subtract line E from line D . . .   **F.** _____

G. Total capital gain portion of distribution. Add lines A and E. Enter here and on Form 4972, line 6. On the dotted line next to line 6, write "NUA" and the amount from line E above. . . . .   **G.** _____

Death Benefit Worksheet (keep for your records)

A. Enter the amount from Form 1099-R, box 3, or, if you are including NUA in taxable income, the amount from line G of the NUA Worksheet   **A.** _____

B. Enter the amount from Form 1099-R, box 2a, plus, if you are including NUA in taxable income, the amount from Form 1099-R, box 6 . .   **B.** _____

C. Divide line A by line B and enter the result as a decimal (rounded to at least three places) . . . .   **C.** _____._____

D. Enter your share of the death benefit exclusion* . . . . . .   **D.** _____

E. Multiply line D by line C . . . .   **E.** _____

F. Subtract line E from line A. Enter here and on Form 4972, line 6 . .   **F.** _____

*Applies only for participants who died before August 21, 1996. If there are multiple recipients of the distribution, the allowable death benefit exclusion must be allocated among the recipients in the same proportion that they share the distribution.

Form 4972 (2004)   Page **4**

Part II

See *Capital Gain Election* on page 3 before completing Part II.

Line 6. Leave this line blank if your distribution does not include a captial gain amount or you are not making the 20% capital gain election, and go to Part III.

Generally, enter on line 6 the amount from Form 1099-R, box 3. However, if you elect to include NUA in your taxable income, use the NUA Worksheet on page 3 to figure the amount to enter. If you are taking a death benefit exclusion (for a participant who died before August 21, 1996), use the Death Benefit Worksheet on page 3 to figure the amount to enter on line 6. The remaining allowable death benefit exclusion should be entered on line 9 if you choose the 10-year tax option.

If any federal estate tax was paid on the lump-sum distribution, you must decrease the capital gain amount by the amount of estate tax applicable to it. To figure this amount, you must complete line C of the Death Benefit Worksheet on page 3, even if you do not take the death benefit exclusion. Multiply the total federal estate tax paid on the lump-sum distribution by the decimal on line C of the Death Benefit Worksheet. The result is the portion of the federal estate tax applicable to the capital gain amount. Then, use that result to reduce the amount in Form 1099-R, box 3, if you do not take the death benefit exclusion, or reduce line F of the Death Benefit Worksheet if you do. Enter the remaining capital gain on line 6. If you elected to include NUA in taxable income, subtract the portion of federal estate tax applicable to the capital gain amount from the amount on line G of the NUA Worksheet. Enter the result on line 6. Enter the remainder of the federal estate tax on line 18.

 If you take the death benefit exclusion and federal estate tax was paid on the capital gain amount, the capital gain amount must be reduced by both the procedures discussed above to figure the correct entry for line 6.

Part III

Line 8. If Form 1099-R, box 2a, is blank, you must first figure the taxable amount. For details on how to do this, see Pub. 575.

If you made the 20% capital gain election, enter only the ordinary income portion of the distribution on this line. The ordinary income portion is the amount from Form 1099-R, box 2a, minus the amount from box 3 of that form. Add the amount from line F of the NUA Worksheet if you included NUA capital gain in the 20% capital gain election.

If you did not make the 20% capital gain election and did not elect to include NUA in taxable income, enter the amount from Form 1099-R, box 2a. If you did not make the 20% capital gain election but did elect to include NUA in your taxable income, add the amount from Form 1099-R, box 2a, to the amount from Form 1099-R, box 6. Enter the total on line 8. On the dotted line next to line 8, write "NUA" and the amount of NUA included.

 Community property laws do not apply in figuring tax on the amount you report on line 8.

Line 9. If you received the distribution because of the plan participant's death and the participant died before August 21, 1996, you may be able to exclude up to $5,000 of the lump sum from your gross income. If there are multiple recipients of the distribution not all of whom are trusts, enter on line 9 the full remaining allowable death benefit exclusion (after the amount taken against the capital gain portion of the distribution by all recipients—see the instructions for line 6) without allocation among the recipients. (The exclusion is in effect allocated among the recipients through the computation under *Multiple recipients of a lump-sum distribution* on page 3.) This exclusion applies to the beneficiaries or estates of common-law employees, self-employed individuals, and shareholder-employees who owned more than 2% of the stock of an S corporation. Pub. 939 gives more information about the death benefit exclusion.

Enter the allowable death benefit exclusion on line 9. But see the instructions for line 6 if you made a capital gain election.

Line 18. A beneficiary who receives a lump-sum distribution because of a plan participant's death must reduce the taxable part of the distribution by any federal estate tax paid on the lump-sum distribution. Do this by entering on line 18 the federal estate tax attributable to the lump-sum distribution. Also see the instructions for line 6.

Lines 24 and 27. Use the following Tax Rate Schedule to complete lines 24 and 27.

Tax Rate Schedule

If the amount on line 23 or 26 is:		Enter on line 24 or 27:	
Over	But not over—		Of the amount over—
$ 0	$1,190	- - - - - 11%	$ 0
1,190	2,270	$130.90 + 12%	1,190
2,270	4,530	260.50 + 14%	2,270
4,530	6,690	576.90 + 15%	4,530
6,690	9,170	900.90 + 16%	6,690
9,170	11,440	1,297.70 + 18%	9,170
11,440	13,710	1,706.30 + 20%	11,440
13,710	17,160	2,160.30 + 23%	13,710
17,160	22,880	2,953.80 + 26%	17,160
22,880	28,600	4,441.00 + 30%	22,880
28,600	34,320	6,157.00 + 34%	28,600
34,320	42,300	8,101.80 + 38%	34,320
42,300	57,190	11,134.20 + 42%	42,300
57,190	85,790	17,388.00 + 48%	57,190
85,790	- - - - -	31,116.00 + 50%	85,790

Paperwork Reduction Act Notice. We ask for the information on this form to carry out the Internal Revenue laws of the United States. You are required to give us the information. We need it to ensure that you are complying with these laws and to allow us to figure and collect the right amount of tax.

You are not required to provide the information requested on a form that is subject to the Paperwork Reduction Act unless the form displays a valid OMB control number. Books or records relating to a form or its instructions must be retained as long as their contents may become material in the administration of any Internal Revenue law. Generally, tax returns and return information are confidential, as required by section 6103.

The time needed to complete this form will vary depending on individual circumstances. The estimated average time is:

Recordkeeping . . . . 52 min.

Learning about the law or the form . . . . 19 min.

Preparing the form . . . 1 hr., 11 min.

Copying, assembling, and sending the form to the IRS . . 20 min.

If you have comments concerning the accuracy of these time estimates or suggestions for making this form simpler, we would be happy to hear from you. See the instructions for the tax return with which this form is filed.

Printed on recycled paper

Tax Rate Schedule for 1986

If the amount on line 30 or 33 is:		Enter on line 31 or 34:			
Over—	But not over—	Amount		Plus percentage	Of the amount over—
$0	$1,190	- - - - - -		11%	$0
1,190	2,270	$130.90	+	12%	1,190
2,270	4,530	260.50	+	14%	2,270
4,530	6,690	576.90	+	15%	4,530
6,690	9,170	900.90	+	16%	6,690
9,170	11,440	1,297.70	+	18%	9,170
11,440	13,710	1,706.30	+	20%	11,440
13,710	17,160	2,160.30	+	23%	13,710
17,160	22,880	2,953.80	+	26%	17,160
22,880	28,600	4,441.00	+	30%	22,880
28,600	34,320	6,157.00	+	34%	28,600
34,320	42,300	8,101.80	+	38%	34,320
42,300	57,190	11,134.20	+	42%	42,300
57,190	85,790	17,388.00	+	48%	57,190
85,790	- - - - -	31,116.00	+	50%	85,790

Form **5329**

Additional Taxes on Qualified Plans (Including IRAs) and Other Tax-Favored Accounts

► Attach to Form 1040.

► See separate instructions.

OMB No. 1545-0203

20**04**

Department of the Treasury
Internal Revenue Service   (99)

Attachment
Sequence No. **29**

Name of individual subject to additional tax. If married filing jointly, see instructions.

Your social security number

Fill in Your Address Only If You Are Filing This Form by Itself and Not With Your Tax Return

Home address (number and street), or P.O. box if mail is not delivered to your home

Apt. no.

City, town or post office, state, and ZIP code

If this is an amended return, check here ► ☐

If you **only** owe the additional 10% tax on early distributions, you may be able to report this tax directly on Form 1040, line 59, without filing Form 5329. See the instructions for Form 1040, line 59.

Part I   **Additional Tax on Early Distributions**

Complete this part if you took a taxable distribution, before you reached age 59½, from a qualified retirement plan (including an IRA) or modified endowment contract (unless you are reporting this tax directly on Form 1040—see above). You may also have to complete this part to indicate that you qualify for an exception to the additional tax on early distributions or for certain Roth IRA distributions (see instructions).

1	Early distributions included in income. For Roth IRA distributions, see instructions	**1**	
2	Early distributions included on line 1 that are not subject to the additional tax (see instructions). Enter the appropriate exception number from the instructions: _____	**2**	
3	Amount subject to additional tax. Subtract line 2 from line 1	**3**	
4	**Additional tax.** Enter 10% (.10) of line 3. Include this amount on Form 1040, line 59 .	**4**	

Caution: *If any part of the amount on line 3 was a distribution from a SIMPLE IRA, you may have to include 25% of that amount on line 4 instead of 10% (see instructions).*

Part II   **Additional Tax on Certain Distributions From Education Accounts**

Complete this part if you included an amount in income, on Form 1040, line 21, from a Coverdell education savings account (ESA) or a qualified tuition program (QTP).

5	Distributions included in income from Coverdell ESAs and QTPs	**5**	
6	Distributions included on line 5 that are not subject to the additional tax (see instructions) . .	**6**	
7	Amount subject to additional tax. Subtract line 6 from line 5	**7**	
8	**Additional tax.** Enter 10% (.10) of line 7. Include this amount on Form 1040, line 59 . .	**8**	

Part III   **Additional Tax on Excess Contributions to Traditional IRAs**

Complete this part if you contributed more to your traditional IRAs for 2004 than is allowable or you had an amount on line 17 of your 2003 Form 5329.

9	Enter your excess contributions from line 16 of your 2003 Form 5329 (see instructions). If zero, go to line 15		**9**	
10	If your traditional IRA contributions for 2004 are less than your maximum allowable contribution, see instructions. Otherwise, enter -0-	**10**		
11	2004 traditional IRA distributions included in income (see instructions)	**11**		
12	2004 distributions of prior year excess contributions (see instructions)	**12**		
13	Add lines 10, 11, and 12		**13**	
14	Prior year excess contributions. Subtract line 13 from line 9. If zero or less, enter -0-		**14**	
15	Excess contributions for 2004 (see instructions)		**15**	
16	Total excess contributions. Add lines 14 and 15		**16**	
17	**Additional tax.** Enter 6% (.06) of the **smaller** of line 16 or the value of your traditional IRAs on December 31, 2004 (including 2004 contributions made in 2005). Include this amount on Form 1040, line 59 . . .		**17**	

Part IV   **Additional Tax on Excess Contributions to Roth IRAs**

Complete this part if you contributed more to your Roth IRAs for 2004 than is allowable or you had an amount on line 25 of your 2003 Form 5329.

18	Enter your excess contributions from line 24 of your 2003 Form 5329 (see instructions). If zero, go to line 23		**18**	
19	If your Roth IRA contributions for 2004 are less than your maximum allowable contribution, see instructions. Otherwise, enter -0- . . .	**19**		
20	2004 distributions from your Roth IRAs (see instructions)	**20**		
21	Add lines 19 and 20		**21**	
22	Prior year excess contributions. Subtract line 21 from line 18. If zero or less, enter -0- . . .		**22**	
23	Excess contributions for 2004 (see instructions)		**23**	
24	Total excess contributions. Add lines 22 and 23		**24**	
25	**Additional tax.** Enter 6% (.06) of the **smaller** of line 24 **or** the value of your Roth IRAs on December 31, 2004 (including 2004 contributions made in 2005). Include this amount on Form 1040, line 59		**25**	

For Paperwork Reduction Act Notice, see page 5 of the instructions.

Cat. No. 13329Q

Form **5329** (2004)

Form 5329 (2004)   Page **2**

Part V   **Additional Tax on Excess Contributions to Coverdell ESAs**
Complete this part if the contributions to your Coverdell ESAs for 2004 were more than is allowable or you had an
amount on line 33 of your 2003 Form 5329.

26	Enter the excess contributions from line 32 of your 2003 Form 5329 (see instructions). If zero, go to line 31	**26**	
27	If the contributions to your Coverdell ESAs for 2004 were less than the maximum allowable contribution, see instructions. Otherwise, enter -0- **27**		
28	2004 distributions from your Coverdell ESAs (see instructions) . . **28**		
29	Add lines 27 and 28 .	**29**	
30	Prior year excess contributions. Subtract line 29 from line 26. If zero or less, enter -0- . . .	**30**	
31	Excess contributions for 2004 (see instructions)	**31**	
32	Total excess contributions. Add lines 30 and 31	**32**	
33	**Additional tax.** Enter 6% (.06) of the **smaller** of line 32 **or** the value of your Coverdell ESAs on December 31, 2004 (including 2004 contributions made in 2005). Include this amount on Form 1040, line 59	**33**	

Part VI   **Additional Tax on Excess Contributions to Archer MSAs**
Complete this part if you or your employer contributed more to your Archer MSAs for 2004 than is allowable or you
had an amount on line 41 of your 2003 Form 5329.

34	Enter the excess contributions from line 40 of your 2003 Form 5329 (see instructions). If zero, go to line 39	**34**	
35	If the contributions to your Archer MSAs for 2004 are less than the maximum allowable contribution, see instructions. Otherwise, enter -0- **35**		
36	2004 distributions from your Archer MSAs from Form 8853, line 10 . **36**		
37	Add lines 35 and 36 .	**37**	
38	Prior year excess contributions. Subtract line 37 from line 34. If zero or less, enter -0- . . .	**38**	
39	Excess contributions for 2004 (see instructions)	**39**	
40	Total excess contributions. Add lines 38 and 39	**40**	
41	**Additional tax.** Enter 6% (.06) of the **smaller** of line 40 **or** the value of your Archer MSAs on December 31, 2004 (including 2004 contributions made in 2005). Include this amount on Form 1040, line 59	**41**	

Part VII   **Additional Tax on Excess Contributions to Health Savings Accounts (HSAs)**
Complete this part if contributions to your HSAs were more than is allowable.

42	Excess contributions for 2004 (see instructions)	**42**	
43	**Additional tax.** Enter 6% (.06) of the **smaller** of line 42 or the value of your HSAs on December 31, 2004 (including 2004 contributions made in 2005). Include this amount on Form 1040, line 59 . . .	**43**	

Part VIII   **Additional Tax on Excess Accumulation in Qualified Retirement Plans (Including IRAs)**
Complete this part if you did not receive the minimum required distribution from your qualified retirement plan.

44	Minimum required distribution for 2004 (see instructions)	**44**	
45	Amount actually distributed to you in 2004	**45**	
46	Subtract line 45 from line 44. If zero or less, enter -0-	**46**	
47	**Additional tax.** Enter 50% (.50) of line 46. Include this amount on Form 1040, line 59 . . .	**47**	

Signature. Complete **only** if you are filing this form by itself and not with your tax return.

Please Sign Here	Under penalties of perjury, I declare that I have examined this form, including accompanying schedules and statements, and to the best of my knowledge and belief, it is true, correct, and complete. Declaration of preparer (other than taxpayer) is based on all information of which preparer has any knowledge.

▶ Your signature _____   ▶ Date _____

Paid Preparer's Use Only	Preparer's signature ▶		Date	Check if self-employed ☐	Preparer's SSN or PTIN
	Firm's name (or yours if self-employed), address, and ZIP code ▶			EIN	
				Phone no. ( )	

Form **5329** (2004)

20**04**

Department of the Treasury
Internal Revenue Service

Instructions for Form 5329

Additional Taxes on Qualified Plans (Including IRAs) and Other Tax-Favored Accounts

Section references are to the Internal Revenue Code unless otherwise noted.

General Instructions

What's New

- If your Form 1099-R has a distribution code 1 in box 7 and you qualify for an exception to the additional 10% tax, you are required to file Form 5329.
- There is an additional 6% tax on excess contributions to health savings accounts.
- Enter exception number 11 on line 2 for certain distributions from section 457 plans.

Purpose of Form

Use Form 5329 to report additional taxes on:
- Individual retirement arrangements (IRAs),
- Other qualified retirement plans,
- Modified endowment contracts,
- Coverdell ESAs,
- Qualified tuition programs (QTPs),
- Archer MSAs, or
- Health savings accounts (HSAs).

Who Must File

You must file Form 5329 if any of the following apply.
- You received an early distribution from a Roth IRA, the amount on Form 8606, line 23, is more than zero, and the amount on Form 5329, line 1, is more than zero.
- You received an early distribution from a qualified retirement plan (other than a Roth IRA) and distribution code 1 is not shown in box 7 of Form 1099-R, Distributions From Pensions, Annuities, Retirement or Profit-Sharing Plans, IRAs, Insurance Contracts, etc.

Note. You do not have to file Form 5329 if distribution code 1 is correctly shown in box 7 of all Forms 1099-R and you owe the additional tax on each Form 1099-R. Instead, see the instructions for Form 1040, line 59, for how to report the additional 10% tax directly on that line.
- You meet an exception to the tax on early distributions and distribution code 1 is shown in box 7 of Form 1099-R.
- You meet an exception to the tax on early distributions from the list on page

2 but box 7 of your Form 1099-R does not indicate an exception or the exception does not apply to the entire distribution.
- You received taxable distributions from Coverdell ESAs or QTPs.
- The contributions for 2004 to your traditional IRAs, Roth IRAs, Coverdell ESAs, Archer MSAs, or HSAs exceed your maximum contribution limit, or you had a tax due from an excess contribution on line 17, 25, 33, or 41 of your 2003 Form 5329.
- You did not receive the minimum required distribution from your qualified retirement plan.

> **TIP** *If you rolled over part or all of a distribution from a qualified retirement plan, the part rolled over is not subject to the additional tax on early distributions. See the instructions for Form 1040, lines 15a and 15b or lines 16a and 16b, or Form 1040A, lines 11a and 11b or 12a and 12b, for how to report the rollover.*

When and Where To File

File Form 5329 with your 2004 Form 1040 by the due date, including extensions, of your Form 1040.

If you do not have to file a 2004 income tax return, complete and file Form 5329 by itself at the time and place you would be required to file Form 1040. Be sure to include your address on page 1 and your signature and the date on page 2. Enclose, but do not attach, a check or money order payable to "United States Treasury" for any taxes due. Write your SSN and "2004 Form 5329" on the check.

Prior tax years. If you are filing Form 5329 for a prior year, you must use that year's version of the form. If you do not have other changes, file Form 5329 by itself (see above). If you have other changes, file Form 5329 for that year with Form 1040X, Amended U.S. Individual Income Tax Return.

Definitions

Qualified retirement plan. A qualified retirement plan includes:

- A qualified pension, profit-sharing, or stock bonus plan (including a 401(k) plan),
- A tax-sheltered annuity contract,
- A qualified annuity plan, and
- An IRA.

For purposes of the additional tax on early distributions, an eligible governmental section 457 deferred compensation plan is treated as a qualified retirement plan, but only to the extent that a distribution is attributable to an amount transferred from a qualified retirement plan (as defined above).

Note. Modified endowment contracts are not qualified retirement plans.

Traditional IRAs. For purposes of Form 5329, a traditional IRA is any IRA, including a simplified employee pension (SEP) IRA, other than a SIMPLE IRA or Roth IRA.

Early distribution. Generally, any distribution from your IRA, other qualified retirement plan, or modified endowment contract before you reach age 59½ is an early distribution.

Rollover. A rollover is a tax-free distribution of assets from one qualified retirement plan that is reinvested in another plan or the same plan. Generally, you must complete the rollover within 60 days following the distribution. Any taxable amount not rolled over must be included in income and may be subject to the additional tax on early distributions.

The IRS may waive the 60-day requirement if failing to waive it would be against equity or good conscience, such as situations where a casualty, disaster, or other events beyond your reasonable control prevented you from meeting the 60-day requirement. Also, the 60-day period may be extended if you had a frozen deposit. See Pub. 590, Individual Retirement Arrangements (IRAs), for details.

Compensation. Compensation includes wages, salaries, tips, bonuses, and other pay you receive for services you perform. It also includes sales commissions, commissions on insurance premiums, and pay based on a percentage of profits. It includes net earnings from self-employment, but only for a trade or business in which your personal services are a material income-producing factor.

For IRAs, treat all taxable alimony received under a decree of divorce or separate maintenance as compensation.

Compensation does not include any amounts received as a pension or annuity and does not include any amount received as deferred compensation.

Taxable compensation is your compensation that is included in gross income reduced by any deductions on Form 1040, lines 30 and 32, but not by any loss from self-employment.

Additional Information

See Pub. 590, Pub. 560, Retirement Plans for Small Business, Pub. 575, Pension and Annuity Income, and Pub. 970, Tax Benefits for Education.

Specific Instructions

Joint returns. If both you and your spouse are required to file Form 5329, complete a separate form for each of you. Include the combined tax on Form 1040, line 59.

Amended return. If you are filing an amended 2004 Form 5329, check the box at the top of page 1 of the form. Do not use the 2004 Form 5329 to amend your return for any other year. Instead, see *Prior tax years* on page 1.

Part I—Additional Tax on Early Distributions

In general, if you receive an early distribution (including an involuntary cashout) from an IRA, other qualified retirement plan, or modified endowment contract, the part of the distribution included in income generally is subject to an additional 10% tax. But see *Exception for Roth IRA Distributions* on this page.

The additional tax on early distributions does not apply to:
• A distribution from a traditional or SIMPLE IRA that was converted to a Roth IRA;
• A distribution of certain excess IRA contributions (see the instructions for lines 15 and 23);

Note. Any related earnings withdrawn with excess contributions are subject to the additional tax on early distributions if you were under age 59½ at the time of the distribution.
• A distribution of excess contributions from a qualified cash or deferred arrangement;

• A distribution of excess aggregate contributions to meet nondiscrimination requirements for employee contributions and matching employer contributions;
• A distribution of excess deferrals; and
• A distribution from an eligible governmental section 457 deferred compensation plan to the extent the distribution is not attributable to an amount transferred from a qualified retirement plan (excluding an eligible section 457 deferred compensation plan).

See the instructions for line 2 on this page for other distributions that are not subject to the tax.

Line 1

Enter the amount of early distributions included in income that you received from:
• A qualified retirement plan, including earnings on withdrawn excess contributions to your IRAs included in income in 2004, or
• A modified endowment contract entered into after June 20, 1988.

Certain prohibited transactions, such as borrowing from your IRA or pledging your IRA assets as security for a loan, are considered to be distributions and may also cause you to owe the additional tax on early distributions. See Pub. 590 for details.

Exception for Roth IRA Distributions

If you received an early distribution from a Roth IRA, first allocate the amount on your 2004 Form 8606, line 19, in the order shown, to the amounts on the lines listed below (to the extent a prior year distribution was not allocable to the amount). Then, include on line 1 of Form 5329 the amount from your 2004 Form 8606, line 25, plus the amount, if any, allocated to the amount on your 2004 Form 8606, line 20 (include this amount, if any, on Form 5329, line 2, and enter the exception number 09), or 2000 Form 8606, line 16, or 2001, 2002, 2003, or 2004 Form 8606, line 18.
• Your 2004 Form 8606, line 20.
• Your 2004 Form 8606, line 22.
• Your 1998 Form 8606, line 16.
• Your 1998 Form 8606, line 15.
• Your 1999 Form 8606, line 16.
• Your 1999 Form 8606, line 15.
• Your 2000 Form 8606, line 16.
• Your 2000 Form 8606, line 15.
• Your 2001 Form 8606, line 18.
• Your 2001 Form 8606, line 17.
• Your 2002 Form 8606, line 18.
• Your 2002 Form 8606, line 17.
• Your 2003 Form 8606, line 18.
• Your 2003 Form 8606, line 17.
• Your 2004 Form 8606, line 18.

• Your 2004 Form 8606, line 17.
• Your 2004 Form 8606, line 25.

Example. You converted $20,000 from a traditional IRA to a Roth IRA in 2000 and converted $10,000 in 2001. Your 2000 Form 8606 had $5,000 on line 15 and $15,000 on line 16 and your 2001 Form 8606 had $3,000 on line 17 and $7,000 on line 18. You made Roth IRA contributions of $2,000 for 2000 and 2001. You did not make any Roth IRA conversions or contributions for 2002 through 2004, or take any Roth IRA distributions before 2004. On July 9, 2004, at age 53, you took a $33,000 distribution from your Roth IRA. Your 2004 Form 8606 shows $33,000 on line 19; $29,000 on line 23 ($33,000 minus $4,000 for your contributions) and $0 on line 25 ($29,000 minus your basis in Roth IRA conversions of $30,000). First, $4,000 of the $33,000 is allocated to your 2004 Form 8606, line 22; then $15,000 to your 2000 Form 8606 line 16; $5,000 to your 2000 Form 8606, line 15; and $7,000 to your 2001 Form 8606, line 18. The remaining $2,000 is allocated to the $3,000 on your 2001 Form 8606, line 17. On line 1, enter $22,000 ($15,000 plus the $7,000 that was allocated to your 2001 Form 8606, line 18). If you take a Roth IRA distribution in 2005, the first $1,000 will be allocated to the $1,000 remaining from your 2001 Form 8606, line 17, and will not be subject to the additional tax on early distributions.

Additional Information. For more details, see *Are Distributions Taxable?* in Pub. 590.

Line 2

The additional tax on early distributions does not apply to the distributions described below. Enter on line 2 the amount that can be excluded. In the space provided, enter the applicable exception number (01-11).

No. Exception

01 Qualified retirement plan distributions due to separation from service in or after the year you reach age 55 (does not apply to IRAs).

02 Distributions made as part of a series of substantially equal periodic payments (made at least annually) for your life (or life expectancy) or the joint lives (or joint life expectancies) of you and your designated beneficiary (if from an employer plan, payments must begin after separation from service).

03 Distributions due to total and permanent disability.

04 Distributions due to death (does not apply to modified endowment contracts).

05 Qualified retirement plan distributions up to (1) the amount you paid for unreimbursed medical expenses during the year minus (2) 7.5% of your adjusted gross income for the year.

06 Qualified retirement plan distributions made to an alternate payee under a qualified domestic relations order (does not apply to IRAs).

07 IRA distributions made to unemployed individuals for health insurance premiums.

08 IRA distributions made for higher education expenses.

09 IRA distributions made for purchase of a first home, up to $10,000.

10 Distributions due to an IRS levy on the qualified retirement plan.

11 Other (see instructions). Also, enter this code if more than one exception applies.

Other. The following exceptions also apply.

• Distributions incorrectly indicated as early distributions by code 1, J, or S in box 7 of Form 1099-R. Include on line 2 the amount you received when you were age 59½ or older.

• Distributions from a section 457 plan, which are not from a rollover from a qualified retirement plan.

• Distributions from a plan maintained by an employer if:

  1. You separated from service by March 1, 1986;

  2. As of March 1, 1986, your entire interest was in pay status under a written election that provides a specific schedule for distribution of your entire interest; and

  3. The distribution is actually being made under the written election.

• Distributions that are dividends paid with respect to stock described in section 404(k).

• Distributions from annuity contracts to the extent that the distributions are allocable to the investment in the contract before August 14, 1982.

For additional exceptions that apply to annuities, see Pub. 575.

Line 4

If any amount on line 3 was a distribution from a SIMPLE IRA received within 2 years from the date you first participated in the SIMPLE IRA plan, you must multiply that amount by 25% instead of 10%. These distributions are included in boxes 1 and 2a of Form 1099-R and are designated with code S in box 7.

Part II—Additional Tax on Certain Distributions From Education Accounts

Line 6

This tax does not apply to distributions:
• Due to the death or disability of the beneficiary;
• Made on account of a tax-free scholarship, allowance, or payment described in section 25A(g)(2);
• From QTPs that were used for the qualified higher education expenses of the beneficiary;
• From QTPs and Coverdell ESAs made because of attendance by the beneficiary at a U.S. military academy. This exception applies only to the extent that the distribution does not exceed the costs of advanced education (as defined in title 10 of the U.S. Code) at the academy, or
• Distributions used for qualified higher education expenses included in income because the expenses were used to figure the Hope and lifetime learning credit.

Enter on line 6 the portion of line 5 that is excluded.

Part III—Additional Tax on Excess Contributions to Traditional IRAs

If you contributed more for 2004 than is allowable or you had an amount on line 17 of your 2003 Form 5329, you may owe this tax. But you may be able to avoid the tax on any 2004 excess contributions (see the instructions for line 15).

Line 9

Enter the amount from line 16 of your 2003 Form 5329 only if the amount on line 17 of your 2003 Form 5329 is more than zero.

Line 10

If you contributed less to your traditional IRAs for 2004 than your contribution limit for traditional IRAs, enter the difference.

If you are not married filing jointly, your contribution limit for traditional IRAs is the smaller of your taxable compensation (see page 1) or $3,000 ($3,500 if age 50 or older at the end of 2004). If you are married filing jointly, your contribution limit is generally $3,000 ($3,500 if age 50 or older at the end of 2004) and your spouse's contribution limit is $3,000 ($3,500 if age 50 or older at the end of 2004). But if the combined taxable compensation for you and your spouse is less than

$6,000 ($6,500 if one spouse is 50 or older at the end of 2004; $7,000 if both spouses are 50 or older at the end of 2004), see *How Much Can Be Contributed?* in Pub. 590 for special rules.

Also include on line 9a or 9b of the IRA Deduction Worksheet in the instructions for Form 1040, line 25, the smaller of (a) Form 5329, line 10, or (b) the excess, if any, of Form 5329, line 9, over the sum of Form 5329, lines 11 and 12.

Line 11

Enter on line 11 any withdrawals from your traditional IRAs that are included in your income. Do not include any withdrawn contributions reported on line 12.

Line 12

Enter any excess contributions to your traditional IRAs for 1976 through 2002 that you had returned to you in 2004 and any 2003 excess contributions that you had returned to you in 2004 after the due date (including extensions) of your 2003 income tax return, that are included on line 9, if:
• You did not claim a deduction for the excess contribution and no traditional IRA deduction was allowable (without regard to the modified AGI limitation) for the excess contribution, and
• The total contributions to your traditional IRAs for the tax year for which the excess contributions were made were not more than: (a) $3,000 for 2003 ($3,500 if age 50 or older at the end of 2003), (b) $3,000 for 2002 ($3,500 if age 50 or older at the end of 2002), (c) $2,000 for years after 1996 and before 2002, or (d) $2,250 for years before 1997. If the total contributions for the year included employer contributions to a SEP, increase that amount by the smaller of the amount of the employer contributions or $40,000 ($35,000 for 2001, or $30,000 for years before 2001).

Line 15

Enter the excess of your contributions to traditional IRAs for 2004 (unless withdrawn—see below) over your contribution limit for traditional IRAs. See the instructions for line 10 to figure your contribution limit for traditional IRAs. Any amount you contribute for the year in which you reach age 70½ or a later year is an excess contribution because your contribution limit is zero. Do not include rollovers in figuring your excess contributions.

You can withdraw some or all of your excess contributions for 2004 and they will not be treated as having been contributed if:

-3-

- You make the withdrawal by the due date, including extensions, of your 2004 tax return,
- You do not claim a traditional IRA deduction for the withdrawn contribution, and
- You withdraw any earnings on the withdrawn contribution and include the earnings in gross income (see the Instructions for Form 8606 for details). Also, if you had not reached age 59½ at the time of the withdrawal, include the earnings as an early distribution on line 1 of Form 5329 for the year in which you report the earnings.

If you timely filed your return without withdrawing the excess contributions, you can still make the withdrawal no later than 6 months after the due date of your tax return, excluding extensions. If you do, file an amended return with "Filed pursuant to section 301.9100-2" written at the top. Report any related earnings for 2004 on the amended return and include an explanation of the withdrawal. Make any other necessary changes on the amended return (for example, if you reported the contributions as excess contributions on your original return, include an amended Form 5329 reflecting that the withdrawn contributions are no longer treated as having been contributed).

Part IV—Additional Tax on Excess Contributions to Roth IRAs

If you contributed more to your Roth IRA for 2004 than is allowable or you had an amount on line 25 of your 2003 Form 5329, you may owe this tax. But you may be able to avoid the tax on any 2004 excess contributions (see the instructions for line 23).

Line 18

Enter the amount from line 24 of your 2003 Form 5329 only if the amount on line 25 of your 2003 Form 5329 is more than zero.

Line 19

If you contributed less to your Roth IRAs for 2004 than your contribution limit for Roth IRAs, enter the difference. Your contribution limit for Roth IRAs is generally your contribution limit for traditional IRAs (see the instructions for line 10) reduced by the amount you contributed to traditional IRAs. But your contribution limit for Roth IRAs may be further reduced or eliminated if your modified AGI for Roth IRA purposes is over:
- $150,000 if married filing jointly or qualifying widow(er),
- $0 if married filing separately and you lived with your spouse at any time in 2004, or

- $95,000 for any other taxpayer.
  See Pub. 590 for details.

Line 20

Generally, enter the amount from Form 8606, line 19 plus any qualified distributions. But if you withdrew the entire balance of all your Roth IRAs, do not enter less than the amount on Form 5329, line 18 (see *Example*).

Example. You contributed $1,000 to a Roth IRA in 2002, your only contribution to Roth IRAs. In 2004, you discovered you were not eligible to contribute to a Roth IRA in 2002. On September 9, 2004, you withdrew $800, the entire balance in the Roth IRA. You must file Form 5329 for 2002 and 2003 to pay the additional taxes for those years. When you complete Form 5329 for 2004, you enter $1,000 (not $800) on line 20, because you withdrew the entire balance.

Line 23

Enter the excess of your contributions to Roth IRAs for 2004 (unless withdrawn—see below) over your contribution limit for Roth IRAs (see the instructions for line 19).

Any amounts converted to a Roth IRA are excess Roth IRA contributions if your modified AGI for Roth IRA purposes is over $100,000 or your filing status is married filing separately and you lived with your spouse at any time in 2004. See *Recharacterizations* in the Instructions for Form 8606 for details. Do not include rollovers in figuring your excess contributions.

You can withdraw some or all of your excess contributions for 2004 and they will not be treated as having been contributed if:
- You make the withdrawal by the due date, including extensions, of your 2004 tax return, and
- You withdraw any earnings on the withdrawn contribution and include the earnings in gross income (see the Instructions for Form 8606 for details). Also, if you had not reached age 59½ at the time of the withdrawal, include the earnings as an early distribution on line 1 of Form 5329 for the year in which you report the earnings.

If you timely filed your return without withdrawing the excess contributions, you can still make the withdrawal no later than 6 months after the due date of your tax return, excluding extensions. If you do, file an amended return with "Filed pursuant to section 301.9100-2" written at the top. Report any related earnings for 2004 on the amended return and include an explanation of the withdrawal. Make any other necessary changes on the amended return (for example, if you reported the contributions as excess contributions

on your original return, include an amended Form 5329 reflecting that the withdrawn contributions are no longer treated as having been contributed).

Part V—Additional Tax on Excess Contributions to Coverdell ESAs

If the contributions to your Coverdell ESAs for 2004 were more than is allowable or you had an amount on line 33 of your 2003 Form 5329, you owe this tax. But you may be able to avoid the tax on any 2004 excess contributions (see the instructions for line 31).

Line 26

Enter the amount from line 32 of your 2003 Form 5329 only if the amount on line 33 of your 2003 Form 5329 is more than zero.

Line 27

Enter the excess, if any, of the maximum amount that can be contributed to your Coverdell ESAs for 2004 (see the instructions for line 31) over the amount actually contributed for 2004.

Line 28

Enter your total distributions from Coverdell ESAs in 2004. Do not include rollovers or returned excess contributions.

Line 31

Enter the excess of the contributions to your Coverdell ESAs for 2004 (not including rollovers) over your contribution limit for Coverdell ESAs. Your contribution limit is the smaller of $2,000 or the sum of the maximum amounts allowed to be contributed by the contributor(s) to your Coverdell ESAs. The maximum contribution may be limited based on the contributor's modified AGI. See Pub. 970 for details.

You can withdraw some or all of the excess contributions for 2004 and they will not be treated as having been contributed if:
- You make the withdrawal before June 1, 2005, and
- You also withdraw any income earned on the withdrawn contribution and include the earnings in gross income for the year in which the contribution was made.

If you filed your return without withdrawing the excess contributions, you can still make the withdrawal, but it must be made before June 1, 2005. If you do, file an amended return. Report any related earnings for 2004 on the amended return and include an explanation of the withdrawal. Make any other necessary changes on the amended return (for example, if you reported the contributions as excess contributions on your original return, include an amended Form 5329 reflecting that the withdrawn contributions are no longer treated as having been contributed).

Part VI—Additional Tax on Excess Contributions to Archer MSAs

If you or your employer contributed more to your Archer MSA for 2004 than is allowable or you had an amount on line 41 of your 2003 Form 5329, you may owe this tax. But you may be able to avoid the tax on any 2004 excess contributions (see the instructions for line 39).

Line 34

Enter the amount from line 40 of your 2003 Form 5329 only if the amount on line 41 of your 2003 Form 5329 is more than zero.

Line 35

If the contribution limit for your Archer MSAs (the smaller of line 5 or line 6 of Form 8853) is greater than the contributions to your Archer MSAs for 2004, enter the difference on line 35. Also include on line 7 of your 2004 Form 8853 the smaller of:
- Form 5329, line 35, or
- The excess, if any, of Form 5329, line 34, over Form 5329, line 36.

Line 39

Enter the excess of your contributions to your Archer MSA for 2004 (from Form 8853, line 4) over your contribution limit (the smaller of line 5 or line 6 of Form 8853). However, you can withdraw some or all of the excess contributions for 2004 and they will not be treated as having been contributed if:
- You make the withdrawal by the due date, including extensions, of your 2004 tax return, and
- You withdraw any income earned on the withdrawn contributions and include the earnings in gross income for the year in which you receive the withdrawn contributions and earnings.

Include the withdrawn contribution and related earnings on Form 8853, lines 8a and 8b.

If you timely filed your return without withdrawing the excess contributions, you can still make the withdrawal no later than 6 months after the due date of your tax return, excluding extensions. If you do, file an amended return with "Filed pursuant to section 301.9100-2" written at the top. Report any related earnings for 2004 on the amended return and include an explanation of the

withdrawal. Make any other necessary changes on the amended return (for example, if you reported the contributions as excess contributions on your original return, include an amended Form 5329 reflecting that the withdrawn contributions are no longer treated as having been contributed).

Also include on line 39 any excess contributions your employer made. See Form 8853 for details.

Part VII—Additional Tax on Excess Contributions to Health Savings Accounts

If the contributions to your health savings account (HSA) exceed your contribution limit, you may owe this tax. However, you may be able to avoid this tax if the excess contributions are timely removed from your account.

Line 42

Enter the excess contributions to your HSA for 2004 (unless withdrawn—see below) over your contribution limit. The instructions for Form 8889 explain how to figure excess contributions.

You can withdraw some or all of the excess contributions for 2004 and they will not be treated as having been contributed if:
- You make the withdrawal by the due date, including extensions, of your 2004 return,
- You do not claim an exclusion from income for the amount of the withdrawn contributions, and
- You also withdraw any earnings on the withdrawn contributions and include the earnings in your gross income.

If you timely filed your return without withdrawing the excess contributions, you can still make the withdrawal no later than 6 months after the due date of your tax return, excluding extensions. If you do, file an amended return with "Filed pursuant to section 301.9100-2" written at the top. Report any related earnings for 2004 on the amended return and include an explanation of the withdrawal. Make any other necessary changes on the amended return (for example, if you reported the contributions as excess contributions on your original return, include an amended Form 5329 reflecting that the withdrawn contributions are no longer treated as having been contributed).

Part VIII—Additional Tax on Excess Accumulation in Qualified Retirement Plans (Including IRAs)

You owe this tax if you do not receive the minimum required distribution from your qualified retirement plan, including an IRA or an eligible section 457 deferred compensation plan. The additional tax is 50% of the excess accumulation—the difference between the amount that was required to be distributed and the amount that was actually distributed.

Required Distributions

IRA (other than a Roth IRA). You must start receiving distributions from your IRA by April 1 of the year following the year in which you reach age 70½. At that time, you can receive your entire interest in the IRA or begin receiving periodic distributions. If you choose to receive periodic distributions, you must receive a minimum required distribution each year. You can figure the minimum required distribution by dividing the account balance of your IRAs (other than Roth IRAs) on December 31 of the year preceding the distribution by the applicable life expectancy. For applicable life expectancies, see Pub. 590.

If the trustee, custodian, or issuer of your IRA informs you of the minimum required distribution, you can use that amount.

If you have more than one IRA, you can take the minimum required distribution from any one or more of the individual IRAs.

For more details on the minimum distribution rules (including examples), see Pub. 590.

Roth IRA. There are no minimum required distributions during the lifetime of the owner of a Roth IRA. Following the death of the Roth IRA owner, required distribution rules apply to the beneficiary. See Pub. 590 for details.

Qualified retirement plans (other than IRAs) and eligible section 457 deferred compensation plans. In general, you must begin receiving distributions from your plan no later than April 1 following the later of (a) the year in which you reach age 70½ or (b) the year in which you retire.

Exception. If you owned more than 5% of the employer maintaining the plan, you must begin receiving distributions no later than April 1 of the year following the year in which you reach age 70½, regardless of when you retire.

Your plan administrator should figure the amount that must be distributed each year.

Note. The IRS may waive this tax if you can show that any shortfall in the amount of withdrawals was due to reasonable error and you are taking appropriate steps to remedy the shortfall. If you believe you qualify for this relief, file Form 5329, pay the tax, and attach a letter of explanation. If the IRS waives the tax, we will send you a refund.

For more details, see Pub. 575.

Paperwork Reduction Act Notice. We ask for the information on this form to carry out the Internal Revenue laws of the United States. You are required to give us the information. We need it to ensure that you are complying with these laws and to allow us to figure and collect the right amount of tax.

You are not required to provide the information requested on a form that is subject to the Paperwork Reduction Act unless the form displays a valid OMB control number. Books or records relating to a form or its instructions must be retained as long as their contents may become material in the administration of any Internal Revenue law. Generally, tax returns and return information are confidential, as required by section 6103.

The time needed to complete and file this form will vary depending on individual circumstances. The estimated average time is: **Recordkeeping,** 2 hr., 2 min.; **Learning about the law or the form,** 32 min.; **Preparing the form,** 2 hr., 17 min.; **Copying, assembling, and sending the form to the IRS,** 13 min.

If you have comments concerning the accuracy of these time estimates or suggestions for making this form simpler, we would be happy to hear from you. You can write to the Internal Revenue Service, Tax Products Coordinating Committee, SE:W:CAR:MP:T:T:SP, 1111 Constitution Ave. NW, IR-6406, Washington, DC 20224. Do not send the form to this address. Instead, see *When and Where To File* on page 1.

Form **5330**
(Rev. August 2004)
Department of the Treasury
Internal Revenue Service

Return of Excise Taxes Related to Employee Benefit Plans
(Under sections 4971, 4972, 4973(a)(3), 4975, 4976, 4977, 4978, 4978A, 4979, 4979A, 4980, and 4980F of the Internal Revenue Code)

OMB No. 1545-0575

Filer tax year beginning _____ , and ending _____ ,

A Name of filer (see page 2 of the instructions)	B Filer's identifying number—EIN or SSN (see instructions)
Number, street, and room or suite no. (If a P.O. box, see page 2 of the instructions)	▶
City or town, state, and ZIP code	E Plan sponsor's EIN
C Name and address of plan sponsor	F Plan year ending
D Name of plan	G Plan number

H Check here if this is an amended return. . . . . ▶ ☐

Part I   Summary of Taxes Due

		FOR IRS USE ONLY		
1	Section 4972 tax on nondeductible contributions to qualified plans (from line 14l) . .	161	**1**	
2	Section 4973(a)(3) tax on excess contributions to section 403(b)(7)(A) custodial accounts (from line 24)	164	**2**	
3	Section 4976 tax on disqualified benefits for funded welfare plans (see instructions) .	200	**3**	
4a	Section 4978 and 4978A tax on certain ESOP dispositions (see instructions). . . .	209	**4a**	
b	The tax on line 4a is a result of the application of: ☐ Sec. 664(g) ☐ Sec. 1042 ☐ Sec. 4978A		**4b**	
5	Section 4979A tax on certain prohibited allocations of qualified ESOP securities (see instructions)	203	**5**	
6a	Section 4975(a) tax on prohibited transactions (from line 25c)	159	**6a**	
b	Section 4975(b) tax on failure to correct prohibited transactions (see Part IV instructions) . . .	224	**6b**	
7a	Section 4971(a) tax on failure to meet minimum funding standards (see instructions) .	163	**7a**	
b	Section 4971(b) tax on failure to correct minimum funding standards (see Part VI instructions) . .	225	**7b**	
8	Section 4977 tax on excess fringe benefits (from line 30d)	201	**8**	
9	Section 4979 tax on excess contributions to certain plans (see instructions)	205	**9**	
10	Section 4980 tax on reversion of qualified plan assets to an employer (from line 34) .	204	**10**	
11	Section 4980F tax on failure to provide notice of significant reduction in future accruals (from line 41)	228	**11**	
12a	Section 4971(f)(1) tax on failure to pay liquidity shortfall (from line 45)	226	**12a**	
b	Section 4971(f)(2) additional tax on failure to correct liquidity shortfall (see Part XI instructions)	227	**12b**	
13a	**Total tax.** Add lines 1 through 12b (see page 4 of the instructions)		**13a**	
b	Enter amount of tax paid with Form 5558 or any other tax paid prior to filing this return. . .		**13b**	
c	**Total tax due.** Subtract line 13b from line 13a. Attach check or money order payable to "United States Treasury." Write your name, identifying number, and "Form 5330, Section(s) _____" on your payment . . . . ▶		**13c**	

Sign Here

Under penalties of perjury, I declare that I have examined this return, including accompanying schedules and statements, and to the best of my knowledge and belief, it is true, correct, and complete. Declaration of preparer (other than taxpayer) is based on all information of which preparer has any knowledge.

▶ _____ Your signature

(____) _____ Telephone number

▶ _____ Date

Paid Preparer's Use Only

Preparer's signature ▶		Date
Firm's name (or yours if self-employed) and address ▶		

For Privacy Act and Paperwork Reduction Act Notice, see page 9 of the instructions.   Cat. No. 11870M   Form **5330** (Rev. 8-2004)

Form 5330 (Rev. 8-2004)   Page **2**

DUE DATE: The taxes listed on this page are due by the last day of the 7th month after the end of the tax year of the filer.

| **Part II** | **Tax on Nondeductible Employer Contributions to Qualified Plans (Section 4972)** |

14a Total contributions for your tax year to your qualified (under section 401(a), 403(a), or 408(k), or 408(p)) plan. . . . .

b Amount allowable as a deduction under section 404 . . . .

c Subtract line 14b from line 14a . . . .

d Enter amount of any prior year nondeductible contributions made for years beginning after 12/31/86 . . . .

e Amount of any prior year nondeductible contributions for years beginning after 12/31/86 returned to you in this tax year or any prior tax year . . .

f Subtract line 14e from line 14d . . . .

g Amount of line 14f carried forward and deductible in this tax year . . .

h Subtract line 14g from line 14f . . . .

i Tentative taxable excess contributions. Add lines 14c and 14h . . . .

j Nondeductible section 4972(c)(6) or (7) contributions exempt from excise tax . . . .

k Taxable excess contributions. Subtract line 14j from line 14i . . . .

l Multiply line 14k by 10%. Enter here and on line 1 . . . . ▶

| **Part III** | **Tax on Excess Contributions to Section 403(b)(7)(A) Custodial Accounts (Section 4973(a)(3))** |

15 Total amount contributed for current year less rollovers (see page 5 of the instructions) . . . .

16 Amount excludable from gross income under section 403(b) (see page 5 of the instructions) . .

17 Current year excess contributions. Subtract line 16 from line 15; but not less than zero . . . .

18 Prior year excess contributions not previously eliminated. If zero, go to line 22a . . . .

19 Contribution credit. If line 16 is more than line 15, enter the excess; otherwise, enter -0-. . . . .

20 Total of all prior years' distributions out of the account included in your gross income under section 72(e) and not previously used to reduce excess contributions . . . .

21 Adjusted prior years' excess contributions. Subtract the total of lines 19 and 20 from line 18 . .

22a Taxable excess contributions. Add lines 17 and 21 . . . .

b Multiply line 22a by 6% . . . .

23a Enter the value of your account as of the last day of the year . . . .

b Multiply line 23a by 6% . . . .

24 **Excess contributions tax.** Enter the lesser of line 22b or line 23b. Enter here and on line 2 . ▶

Form **5330** (Rev. 8-2004)

Form 5330 (Rev. 8-2004)   Page **3**

DUE DATE: Section 4975 taxes are due by the last day of the 7th month after the end of the tax year of the filer.

| **Part IV** | **Tax on Prohibited Transactions (Section 4975)** (see instructions) |

25a Is the excise tax a result of a prohibited transaction that was (check one or more):
☐ discrete   ☐ other than discrete (a lease or a loan)

b Complete the table below to disclose the prohibited transactions and figure the initial tax (see instructions).

(a) Transaction number	**(b)** Date of transaction (see page 6 of the instructions)	**(c)** Description of prohibited transaction	**(d)** Amount involved in prohibited transaction (see page 6 of the instructions)	**(e)** Initial tax on prohibited transaction (multiply each transaction in column (c) by the appropriate rate (see page 6 of the instructions))
(i)				
(ii)				
(iii)				
(iv)				
(v)				
(vi)				
(vii)				
(viii)				
(ix)				
(x)				

25c Add amounts in column (e). Enter here and on line 6a . . . . ▶

26 Have you corrected **all** of the prohibited transactions that you are reporting on this return? (See page 7
of the instructions) . . . . ☐ **Yes** ☐ **No**
If "Yes," complete Part V. If "No," complete Part V and see page 7 of the instructions.

Form **5330** (Rev. 8-2004)

Form 5330 (Rev. 8-2004) Page **4**

Part V   Schedule of Other Participating Disqualified Persons and Description of Correction (see instructions)

27 Complete the schedule of other participating disqualified persons and description of correction (see instructions)

(a) Item no. from Part IV	(b) Name and address of disqualified person	(c) EIN or SSN	(d) Date of correction	(e) Description of correction

Form **5330** (Rev. 8-2004)

Form 5330 (Rev. 8-2004)   Page **5**

DUE DATE: See **When To File** on page 1 of the instructions for taxes due under sections 4971, 4977, 4979, 4980, 4971(f), and 4980F.

Part VI   **Tax on Failure To Meet Minimum Funding Standards (Section 4971(a) and 4971(b))**

28	Accumulated funding deficiency in the plan's minimum funding standard account (see page 7 of the instructions). . . . .
29	Multiply line 28 by tax rate (see instructions on page 7 for applicable tax rates). Enter here and on line 7a . . . . ▶

Part VII   **Tax on Excess Fringe Benefits (Section 4977)**

30a	Did you make an election to be taxed under section 4977?. . . . . . . ☐ Yes ☐ No
b	If "Yes," enter the calendar year in which the excess fringe benefits were paid ▶ _____
c	If line 30a is "Yes," enter the excess fringe benefits on this line (see page 8 of the instructions). .
d	Enter 30% of line 30c on this line and on line 8 . . . . ▶

Part VIII   **Tax on Excess Contributions to Certain Plans (Section 4979)**

31a	Enter the amount of any excess contributions under a cash or deferred arrangement that is part of a plan qualified under section 401(a), 403(a), 403(b), 408(k), 501(c)(18) or excess aggregate contributions described in section 401(m) . . . .
b	Multiply line 31a by 10%. Enter here and on line 9. . . . . ▶

Part IX   **Tax on Reversion of Qualified Plan Assets to an Employer (Section 4980)** (See page 8 of instructions)

32	Date reversion occurred ▶ month _____ day _____ year _____
33a	Employer reversion amount _____ b Excise tax rate _____ %
34	Multiply line 33a by line 33b and enter the amount here and on line 10 . . . . ▶
35	Explain below why you qualify for a rate other than 50%:

Part X   **Tax on Failure to Provide Notice of Significant Reduction in Future Accruals (Section 4980F)**

36	Enter the number of applicable individuals who were not provided ERISA section 204(h) notice. ▶
37	Enter the effective date of the amendment . . . . ▶
38	Enter the number of days in the noncompliance period . . . . ▶
39	Enter the total number of failures to provide ERISA section 204(h) notice (see page 8 of the instructions) . . . . ▶
40	Provide a brief description of the failure, and of the correction made, if any

----

41	Multiply line 39 by $100. Enter here and on line 11. . . . .

Part XI   **Tax on Failure to Pay Liquidity Shortfall (Section 4971(f)(1))**

		1st Quarter	2nd Quarter	3rd Quarter	4th Quarter	Total
42	Amount of shortfall . . .					
43	Shortfall paid by the due date					
44	Net shortfall amount . . .					
45	Multiply line 44 (total column) by 10% (5% for multiemployer plans). Enter here and on line 12a ▶					

⊕ Printed on recycled paper   Form **5330** (Rev. 8-2004)

Instructions for Form 5330

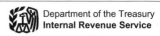

Department of the Treasury
Internal Revenue Service

(Rev. October 2004)

Return of Excise Taxes
Related to Employee Benefit Plans

Section references are to the Internal Revenue Code unless otherwise noted.

General Instructions

What's New

- For securities in an S corporation, section 4979A imposes an excise tax on the allocation or the ownership of the amount involved in (a) any transaction where a disqualified person owns a synthetic equity in any nonallocation year, or (b) any transaction involving employer securities that violates section 409(p) or a nonallocation year.
- Under section 409(p)(7), the Secretary of the Treasury may, through regulations or other guidance of general applicability, provide that a nonallocation year occurs in any case, in which the principal purpose of the ownership structure of an S corporation constitutes an avoidance or evasion of section 409(p).
- References to section 4978B have been deleted.
- These instructions have been reorganized to be consistent with the revised Form 5330.

Purpose of Form

File Form 5330 to report the tax on:
- A minimum funding deficiency (section 4971).
- Nondeductible contributions to qualified plans (section 4972).
- Excess contributions to a section 403(b)(7)(A) custodial account (section 4973(a)(3)).
- A prohibited transaction (section 4975).
- A disqualified benefit provided by funded welfare plans (section 4976).
- Excess fringe benefits (section 4977).
- Certain ESOP dispositions (sections 4978 and 4978A).
- Excess contributions to plans with cash or deferred arrangements (section 4979).
- Certain prohibited allocations of qualified securities by an ESOP (section 4979A).
- Reversions of qualified plan assets to employers (section 4980).
- A failure to pay liquidity shortfall (section 4971(f)).
- A failure of applicable plans reducing future benefit accruals to satisfy notice requirements (section 4980F).

Who Must File

A Form 5330 must be filed by:

1. Any employer who is liable for the tax under section 4971 for failure to meet the minimum funding standards under section 412 (liability for tax in the case of an employer who is a party to a collective bargaining agreement, see section 413(b)(6)).

2. Any employer who is liable for the tax under section 4971(f) for a failure to meet the liquidity requirement of section 412(m)(5).

3. Any employer who is liable for the tax under section 4972 for nondeductible contributions to qualified plans.

4. Any individual who is liable for the tax under section 4973(a)(3) because an excess contribution to a section 403(b)(7)(A) custodial account was made for them and that excess has not been eliminated as specified in sections 4973(c)(2)(A) and (B).

5. Any disqualified person who is liable for the tax under section 4975 for participating in a prohibited transaction (other than a fiduciary acting only as such), or an individual (or his or her beneficiary) who engages in a prohibited transaction with respect to his or her individual retirement account for each tax year or part of a tax year in the "taxable period" applicable to such prohibited transaction.

6. Any employer who is liable for the tax under section 4976 for maintaining a funded welfare benefit plan that provides a disqualified benefit during any tax year.

7. Any employer who pays excess fringe benefits and has elected to be taxed under section 4977 on such payments.

8. Any employer or worker-owned cooperative (as defined in section 1042(c)(2)) that maintains an ESOP that disposes of the qualified securities (as defined in section 1042(c)(1)) or section 133 securities within the specified 3-year period.

9. Any employer who is liable for the tax under section 4979 on excess contributions to plans with a cash or deferred arrangement, etc.

10. Any employer or worker-owned cooperative that made the written

statement described in section 664(g)(1)(E) or 1042(b)(3)(B) and made an allocation prohibited under section 409(n) of qualified securities of an ESOP taxable under section 4979A or any employer or worker-owned cooperative who made an allocation of S corporation stock of an ESOP prohibited under section 409(p) taxable under section 4979A.

11. Any employer who receives an employer reversion from a deferred compensation plan that is taxable under section 4980.

12. Any employer or multiemployer plan liable for the tax under section 4980F for failure to give notice of a significant reduction in the rate of future benefit accrual.

A Form 5330 and tax payment is required:
- For each year that you fail to meet the minimum funding standards under section 412 or contribute an excess amount to your section 403(b)(7)(A) custodial account.
- For each year that any of the items in 2 or 3, or 5 through 10, or 12 above apply.
- For a reversion of plan assets from a qualified plan that is taxable under section 4980.
- For each year (or part of a year) in the "taxable period" applicable to a prohibited transaction. See the instructions for Part IV, line 25b, columns (d) and (e), for a definition of taxable period.

When To File

File one Form 5330 to report excise taxes with the same filing due date. One Form 5330 may be filed to report one or more of these taxes. However, if the taxes are from separate plans, file separate forms for each plan.

Generally, the filing of a Form 5330 starts the statute of limitations running only with respect to the particular excise tax(es) reported on that Form 5330. However, statutes of limitations with respect to the prohibited transaction excise tax(es) are based on the filing of the applicable Form 5500. Use Table 1 to determine the due date of Form 5330.

Cat. No. 11871X

Table 1. Excise Tax Due Dates

If the taxes due are under section . . .	Then file Form 5330 by the last day of the . . .
4972	7th month after the end of the tax year of the employer or other person who must file this return.
4973(a)(3)	7th month after the end of the tax year of the employer or other person who must file this return.
4975	7th month after the end of the tax year of the employer or other person who must file this return.
4976	7th month after the end of the tax year of the employer or other person who must file this return.
4978	7th month after the end of the tax year of the employer or other person who must file this return.
4978A	7th month after the end of the tax year of the employer or other person who must file this return.
4979A	7th month after the end of the tax year of the employer or other person who must file this return.
4971	7th month after the end of the employer's tax year or 8½ months after the last day of the plan year that ends with or within the filer's tax year.
4971(f)	7th month after the end of the employer's tax year or 8½ months after the last day of the plan year that ends with or within the filer's tax year.
4977	7th month after the end of the calendar year in which the excess fringe benefits were paid to your employees.
4979	15th month after the close of the plan year to which the excess contributions or excess aggregate contributions relate.
4980	month following the month in which the reversion occurred.
4980F	month following the month in which the failure occurred.

If the filing due date falls on a Saturday, Sunday, or legal holiday, the return may be filed on the next business day.

Extension. File Form 5558, Application for Extension of Time to File Certain Employee Plan Returns, to request an extension of time to file. If approved, you may be granted an extension of up to 6 months.

Caution: Form 5558 does not extend the time to pay your taxes. See the instructions for Form 5558.

Where To File

 File Form 5330 with the: Internal Revenue Service Center, Ogden, UT 84201.

Private delivery services. You can use certain private delivery services designated by the IRS to meet the "timely mailing as timely filing/paying" rule for tax returns and payments. The most recent list of designated private delivery services was published by the IRS in September 2002 and includes only the following:

• Airborne Express (Airborne): Overnight Air Express Service, Next Afternoon Service, Second Day Service.
• DHL Worldwide Express (DHL): DHL "Same Day" Service, DHL USA Overnight.
• Federal Express (FedEx): FedEx Priority Overnight, FedEx Standard Overnight, FedEx 2Day, FedEx International Priority, and FedEx International First.
• United Parcel Service (UPS): UPS Next Day Air, UPS Next Day Air Saver, UPS 2nd Day Air, UPS 2nd Day Air A.M., UPS Worldwide Express Plus, and UPS Worldwide Express.

The private delivery service can tell you how to get written proof of the mailing date.

Interest and Penalties

Interest. Interest is charged on taxes not paid by the due date even if an extension of time to file is granted. Interest is also charged on penalties imposed for failure to file, negligence, fraud, gross valuation overstatements, and substantial understatements of tax from the due date (including extensions) to the date of payment. The interest charge is figured at a rate determined under section 6621.

Penalty for late filing of return. If you do not file a return by the due date, including extensions, you may have to pay a penalty of 5% of the unpaid tax for each month or part of a month the return is late, up to a maximum of 25% of the unpaid tax. The minimum penalty for a return that is more than 60 days late is the smaller of the tax due or $100. The penalty will not be imposed if you can show that the failure to file on time was due to reasonable cause. If you file late, you must attach a statement to Form 5330 explaining the reasonable cause.

Penalty for late payment of tax. If you do not pay the tax when due, you may have to pay a penalty of ½ of 1% of the unpaid tax for each month or part of a month the tax is not paid, up to a maximum of 25% of the unpaid tax. The penalty will not be imposed if you can show that the failure to pay on time was due to reasonable cause.

Interest and penalties for late filing and late payment will be billed separately after the return is filed.

Claim for Refund or Credit/ Amended Return

File an amended Form 5330 for any of the following:
• To claim a refund of overpaid taxes reportable on Form 5330;
• For a credit for overpaid taxes; or
• To report additional taxes due within the same tax year of the filer if those taxes have the same due date as those previously reported. Check the box in item H on page 1 of the return and report the correct amount of taxes in Parts II through XI, as appropriate, and on lines 1 through 13a of Part I. See instructions for lines 13a through 13c.

If you file an amended return to claim a refund or credit, the claim must state in detail the reasons for claiming the refund. In order to promptly consider your claim, you must explain why you are filing the claim and provide the appropriate supporting evidence. See Regulations section 301.6402-2 for more details.

Specific Instructions

Filer tax year. Enter the tax year of the employer, entity, or individual on whom the tax is imposed.

Item A. Name and address of filer. Enter the name and address of the employer, individual, or other entity who is liable for the tax.

Include the suite, room, or other unit numbers after the street number. If the Post Office does not deliver mail to the street address and you have a P.O. box, show the box number instead of the street address.

Item B. Filer's identifying number. Enter the identifying number of an individual (other than a sole proprietor with an employer identification number (EIN)) is his or her social security number. The identifying number of all others is their EIN.

Item C. Name and address of plan sponsor. The term "plan sponsor" means:

1. The employer, for an employee benefit plan that a single employer established or maintains;
2. The employee organization in the case of a plan of an employee organization; or
3. The association, committee, joint board of trustees, or other similar group

of representatives of the parties who establish or maintain the plan, if the plan is established or maintained jointly by one or more employers and one or more employee organizations, or by two or more employers.

Include the suite, room, or other unit numbers after the street number. If the Post Office does not deliver mail to the street address and you have a P.O. box, show the box number instead of the street address.

Item D. Name of plan. Enter the formal name of the plan, group insurance arrangement, or enough information to identify the plan. This should be the same name indicated on the Form 5500 series return/report filed for the plan.

Item E. Plan sponsor's EIN. Enter the nine-digit EIN assigned to the plan sponsor. This should be the same number used to file the Form 5500 series return/report.

Item F. Plan year ending. Plan year means the calendar or fiscal year on which the records of the plan are kept. Enter four digits in year-month order. This number assists the IRS in properly identifying the plan and time period for which the Form 5330 is being filed. For example, a plan year ended March 31, 2004, should be shown as 0403.

Item G. Plan number. Enter the three-digit number that the employer or plan administrator assigned to the plan.

Item H. Amended return. If you are filing an amended Form 5330, check the box on this line, and see the instructions for lines 13a through 13c. Also see *Claim for Refund or Credit/ Amended Return.*

Filer's signature. Please sign and date the form. Also enter a daytime phone number where you can be reached.

Preparer's signature. Anyone who prepares your return and does not charge you should not sign your return. For example, a regular full-time employee or your business partner who prepares the return should not sign.

Generally, anyone who is paid to prepare a return must sign it and fill in the *Paid Preparer's Use Only* area.

The paid preparer must complete the required preparer information and—
• Sign the return by hand, in the space provided for the preparer's signature (signature stamps and labels are not acceptable).
• Give a copy of the return to the filer.

Part I — Summary of Taxes Due

Line 3. Section 4976 – Tax on Disqualified Benefits for Funded

Welfare Plans. Section 4976 imposes an excise tax on employers who maintain a funded welfare benefit plan that provides a disqualified benefit during any tax year. The tax is 100% of the disqualified benefit.

Generally, a "disqualified benefit" is any of the following:
• Any post-retirement medical benefit or life insurance benefit provided for a key employee unless the benefit is provided from a separate account established for the key employee under section 419A(d);
• Any post-retirement medical benefit or life insurance benefit unless the plan meets the nondiscrimination requirements of section 505(b) for those benefits; or
• Any portion of the fund that reverts to the benefit of the employer.

Enter on line 3, the total amount of the disqualified benefit.

Line 4a and 4b. Section 4978 and 4978A – Tax on Certain ESOP Dispositions

Section 4978. Section 4978 imposes an excise tax on dispositions of securities acquired in a sale to which section 1042 applied, or in a qualified gratuitous transfer to which section 664(g) applied, if the dispositions take place within 3 years after the date of the acquisition of qualified securities (as defined in section 1042(c)(1) or a section 664(g) transfer).

The tax is 10% of the amount realized on the disposition of the qualified securities if an ESOP or eligible worker-owned cooperative (as defined in section 1042(c)(2)) disposes of the qualified securities within the 3-year period described above, and either of the following applies:
• The total number of shares held by that plan or cooperative after the disposition is less than the total number of employer securities held immediately after the sale, or
• Except to the extent provided in regulations, the value of qualified securities held by the plan or cooperative after the disposition is less than 30% of the total value of all employer securities as of the disposition (60% of the total value of all employer securities in the case of any qualified employer securities acquired in a qualified gratuitous transfer to which section 664(g) applied).

See section 4978(b)(2) for the limitation on the amount of tax.

The section 4978 tax must be paid by the employer or the eligible worker-owned cooperative that made the written statement described in section 1042(b)(3)(B) on dispositions that occurred during their tax year.

The section 4978 tax does not apply to a distribution of qualified securities or sale of such securities if any of the following occurs:
• The death of the employee;
• The retirement of the employee after the employee has reached age 59½;
• The disability of the employee (within the meaning of section 72(m)(7)); or
• The separation of the employee from service for any period that results in a 1-year break in service (as defined in section 411(a)(6)(A)).

For purposes of section 4978, an exchange of qualified securities in a reorganization described in section 368(a)(1) for stock of another corporation will not be treated as a disposition.

 For section 4978 excise taxes, the amount entered on Part I, line 4a is the amount realized on the disposition of qualified securities multiplied by 10%. Also check the appropriate box on line 4b.

Section 4978A does not apply to the estate of a person who died after December 19, 1989.

Section 4978A. This section imposes a tax on certain transactions involving qualified employer securities. Qualified employer securities for purposes of this tax are defined in section 2057(d) as in effect prior to December 19, 1989.

Section 4978A taxes any disposition of qualified employer securities acquired on or before December 20, 1989, if the disposition of the qualified securities takes place within 3 years after the date the ESOP or eligible worker-owned cooperative acquired the qualified securities.

The section 4978A tax also applies to dispositions of qualified securities that occur after the 3-year period if the qualified securities were not allocated to participants' accounts or the proceeds from the disposition were not allocated to the participants' accounts.

For section 4978A excise taxes, the amount entered on Part I, line 4a is 30% of the amount realized on the disposition or 30% of the amount repaid on the loan, whichever applies. Also check the appropriate box on line 4b.

Line 5. Section 4979A – Tax on Certain Prohibited Allocations of Qualified ESOP Securities. For plan years beginning before January 1, 2005, section 4979A imposes a 50% tax of the allocated amounts involved in:

1. An allocation described in section 664(g)(5)(A). Section 664(g)(5)(A), prohibits any portion of the assets of the ESOP attributable to

securities acquired by the plan in a qualified gratuitous transfer to be allocated to the account of:

a. Any person related to the decedent (within the meaning of section 267(b)) or a member of the decedent's family (within the meaning of section 2032A(e)(2), or

b. Any person who, at the time of the allocation, or at any time during the 1-year period ending on the date of the acquisition of qualified employer securities by the plan, is a 5-percent shareholder of the employer maintaining the plan.

2. A prohibited allocation of qualified securities by an ESOP or eligible worker-owned cooperative. A "prohibited allocation" is any allocation of qualified securities acquired in a non-recognition-of-gain sale under section 1042 which violates section 409(n).

Under section 409(n), an ESOP or worker-owned cooperative cannot allow any portion of assets, attributable to employer securities acquired in a section 1042 sale, to accrue or be allocated (directly or indirectly) to the taxpayer involved in the transaction (or any person related to the taxpayer) during the nonallocation period. For purposes of section 409(n), relationship to the taxpayer is defined under section 267(b).

The nonallocation period is the period beginning on the date the qualified securities are sold and ends on the later of:
- 10 years after the date of sale; or
- The date on which the final payment is made if acquisition indebtedness was incurred at the time of sale.

The employer sponsoring the plan, or the eligible worker-owned cooperative is responsible for paying the tax.

Prohibited allocations of securities in an S corporation.

 Generally, the prohibited allocation rules for securities in an S corporation are effective for plan years beginning after December 31, 2004; however, these rules are effective for plan years ending after March 14, 2001, if:

- *The ESOP was established after March 14, 2001, or*
- *The ESOP was established on or before March 14, 2001, and the employer maintaining the plan was **not** an S corporation.*

For securities in an S corporation, section 4979A imposes a tax on the allocation or the ownership equal to 50% of the amount involved in the following transactions.

1. Any synthetic equity owned by a disqualified person in any nonallocation year. "Synthetic equity " means any stock option, warrant, restricted stock, deferred issuance stock right, or similar interest or right that gives the holder the right to acquire or receive stock of the S corporation in the future. Synthetic equity may also include a stock appreciation right, phantom stock unit, or similar right to a future cash payment based on the value of the stock or appreciation. Synthetic equity also includes nonqualified deferred compensation as described in section 1.409(p)-1T(f)(2)(iv) of the Regulations, disregarding nonqualified deferred compensation that is distributed on or before July 21, 2004. The amount involved is the value of the shares on which the synthetic equity is based or the present value of the nonqualified deferred compensation. For additional information on the treatment of synthetic equity, see section 409(p)(5).

2. Any allocation of employer securities in a nonallocation year violating section 409(p). The amount involved is the amount allocated to the account of any person in violation of section 409(p)(1).

3. In the first nonallocation year the amount involved includes the total value of all the deemed-owned shares of all disqualified persons.

A "nonallocation year" means a plan year where the ESOP, at any time during the year, holds employer securities in an S corporation, and disqualified persons own at least:
- 50 percent of the number of outstanding shares of the S corporation (including deemed-owned ESOP shares), or
- 50 percent of the aggregate number of outstanding shares of stock (including deemed-owned ESOP shares) and synthetic equity in the S corporation.

For purposes of determining a nonallocation year, the attribution rules of section 318(a) will apply; however, the option rule of section 318(a)(4) will not apply. Additionally, the attribution rules defining family member is modified to include the individual's:
- Spouse.
- Ancestor or lineal descendant of the individual or the individual's spouse.
- A brother or sister of the individual or of the individual's spouse and any lineal descendant of the brother or sister.

A spouse of an individual who is legally separated from an individual under a decree of divorce or separate maintenance is not treated as the individual's spouse.

An individual is a disqualified person if:

- The total number of shares owned by the person and the members of the person's family is at least 20% of the deemed-owned of shares (as defined in section 409(p)(4)(C)) in the S corporation, or
- The person owns at least 10% of the deemed-owned shares (as defined in section 409(p)(4)(C)) in the S corporation.

 Under section 409(p)(7), the Secretary of the Treasury may, through regulations or other guidance of general applicability, provide that a nonallocation year occurs in any case in which the principal purpose of the ownership structure of an S corporation constitutes an avoidance or evasion of section 409(p). For a description of situations where the definition of nonallocation year was considered, see Revenue Ruling 2004-4, 2004-6 I.R.B. 414.

 For section 4979A excise taxes, the amount entered on Part I, line 5 is 50% of the amount involved as described in items 1 through 3, under *Prohibited allocations of securities in an S corporation*, above.

Lines 13a through 13c. If you are filing an amended Form 5330 and you paid tax with your original return and those taxes have the same due date as those previously reported, check the box in item H and enter the tax reported on your original return in the entry space for line 13b. If you file Form 5330 for a claim for refund or credit, show the amount of overreported tax in parentheses on line 13c. Otherwise, show the amount of additional tax due on line 13c and include the payment with the amended Form 5330.

Make your check or money order payable to the "United States Treasury" for the full amount due. Attach the payment to your return. Write your name, identifying number, and "Form 5330, Section ____" on your payment.

Part II (Section 4972)

Tax on Nondeductible Employer Contributions to Qualified Plans

Section 4972 imposes an excise tax on employers who make nondeductible contributions to their qualified plans. A "qualified plan" for purposes of this tax means any plan qualified under section 401(a), any annuity plan qualified under section 403(a), and any simplified employee pension plan qualified under section 408(k) or 408(p). The term "qualified plan" does not include certain governmental plans and certain plans maintained by tax-exempt organizations.

The nondeductible contributions are computed as of the end of the employer's tax year. The current year nondeductible contributions are equal to the amount contributed during the employer's tax year over the amount of contributions allowable as a deduction under section 404. In addition, prior year nondeductible contributions continue to be subject to this tax annually until eliminated by either distributions to the employer of the amount of nondeductible contributions, or a carryforward deduction in years after the nondeductible contributions are made.

Although pre-1987 nondeductible contributions are not subject to this excise tax, they are taken into account to determine the extent to which post-1986 contributions are deductible. See section 4972 and Publication 560, Retirement Plans for Small Business, for details.

Defined benefit plans exception. Generally, contributions up to the current unfunded liability of a defined benefit plan are deductible, regardless of the number of participants in the plan. In addition, when determining the amount of nondeductible contributions for any tax year, an employer may elect, for that tax year, not to include any contributions to a defined benefit plan except to the extent they exceed the full-funding limitation (as defined in section 412(c)(7), determined without regard to section 412(c)(7)(A)(i)(l)). When determining the amount of nondeductible contributions, the deductible limits under section 404(a)(7) must be applied first to contributions to defined contribution plans and then to contributions to defined benefit plans. This election applies to terminated and ongoing plans. An employer making this election cannot also benefit from the exceptions for terminating plans and for certain contributions to defined contribution plans under section 4972(c)(6).

Defined contribution plans exception. Employer contributions to one or more defined contribution plans that are nondeductible because they exceed the combined plan deduction limits of section 404(a)(7), are not subject to the 10% excise tax to the extent the contributions do not exceed the greater of:
- 6% of compensation (within the meaning of section 404(a) and as adjusted under section 404(a)(12)) paid or accrued (during the taxable year in which the contributions were made) to beneficiaries under plans, or
- The sum of the amount of contributions described in sections 401(m)(4)(A) and 402(g)(3)(A), or

- Contributions to a SIMPLE 401(k) or a SIMPLE IRA that are considered nondeductible because they are not made in connection with the employer's trade or business.

The combined plan deduction limits are first applied to contributions to the defined benefit plan and then to the defined contribution plan.

Restorative payments to a defined contribution plan are not considered nondeductible contributions if the payments are made to restore some or all of the plan's losses due to an action (or a failure to act) that creates a reasonable risk of liability for breach of fiduciary duty. Amounts paid in excess of the amount of the loss are not considered restorative payments.

Part III (Section 4973(a)(3))

Tax on Excess Contributions to Section 403(b)(7)(A) Custodial Accounts

Line 15. Reduce total current year contributions by any rollover contributions described in sections 403(b)(8) or 408(d)(3)(A).

Line 16. The amount you will enter on line 16 is the amount excludable under section 415(c) (limit on annual additions). Figure the amount to enter on line 16 using Table 2.

 To determine the amount excludable for years prior to January 1, 2002, see Publication 571, Tax-Sheltered Annuity (403(b)) Plans, for the specific year.

Table 2. Limit on Annual Additions

1. Enter your includible compensation for your most recent year of service* . . . . . **1.**_____
2. Maximum* **2.** $41,000
3. Enter the lesser of line 1 or line 2. This is your limit on annual additions. Enter this amount on line 16, Part III . . **3.**_____
*For more information, see Publication 571 for the year the excess contribution is being calculated.

 The limitation on line 2 ($41,000 for 2004) of Table 2, under section 415(c)(1)(A), is subject to changes in the cost-of-living as described in section 415(d). Currently, the dollar limit for a calendar year as adjusted annually for cost-of-living increases is published during the fourth quarter of the prior calendar year in the Internal Revenue Bulletin.

Part IV (Section 4975)

Tax on Prohibited Transactions

Section 4975 imposes an excise tax on a disqualified person that engages in a prohibited transaction with the plan.

Plan. For purposes of prohibited transactions (section 4975), the term "plan" means any of the following:
- A trust described in section 401(a) that forms part of a plan.
- A plan described in section 403(a), and that trust or plan is exempt from tax under section 501(a).
- An individual retirement account described in section 408(a).
- An individual retirement annuity described in section 408(b).
- An Archer MSA described in section 220(d).
- A Coverdell education savings account described in section 530.
- A Health Savings Account described in section 223(d).
- A trust described in section 501(c)(22).

 If the IRS determined at any time that your plan was a "plan" as defined above, it will always remain subject to the excise tax on prohibited transactions (section 4975). This also applies to the tax on minimum funding deficiencies (section 4971).

Disqualified person. A "disqualified person" is any person who is:
1. A fiduciary.
2. A person providing services to the plan.
3. An employer, any of whose employees are covered by the plan.
4. An employee organization, any of whose members are covered by the plan.
5. Any direct or indirect owner of 50% or more of:
   a. The combined voting power of all classes of stock entitled to vote, or the total value of shares of all classes of stock of a corporation,
   b. The capital interest or the profits interest of a partnership, or
   c. The beneficial interest of a trust or unincorporated enterprise, which is an employer or an employee organization described in 3, or 4 above. A limited liability company should be treated as a corporation, or a partnership, depending on how the organization is treated for federal tax purposes.
6. A member of the family of any individual described in 1, 2, 3, or 5. Member of a family is the spouse, ancestor, lineal descendant, and any spouse of a lineal descendant.
7. A corporation, partnership, or trust or estate of which (or in which) any direct or indirect owner holds 50% or more of the interest described in 5a,

5b, or 5c. For purposes of 7, the beneficial interest of the trust or estate is owned directly or indirectly, or held by persons described in 1 through 5.

8. An officer, director (or an individual having powers or responsibilities similar to those of officers or directors), a 10% or more shareholder or highly compensated employee (earning 10% or more of the yearly wages of an employer) of a person described in 3, 4, 5, or 7.

9. A 10% or more (in capital or profits) partner or joint venturer of a person described in 3, 4, 5, or 7.

10. Any disqualified person, as described in 1 through 9 above, who is a disqualified person with respect to any plan to which a section 501(c)(22) trust applies, is permitted to make payments under section 4223 of ERISA.

Prohibited transaction. A "prohibited transaction" is any direct or indirect:

1. Sale or exchange, or leasing of any property between a plan and a disqualified person; or a transfer of real or personal property by a disqualified person to a plan where the property is subject to a mortgage or similar lien placed on the property by the disqualified person within 10 years prior to the transfer, or the property transferred is subject to a mortgage or similar lien which the plan assumes.

2. Lending of money or other extension of credit between a plan and a disqualified person.

3. Furnishing of goods, services, or facilities between a plan and a disqualified person.

4. Transfer to, or use by or for the benefit of, a disqualified person of income or assets of a plan.

5. Act by a disqualified person who is a fiduciary whereby he or she deals with the income or assets of a plan in his or her own interest or account.

6. Receipt of any consideration for his or her own personal account by any disqualified person who is a fiduciary from any party dealing with the plan connected with a transaction involving the income or assets of the plan.

Exemptions. See sections 4975(d), 4975(f)(6)(B)(ii), and 4975(f)(6)(B)(iii) for specific exemptions to prohibited transactions. Also see section 4975(c)(2) for certain other transactions or classes of transactions that may be exempt.

Line 25a. Check the box that best characterizes the prohibited transaction for which an excise tax is being paid. A prohibited transaction is discrete unless it is of an ongoing nature. Transactions involving the use of money (loans, etc.) or other property (rent, etc.) are of an

ongoing nature and will be treated as a new prohibited transaction on the first day of each succeeding tax year or part of a tax year that is within the taxable period.

Line 25b, Column (b). List the date of all prohibited transactions that took place in connection with a particular plan during the current tax year. Also list the date of all prohibited transactions that took place in prior years unless either the transaction was corrected in a prior tax year or the section 4975(a) tax was assessed in the prior tax year. A disqualified person who engages in a prohibited transaction must file a separate Form 5330 to report the excise tax due under section 4975 for each tax year.

Line 25b, Columns (d) and (e). The "amount involved" in a prohibited transaction means the greater of the amount of money and the fair market value (FMV) of the other property given, or the amount of money and the FMV of the other property received. However, for services described in sections 4975(d)(2) and (10), the amount involved only applies to excess compensation. Fair market value must be determined as of the date on which the prohibited transaction occurs. If the use of money or other property is involved, the amount involved is the greater of the amount paid for the use or the FMV of the use for the period for which the money or other property is used. In addition, transactions involving the use of money or other property will be treated as giving rise to a prohibited transaction occurring on the date of the actual transaction plus a new prohibited transaction on the first day of each succeeding tax year or portion of a succeeding tax year which is within the taxable period. The "taxable period " is the period of time beginning with the date of the prohibited transaction and ending with the earliest of:

1. The date correction is completed,
2. The date of the mailing of a notice of deficiency, or
3. The date on which the tax under section 4975(a) is assessed.

See the instruction for *Additional tax for failure to correct the prohibited transaction,* under Part IV for the definition of correction.

 Temporary Regulations section 141.4975-13 states that, until final regulations are written under section 4975(f), the definitions of "amount involved" and "correction" found in Regulations section 53.4941(e)-1 will apply.

Column (e). The initial tax on a prohibited transaction is 15% of the amount involved in each prohibited transaction for each year or part of a

year in the taxable period. Multiply the amount in column (d) by 15%.

Example. The following example of a prohibited transaction does not cover all types of prohibited transactions. For more examples, see Regulations section 53.4941(e)-1(b)(4).

A disqualified person borrows money from a plan in a prohibited transaction under section 4975. The FMV of the use of the money and the actual interest on the loan is $1,000 per month (the actual interest is paid in this example). The loan was made on July 1, 2003, (date of transaction) and repaid on December 31, 2004 (date of correction). The disqualified person's taxable year is the calendar year. On July 31, 2005, the disqualified person files a delinquent Form 5330 for the 2003 plan year and a timely Form 5330 for the 2004 plan year. No Notice of Deficiency with respect to the tax imposed by section 4975(a) has been mailed to the disqualified person and no assessment of such tax has been made before the time the disqualified person filed the Forms 5330.

When a loan is a prohibited transaction, the loan is treated as giving rise to a prohibited transaction on the date the transaction occurs, and an additional prohibited transaction on the first day of each succeeding taxable year (or portion of a taxable year) within the taxable period that begins on the date the loan occurs. Each prohibited transaction has its own separate taxable period which begins on the date the prohibited transaction occurred or is deemed to occur and ends on the date of the correction. The taxable period that begins on the date the loan occurs runs from July 1, 2003, (date of loan) through December 31, 2004 (date of correction). Therefore, in this example, there are two prohibited transactions, the first occurring on July 1, 2003, and the second occurring on January 1, 2004.

Section 4975(a) imposes a 15% excise tax on the amount involved for each taxable year or part thereof in the taxable period of each prohibited transaction.

The amount involved to be reported on column (d) of Form 5330 filed for 2003 is $6,000 (6 months × $1,000). The amount of tax due is $900 ($6,000 ×15%). (Any interest and penalties imposed for the delinquent filing of the Form 5330 for 2003 will be billed separately to the disqualified person.)

The taxable period for the second prohibited transaction runs from January 1, 2004, through December 31, 2004 (date of correction). Because there are two prohibited transactions with taxable periods running during

Figure 1. 2003 Example

Part IV —Tax on Prohibited Transactions (section 4975)

(a) Transaction number	(b) Date of transaction (see page 6 of the instructions)	(c) Description of prohibited transaction	(d) Amount involved in prohibited transaction (see page 6 of the instructions)	(e) Initial tax on prohibited transaction (multiply each transaction in column (d) by the appropriate rate (see page 6 of the instructions))
(i)	7–1–03	Loan	$6,000	$900
(ii)				
(iii)				
25c. Add amounts in column (e). Enter here and on line 6a . . . . ▶				$900

Figure 2. 2004 Example

Part IV —Tax on Prohibited Transactions (section 4975)

(a) Transaction number	(b) Date of transaction (see page 6 of the instructions)	(c) Description of prohibited transaction	(d) Amount involved in prohibited transaction (see page 6 of the instructions)	(e) Initial tax on prohibited transaction (multiply each transaction in column (d) by the appropriate rate (see page 6 of the instructions))
(i)	7–1–03	Loan	$6,000	$900
(ii)	1–1–04	Loan	$12,000	$1,800
(iii)				
25c. Add amounts in column (e). Enter here and on line 6a . . . . ▶				$2,700

2004, the section 4975(a) tax is due for the 2004 taxable year for both prohibited transactions. The excise tax to be reported on the Form 5330 filed for 2004 would include both the prohibited transaction of July 1, 2003, with an amount involved of $6,000, resulting in a tax due of $900 ($6,000 × 15%) and the second prohibited transaction of January 1, 2004, with an amount involved of $12,000 (12 months × $1,000), resulting in a tax due of $1,800 ($12,000 × 15%). Line 25b of the Forms 5330 would be completed as shown in Figures 1 and 2.

 When a loan from a qualified plan that is a prohibited transaction spans successive taxable years, and thus constitutes multiple prohibited transactions, and during those years the first tier prohibited transaction excise tax rate changes, the first tier excise tax liability for each prohibited transaction is the sum of the products resulting from multiplying the amount involved for each year in the taxable period for that prohibited transaction by the excise tax rate in effect at the beginning of that taxable period. For more information see Revenue Ruling 2002-43, 2002-2 I.R.B. 85. Unlike the previous example, the example in Rev. Rul. 2002-43 contains unpaid interest.

Additional tax for failure to correct the prohibited transaction (Section 4975(b)). To avoid liability for additional taxes and penalties, and in some cases further initial taxes, a correction must be made within the taxable period. The term "correction" is defined as undoing the prohibited transaction to the extent possible, but in any case placing the plan in a financial position not worse than that in which it would be if the disqualified person were acting under the highest fiduciary standards.

If the initial tax is not corrected within the taxable period, an additional tax equal to 100% of the amount involved will be imposed under section 4975(b). Any disqualified person who participated in the prohibited transaction (other than a fiduciary acting only as such) must pay this tax imposed by section 4975(b). Report the additional tax on line 6b.

Line 26. If the "No" box is checked on line 26, there has not been a correction of all of the prohibited transactions by the end of the tax year for which this Form 5330 is being filed. Attach a statement indicating when correction has been or will be made.

Part V

Schedule of Other Participating Disqualified Persons and Description of Correction

If more than one disqualified person participated in the same prohibited transaction, list on this schedule the name, address, and the social security number or employer identification number of each disqualified person, other than the disqualified person who files this return.

Line 27. For all transactions complete columns (a), (b), and (c). If the transaction has been corrected, complete columns (a) through (e). If additional space is needed you may attach a statement fully explaining the correction and identifying persons involved in the prohibited transaction.

Part VI (Section 4971(a) and (b))

Tax on Failure To Meet Minimum Funding Standards

Section 4971(a) imposes a 10% tax (5% for multiemployer plans) on the amount of the accumulated funding deficiency determined as of the end of the plan year.

If a plan fails to meet the funding requirements of section 412, the employer and all controlled group members will be subject to the excise taxes under sections 4971(a) and (b).

Except in the case of a multiemployer plan, all members of a controlled group are jointly and severally liable for this tax. A "controlled group" in this case means a controlled group of corporations (section 414(b)), a group of trades or businesses under common control (section 414(c)), an affiliated service group (section 414(m)), and any other group treated as a single employer under section 414(o).

If the IRS determined at any time that your plan was a "plan" as defined in Part IV (Section 4975), it will always remain subject to the excise tax on failure to meet minimum funding standards.

Line 28. If your plan has an accumulated funding deficiency as defined in section 412(a) (section 418B if this is a multiemployer plan in reorganization), complete line 28.

Line 29. Multiply line 28 by the applicable tax rate shown below and enter the result on line 29.
- 10% for plans (other than multiemployer plans), or
- 5% for all multiemployer plans.

Additional tax for failure to correct the accumulated funding deficiency. When an initial tax is imposed by section 4971(a) on an accumulated funding deficiency and the accumulated funding deficiency is not corrected within the taxable period, an additional tax equal to 100% of the accumulated funding deficiency to the extent not corrected is imposed by section 4971(b).

The "taxable period" is the period beginning with the end of the plan year where there is an accumulated funding deficiency and ending on the earlier of:
- The date the notice of deficiency for the section 4971(a) excise tax is mailed, or
- The date the section 4971(a) excise tax is assessed.

Report the tax for failure to correct the accumulated funding deficiency on line 7b.

Part VII (Section 4977)

Tax on Excess Fringe Benefits

If you made an election to be taxed under section 4977 to continue your nontaxable fringe benefit policy that was in existence on or after January 1, 1984, check the "Yes" box on line 30a and complete lines 30b through 30d.

Line 30c. The excess fringe benefits are figured by subtracting 1% of the aggregate compensation paid by you to your employees during the calendar year that was includable in their gross income from the aggregate value of the nontaxable fringe benefits under sections 132(a)(1) and 132(a)(2).

Part VIII (Section 4979)

Tax on Excess Contributions to Certain Plans

Section 4979. Any employer who maintains a plan described in section 401(a), 403(a), 403(b), 408(k), or 501(c)(18) may be subject to an excise tax on the excess aggregate contributions made on behalf of highly compensated employees. The employer may also be subject to an excise tax on the excess contributions to a cash or deferred arrangement connected with the plan.

The tax is on the excess contributions and the excess aggregate contributions made to or on behalf of the highly compensated employees (as defined in section 414(q)).

A highly compensated employee generally is an employee who:
1. Was a 5-percent owner at any time during the year or the preceding year, or,
2. For the preceding year had compensation from the employer in excess of a dollar amount for the year ($90,000 for 2004) and, if the employer so elects, was in the top-paid group for the preceding year.

An employee is in the top-paid group for any year if the employee is in the group consisting of the top 20 percent of the employees of the employer when ranked on the basis of compensation paid. An employee (who is not a 5-percent owner) who has compensation in excess of $90,000 is not a highly compensated employee if the employer elects the top-paid group limitation and the employee is not a member of the top-paid group.

The "excess contributions" subject to the section 4979 excise tax are equal to the amount by which employer contributions actually paid over to the trust exceed the employer contributions that could have been made without violating the special nondiscrimination requirements of section 401(k)(3).

The "excess aggregate contributions" subject to the section 4979 excise tax are equal to the amount by which the aggregate matching contributions of the employer and the employee contributions (and any qualified nonelective contribution or elective contribution taken into account in computing the contribution percentage under section 401(m)) actually made on behalf of the highly compensated employees for each plan year exceed the maximum amount of the contributions permitted in the contribution percentage computation under section 401(m)(2)(A).

However, there is no excise tax liability if the excess contributions or the excess aggregate contributions and any income earned on the contributions are distributed (or, if forfeitable, forfeited) to the participants for whom the excess contributions were made within 2½ months after the end of the plan year.

Part IX (Section 4980)

Tax on Reversion of Qualified Plan Assets to an Employer

An employer reversion is the amount of cash and the FMV of property received, directly, or indirectly by an employer from a qualified plan. Reversions do not include any amount distributed to or on behalf of any employee (or beneficiaries).

If a defined benefit plan is terminated, and an amount in excess of 25% of the maximum amount otherwise available for reversion is transferred from the terminating defined benefit plan to a defined contribution plan, the amount transferred is not treated as an employer reversion for purposes of section 4980. However, the amount the employer receives is subject to the 20% excise tax. For additional information, see Rev. Rul. 2003-85, 2003-32 I.R.B. 291.

Section 4980. Include on lines 34 and 10 the section 4980 tax on employer reversions from a qualified plan. The reversion excise tax is either 50% or 20%. The excise tax rate is 50% if the employer does not (1) establish or maintain a qualified replacement plan following the plan termination or (2) provides certain pro-rata benefit increases in connection with the plan termination. See section 4980(d)(1)(A) or (B) for more information.

If you owe the section 4980 tax, enter the date of the reversion on line 32 and the reversion amount and applicable excise tax rate on line 33a and b. If you use a tax percentage other than 50%, explain on line 35 why you qualify to use a rate other than 50%.

Part X (Section 4980F)

Tax on Failure to Provide Notice of Significant Reduction in Future Accruals

Section 4980F imposes on an employer (or, in the case of a multiemployer plan, the plan) an excise tax of $100 per day per each applicable individual and each employee organization representing participants who are applicable individuals for each day of the noncompliance period for the failure to give notice of plan amendments that provide for a significant reduction in the rate of future benefit accrual or the elimination or significant reduction of an early retirement benefit or retirement-type subsidy. This notice is called a "section 204(h) notice" because the same notice requirement appears at section 204(h) of ERISA.

An "applicable individual" is a participant in the plan, or an alternate payee of a participant under a qualified domestic relations order, whose rate of future benefit accrual (or early retirement benefit or retirement-type subsidy) under the plan may reasonably be expected to be significantly reduced.

Whether a participant or alternate payee is an applicable individual is determined on a typical business day that is reasonably approximate to the time the section 204(h) notice is provided (or at the latest date for providing section 204(h) notice, if earlier), based on all relevant facts and circumstances. For more information in determining whether an individual is a participant or alternate payee see Regulations section 54.4980F-1, Q&A 10.

The "noncompliance period" is the period beginning on the date the failure first occurs and ending on the date the notice of the failure is provided or the failure is corrected.

Exceptions. Section 4980F excise tax will not be imposed for a failure during any period in which:

1. Any person subject to liability for the tax did not know that the failure existed and exercised reasonable diligence to meet the notice requirement. A person is considered to have exercised reasonable diligence, but did not know the failure existed, only if:

a. The responsible person exercised reasonable diligence in attempting to deliver section 204(h), notice to applicable individuals by the latest date permitted. Generally, the section 204(h) notice must be provided at least 45 days before the effective date the section 204(h) amendments take effect. For exceptions to this rule see Regulations section 54.4980F-1, Q&A 9.

b. At the latest date permitted for delivery of section 204(h) notice, the person reasonably believes that section 204(h) notice was actually delivered to each applicable individual by that date.

2. Any person subject to liability for the tax exercised reasonable diligence to meet the notice requirement and corrects the failure within 30 days after the employer (or other person responsible for the tax) knew, or exercising reasonable diligence would have known, that the failure existed.

If the person subject to liability for the excise tax exercised reasonable diligence to meet the notice requirement, the total excise tax imposed during a taxable year of the employer will not exceed $500,000.

Furthermore, in the case of a failure due to reasonable cause and not to willful neglect, the Secretary of the Treasury is authorized to waive the excise tax to the extent that the payment of the tax would be excessive relative to the failure involved. See Rev. Proc. 2004-4, 2004-1 I.R.B. 125 for procedures to follow in applying for a waiver of part or all of the excise tax due to reasonable cause. You can find Rev. Proc. 2004-4 at *www.irs.gov/pub/ irs-irbs/irb04-01.pdf* .

Line 39. A failure occurs on any day that any applicable individual is not provided section 204(h) notice. For more information in determining whether an individual is a participant or alternate payee, see Regulations section 54.4980F-1, Q&A 10.

Example: There are 1000 applicable individuals (AI). The plan administrator fails to give section 204(h) notice to 100 applicable individuals for 60 days, and to 50 of those applicable individuals for an additional 30 days. In this case there are 7,500 failures ((100 AI x 60 days) + (50 AI x 30 days) = 7,500).

Part XI (Section 4971(f))

Tax on Failure to Pay Liquidity Shortfall

Section 4971(f)(1). If your plan has a liquidity shortfall for which an excise tax under section 4971(f)(1) is imposed for any quarter of the plan year, complete lines 42 through 45.

Line 42. Include on line 42 the amount of the liquidity shortfall(s) for each quarter of the plan year.

Line 43. Include on line 43 the amount of any contributions made to the plan by the due date of the required quarterly installment(s) which partially "corrected" the liquidity shortfall(s) reported on line 42.

Line 44. Include on line 44 the net amount of the liquidity shortfall (subtract line 43 from line 42).

Additional tax for failure to correct liquidity shortfall. If the plan has a liquidity shortfall as of the close of any quarter and as of the close of the following 4 quarters, an additional tax will be imposed under section 4971(f)(2) equal to the amount on which tax was imposed by section 4971(f)(1) for such quarter. Report the additional tax on line 12b.

Privacy Act and Paperwork Reduction Act Notice. We ask for the information on this form to carry out the

Internal Revenue laws of the United States. This form is required to be filed under sections 4971, 4972, 4973, 4975, 4976, 4977, 4978, 4978A, 4979, 4979A, 4980, and 4980F of the Internal Revenue Code. Section 6109 requires you to provide your taxpayer identification number (SSN or EIN). If you fail to provide this information in a timely manner, you may be liable for penalties and interest. Routine uses of this information include giving it to the Department of Justice for civil and criminal litigation, and cities, states, and the District of Columbia for use in administering their tax laws. We may also disclose this information to federal and state or local agencies to enforce federal nontax criminal laws and to combat terrorism. The authority to disclose information to combat terrorism expired on December 31, 2003. Legislation is pending that would reinstate this authority.

You are not required to provide the information requested on a form that is subject to the Paperwork Reduction Act unless the form displays a valid OMB control number. Books or records relating to a form or its instructions must be retained as long as their contents may become material in the administration of any Internal Revenue law. Generally, tax returns and return information are confidential, as required by Code section 6103.

The time needed to complete and file this form will vary depending on individual circumstances. The estimated average time is:

Recordkeeping . . .	25 hr., 27 min.
Learning about the law or the form . . .	11 hr., 59 min.
Preparing and sending the form to the IRS	14 hr., 11 min.

If you have comments concerning the accuracy of these time estimates or suggestions for making this form simpler, we would be happy to hear from you. You can write to the Internal Revenue Service, Tax Products Coordinating Committee, SE:W:CAR:MP:T:T:SP, 1111 Constitution Ave., NW, Washington, DC 20224. **Do not** send this form to this address. Instead, see **Where To File** on page 2.

☐ VOID   ☐ CORRECTED

TRUSTEE'S or ISSUER'S name, street address, city, state, and ZIP code	1 IRA contributions (other than amounts in boxes 2–4 and 8–10) $	OMB No. 1545-0747 **2004** Form **5498**	**IRA Contribution Information**
	2 Rollover contributions $		

TRUSTEE'S or ISSUER'S Federal identification no.	PARTICIPANT'S social security number	3 Roth IRA conversion amount $	4 Recharacterized contributions $	**Copy C**
PARTICIPANT'S name		5 Fair market value of account $	6 Life insurance cost included in box 1 $	**For Trustee or Issuer** For Privacy Act and Paperwork Reduction Act Notice, see the **2004 General Instructions for Forms 1099, 1098, 5498, and W-2G.**
Street address (including apt. no.)		7 IRA ☐ SEP ☐ SIMPLE Roth IRA ☐		
City, state, and ZIP code		8 SEP contributions $	9 SIMPLE contributions $	
Account number (optional)		10 Roth IRA contributions $	11 Check if RMD for 2005 ☐	

Form **5498**   Department of the Treasury - Internal Revenue Service

Form **8606**

Department of the Treasury
Internal Revenue Service (99)

Nondeductible IRAs

▶ See separate instructions.

▶ **Attach to Form 1040, Form 1040A, or Form 1040NR.**

OMB No. 1545-1007

20**04**

Attachment
Sequence No. **48**

Name. If married, file a separate form for each spouse required to file Form 8606. See page 5 of the instructions.

Your social security number

**Fill in Your Address Only
if You Are Filing This
Form by Itself and Not
With Your Tax Return**

Home address (number and street, or P.O. box if mail is not delivered to your home)

Apt. no.

City, town or post office, state, and ZIP code

Part I   **Nondeductible Contributions to Traditional IRAs and Distributions From Traditional, SEP, and SIMPLE IRAs**

Complete this part only if:

- You made nondeductible contributions to a traditional IRA for 2004,
- You took distributions from a traditional, SEP, or SIMPLE IRA in 2004 (other than a rollover, conversion, recharacterization, or return of certain contributions) **and** you made nondeductible contributions to a traditional IRA in 2004 or an earlier year, **or**
- You converted part, but not all, of your traditional, SEP, and SIMPLE IRAs to Roth IRAs in 2004 (excluding any portion you recharacterized) **and** you made nondeductible contributions to a traditional IRA in 2004 or an earlier year.

1	Enter your nondeductible contributions to traditional IRAs for 2004, including those made for 2004 from January 1, 2005, through April 15, 2005 (see page 5 of the instructions)	**1**	
2	Enter your total basis in traditional IRAs (see page 5 of the instructions)	**2**	
3	Add lines 1 and 2	**3**	

> **In 2004, did you take a distribution from traditional, SEP, or SIMPLE IRAs or make a Roth IRA conversion?**   —— **No** ——▶ Enter the amount from line 3 on line 14. Do not complete the rest of Part I.
>
>   —— **Yes** ——▶ Go to line 4.

4	Enter those contributions included on line 1 that were made from January 1, 2005, through April 15, 2005	**4**	
5	Subtract line 4 from line 3	**5**	
6	Enter the value of **all** your traditional, SEP, and SIMPLE IRAs as of December 31, 2004, plus any outstanding rollovers (see page 6 of the instructions)	**6**	
7	Enter your distributions from traditional, SEP, and SIMPLE IRAs in 2004. **Do not** include rollovers, conversions to a Roth IRA, certain returned contributions, or recharacterizations of traditional IRA contributions (see page 6 of the instructions)	**7**	
8	Enter the net amount you converted from traditional, SEP, and SIMPLE IRAs to Roth IRAs in 2004. **Do not** include amounts converted that you later recharacterized (see page 6 of the instructions). Also enter this amount on line 16	**8**	
9	Add lines 6, 7, and 8	**9**	
10	Divide line 5 by line 9. Enter the result as a decimal rounded to at least 3 places. If the result is 1.000 or more, enter "1.000" . . .	**10** ✕ .
11	Multiply line 8 by line 10. This is the nontaxable portion of the amount you converted to Roth IRAs. Also enter this amount on line 17 . . .	**11**	
12	Multiply line 7 by line 10. This is the nontaxable portion of your distributions that you did not convert to a Roth IRA	**12**	
13	Add lines 11 and 12. This is the nontaxable portion of all your distributions	**13**	
14	Subtract line 13 from line 3. This is **your total basis in traditional IRAs for 2004 and earlier years**	**14**	
15	**Taxable amount.** Subtract line 12 from line 7. Also include this amount on Form 1040, line 15b; Form 1040A, line 11b; or Form 1040NR, line 16b	**15**	

Note: *You may be subject to an additional 10% tax on the amount on line 15 if you were under age 59½ at the time of the distribution (see page 7 of the instructions).*

For Paperwork Reduction Act Notice, see page 8 of the instructions.   Cat. No. 63966F   Form **8606** (2004)

Form 8606 (2004)   Page **2**

Part II   2004 Conversions From Traditional, SEP, or SIMPLE IRAs to Roth IRAs

Complete this part if you converted part or all of your traditional, SEP, and SIMPLE IRAs to a Roth IRA in 2004 (excluding any portion you recharacterized).

Caution: *If your modified adjusted gross income is over $100,000 **or** you are married filing separately and you lived with your spouse at any time in 2004, you **cannot** convert any amount from traditional, SEP, or SIMPLE IRAs to Roth IRAs for 2004. If you erroneously made a conversion, you must recharacterize (correct) it (see page 7 of the instructions).*

16	If you completed Part I, enter the amount from line 8. Otherwise, enter the net amount you converted from traditional, SEP, and SIMPLE IRAs to Roth IRAs in 2004. **Do not** include amounts you later recharacterized back to traditional, SEP, or SIMPLE IRAs in 2004 or 2005 (see page 7 of the instructions)	**16**
17	If you completed Part I, enter the amount from line 11. Otherwise, enter your basis in the amount on line 16 (see page 7 of the instructions)	**17**
18	**Taxable amount.** Subtract line 17 from line 16. Also include this amount on Form 1040, line 15b; Form 1040A, line 11b; or Form 1040NR, line 16b	**18**

Part III   Distributions From Roth IRAs

Complete this part only if you took a distribution from a Roth IRA in 2004 (other than a rollover, recharacterization, or return of certain contributions—see page 7 of the instructions).

19	Enter your total nonqualified distributions from Roth IRAs in 2004 including any qualified first-time homebuyer distributions (see page 7 of the instructions)	**19**
20	Qualified first-time homebuyer expenses (see page 7 of the instructions). **Do not** enter more than $10,000	**20**
21	Subtract line 20 from line 19. If zero or less, enter -0- and skip lines 22 through 25	**21**
22	Enter your basis in Roth IRA contributions (see page 7 of the instructions)	**22**
23	Subtract line 22 from line 21. If zero or less, enter -0- and skip lines 24 and 25. If more than zero, you may be subject to an additional tax (see page 8 of the instructions)	**23**
24	Enter your basis in Roth IRA conversions (see page 8 of the instructions)	**24**
25	**Taxable amount.** Subtract line 24 from line 23. If zero or less, enter -0-. Also include this amount on Form 1040, line 15b; Form 1040A, line 11b; or Form 1040NR, line 16b	**25**

Sign Here Only if You Are Filing This Form by Itself and Not With Your Tax Return	Under penalties of perjury, I declare that I have examined this form, including accompanying attachments, and to the best of my knowledge and belief, it is true, correct, and complete.

▶ _____   ▶ _____
　　Your signature   Date

Form **8606** (2004)

✸ *Printed on recycled paper*

20**04**

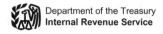 Department of the Treasury
Internal Revenue Service

Instructions for Form 8606

Nondeductible IRAs

Section references are to the Internal Revenue Code unless otherwise noted.

General Instructions

Purpose of Form

Use Form 8606 to report:
- Nondeductible contributions you made to traditional IRAs,
- Distributions from traditional, SEP, or SIMPLE IRAs, if you have ever made nondeductible contributions to traditional IRAs,
- Distributions from Roth IRAs, and
- Conversions from traditional, SEP, or SIMPLE IRAs to Roth IRAs.

Additional information. See Pub. 590, Individual Retirement Arrangements (IRAs), for more details.

 If you received distributions from a traditional, SEP, or SIMPLE IRA in 2004 and you have never made nondeductible contributions to traditional IRAs, do not report the distributions on Form 8606. Instead, see the instructions for Form 1040, lines 15a and 15b; Form 1040A, lines 11a and 11b; or Form 1040NR, lines 16a and 16b. Also, to find out if any of your contributions to traditional IRAs are deductible, see the instructions for Form 1040, line 25; Form 1040A, line 17; or Form 1040NR, line 25.

Who Must File

File Form 8606 if any of the following apply.
- You made nondeductible contributions to a traditional IRA for 2004.
- You received distributions from a traditional, SEP, or SIMPLE IRA in 2004 (other than a rollover, conversion, recharacterization, or return of certain contributions) and your basis in traditional IRAs is more than zero.
- You converted an amount from a traditional, SEP, or SIMPLE IRA to a Roth IRA in 2004 (unless you recharacterized the entire conversion—see page 3).
- You received distributions from a Roth IRA in 2004 (other than a

rollover, recharacterization, or return of certain contributions—see page 7).

Note. If you recharacterized a 2004 Roth IRA contribution as a traditional IRA contribution, or vice versa, treat the contribution as having been made to the second IRA, not the first IRA. See page 3.

 You do not have to file Form 8606 solely to report regular contributions to Roth IRAs. But see What Records Must I Keep? *on page 5.*

When and Where To File

File Form 8606 with your 2004 Form 1040, 1040A, or 1040NR. If you are not required to file an income tax return but are required to file Form 8606, sign Form 8606 and send it to the Internal Revenue Service at the same time and place you would otherwise file Form 1040, 1040A, or 1040NR.

Definitions

Deemed IRAs

A qualified employer plan (retirement plan) can maintain a separate account or annuity under the plan (a deemed IRA) to receive voluntary employee contributions. If in 2004 you had a deemed IRA, use the rules for either a traditional IRA or a Roth IRA depending on which type it was. See Pub. 590 for more details.

Traditional IRAs

For purposes of Form 8606, a traditional IRA is an individual retirement account or an individual retirement annuity other than a SEP, SIMPLE, or Roth IRA.

Contributions. An overall contribution limit applies to traditional IRAs and Roth IRAs. See page 2. Contributions to a traditional IRA may be fully deductible, partially deductible, or completely nondeductible.

Basis. Your basis in traditional IRAs is the total of all your nondeductible contributions to traditional IRAs minus the total of all your nontaxable distributions, adjusted if necessary (see the instructions for line 2 on page 5). Keep track of your basis to figure the nontaxable part of your future distributions.

SEP IRAs

A simplified employee pension (SEP) is an employer-sponsored plan under which an employer can make contributions to traditional IRAs for its employees. If you make contributions to that IRA (excluding employer contributions you make if you are self-employed), they are treated as contributions to a traditional IRA and may be deductible or nondeductible. SEP IRA distributions are reported in the same manner as traditional IRA distributions.

SIMPLE IRAs

Your participation in your employer's SIMPLE IRA plan does not prevent you from making contributions to a traditional, SEP, or Roth IRA.

Roth IRAs

A Roth IRA is similar to a traditional IRA, but has the following features.
- Contributions are never deductible.
- Contributions can be made after the owner reaches age 70½.
- No minimum distributions are required during the Roth IRA owner's lifetime.
- Qualified distributions are not includible in income.

Qualified distribution. Generally, a qualified distribution is any distribution made:

- On or after age 59½,
- Upon death,
- Due to disability, or
- For qualified first-time homebuyer expenses.

Exception. Any distribution made during the 5-year period beginning with the first year for which you made a Roth IRA contribution or conversion

Cat. No. 25399E

is not a qualified distribution, and may be taxable.

Contributions. You can contribute to a Roth IRA for 2004 only if your 2004 modified adjusted gross income (AGI) for Roth IRA purposes is less than:
- $10,000 if married filing separately and you lived with your spouse at any time in 2004,
- $160,000 if married filing jointly or qualifying widow(er), or
- $110,000 if single, head of household, or if married filing separately and you did not live with your spouse at any time in 2004.

Use the Maximum Roth IRA Contribution Worksheet below to figure the maximum amount you can contribute to a Roth IRA for 2004. If you are married filing jointly, complete the worksheet separately for you and your spouse.

 If you contributed too much, see Recharacterizations *on page 3.*

Modified AGI for Roth IRA purposes. First, figure your AGI (Form 1040, line 37; Form 1040A, line 22; or Form 1040NR, line 34). Then, refigure it by:

1. Subtracting any amount due to Roth IRA conversions included on Form 1040, line 15b; Form 1040A, line 11b; or Form 1040NR, line 16b; and

2. Adding the total of the following.

a. IRA deduction from Form 1040, line 25; Form 1040A, line 17; or Form 1040NR, line 25.

b. Student loan interest deduction from Form 1040, line 26; Form 1040A, line 18; or Form 1040NR, line 26.

c. Tuition and fees deduction from Form 1040, line 27, or Form 1040A, line 19.

d. Exclusion of interest from Form 8815, Exclusion of Interest From Series EE and I U.S. Savings Bonds Issued After 1989.

e. Exclusion of employer-provided adoption benefits from Form 8839, Qualified Adoption Expenses.

f. Foreign earned income exclusion from Form 2555, Foreign Earned Income, or Form 2555-EZ, Foreign Earned Income Exclusion.

g. Foreign housing exclusion or deduction from Form 2555.

 When figuring modified AGI for Roth IRA purposes, you may have to refigure items based on modified AGI, such as taxable social security benefits and passive activity losses allowed under the special allowance for rental real estate activities. See Can You Contribute to a Roth IRA? *in Pub. 590 for details.*

Distributions. See the instructions for Part III beginning on page 7.

Overall Contribution Limit for Traditional and Roth IRAs

If you are not married filing jointly, your limit on contributions to traditional and Roth IRAs is the smaller of $3,000 ($3,500 if age 50 or older at the end of 2004) or your taxable compensation (defined below). If you are married filing jointly, your contribution limit is generally $3,000 ($3,500 if age 50 or older at the end of 2004) and your spouse's contribution limit is $3,000 ($3,500 if age 50 or older at the end of 2004) as well. But if the combined taxable compensation of both you and your spouse is less than $6,000 ($6,500 if one spouse is 50 or older at the end of 2004; $7,000 if both spouses are 50 or older at the end of 2004), see Pub. 590 for special rules. This limit does not apply to employer contributions to a SEP or SIMPLE IRA.

 The amount you can contribute to a Roth IRA may also be limited by your modified AGI (see Contributions *and the Maximum Roth IRA Contribution Worksheet on this page).*

Taxable compensation includes the following.
- Wages, salaries, tips, etc. If you received a distribution from a nonqualified deferred compensation plan or nongovernmental section 457 plan that is included in box 1 of your Form W-2, do not include that distribution in taxable compensation. The distribution should be shown in box 11 of your Form W-2. If it is not, contact your employer for the amount of the distribution.
- Self-employment income. If you are self-employed (a sole proprietor or a partner), taxable compensation is your net earnings from your trade or business (provided your personal services are a material income-producing factor) reduced by your deduction for contributions made on your behalf to retirement plans

Maximum Roth IRA Contribution Worksheet (keep for your records)

Caution: *If married filing jointly and the combined taxable compensation (defined on this page) for you and your spouse is less than $6,000 ($6,500 if one spouse is 50 or older at the end of 2004; $7,000 if both spouses are 50 or older at the end of 2004),* **do not** *use this worksheet. Instead, see Pub. 590 for special rules.*

1 If married filing jointly, enter $3,000 ($3,500 if age 50 or older at the end of 2004). All others, enter the **smaller** of $3,000 ($3,500 if age 50 or older at the end of 2004) or your taxable compensation (defined on this page)	**1** _____
2 Enter your total contributions to traditional IRAs for 2004 . .	**2** _____
3 Subtract line 2 from line 1	**3** _____
4 Enter: $160,000 if married filing jointly or qualifying widow(er); $10,000 if married filing separately and you lived with your spouse at any time in 2004. All others, enter $110,000	**4** _____
5 Enter your modified AGI for Roth IRA purposes (see above)	**5** _____
6 Subtract line 5 from line 4. If zero or less, **stop here;** you may not contribute to a Roth IRA for 2004. See **Recharacterizations** on page 3 if you made Roth IRA contributions for 2004	**6** _____
7 If line 4 above is $110,000, enter $15,000; otherwise, enter $10,000. If line 6 is more than or equal to line 7, skip lines 8 and 9 and enter the amount from line 3 on line 10	**7** _____
8 Divide line 6 by line 7 and enter the result as a decimal (rounded to at least 3 places). If the result is 1.000 or more, enter 1.000	**8** _____
9 Multiply line 1 by line 8. If the result is not a multiple of $10, increase it to the next multiple of $10 (for example, increase $490.30 to $500). Enter the result, but not less than $200 . .	**9** _____
10 **Maximum 2004 Roth IRA Contribution.** Enter the **smaller** of line 3 or line 9. See **Recharacterizations** on page 3 if you contributed more than this amount to Roth IRAs for 2004	**10** _____

and the deduction allowed for one-half of your self-employment tax.
- Alimony and separate maintenance.

See Pub. 590 for details.

Note. Rollovers and Roth IRA conversions do not affect your contribution limit.

Recharacterizations

Generally, you can recharacterize (correct) an IRA contribution or Roth IRA conversion by making a trustee-to-trustee transfer from one IRA to another type of IRA. Trustee-to-trustee transfers are made directly between financial institutions or within the same financial institution. You generally must make the transfer by the due date of your return (including extensions) and reflect it on your return. However, if you timely filed your return without making the transfer, you can make the transfer within 6 months of the due date of your return, excluding extensions. If necessary, file an amended return reflecting the transfer (see page 5). Write "Filed pursuant to section 301.9100-2" on the amended return.

Reporting recharacterizations. Any recharacterized conversion will be treated as though the conversion had not occurred. Any recharacterized contribution will be treated as having been originally contributed to the second IRA, not the first IRA. The amount transferred must include related earnings or be reduced by any loss. In most cases, the related earnings that you must transfer are figured by your IRA trustee or custodian. If you need to figure the related earnings, see *How Do You Recharacterize a Contribution* in Pub. 590. Any earnings or loss that occurred in the first IRA will be treated as having occurred in the second IRA. You may not deduct any loss that occurred while the funds were in the first IRA. Also, you cannot take a deduction for a contribution to a traditional IRA if the amount is later recharacterized. See below for how to report the three different types of recharacterizations, including the statement that must be attached to your return explaining the recharacterization.

1. You converted an amount from a traditional, SEP, or SIMPLE IRA to a Roth IRA in 2004 and later recharacterized all or part of the amount back to a traditional, SEP, or

SIMPLE IRA. If you only recharacterized part of the amount converted, report the amount not recharacterized on Form 8606. If you recharacterized the entire amount, do not report the recharacterization on Form 8606. In either case, attach a statement to your return explaining the recharacterization and include the amount converted from the traditional, SEP, or SIMPLE IRA in the total on Form 1040, line 15a; Form 1040A, line 11a; or Form 1040NR, line 16a. If the recharacterization occurred in 2004, also include the amount transferred back from the Roth IRA on that line. If the recharacterization occurred in 2005, report the amount transferred only in the attached statement, and not on your 2004 or 2005 tax return (a 2005 Form 1099-R should be sent to you by January 31, 2006, stating that you made a recharacterization of an amount converted in the prior year).

Example. You are married filing jointly and converted $20,000 from your traditional IRA to a new Roth IRA on May 21, 2004. On April 8, 2005, you determine that your 2004 modified AGI for Roth IRA purposes will exceed $100,000, and you are not allowed to make a Roth IRA conversion. The value of the Roth IRA on that date is $19,000. You recharacterize the conversion by transferring that entire amount to a traditional IRA in a trustee-to-trustee transfer. You report $20,000 on Form 1040, line 15a. You do not include the $19,000 on line 15a because it did not occur in 2004 (you also do not report that amount on your 2005 return because it does not apply to the 2005 tax year). You attach a statement to Form 1040 explaining that you made a conversion of $20,000 from a traditional IRA on May 21, 2004, and that you recharacterized the entire amount, which was then valued at $19,000, back to a traditional IRA on April 8, 2005, because your 2004 modified AGI for Roth IRA purposes exceeded $100,000.

2. You made a contribution to a traditional IRA and later recharacterized part or all of it to a Roth IRA. If you recharacterized only part of the contribution, report the nondeductible traditional IRA portion of the remaining contribution, if any, on Form 8606, Part I. If you recharacterized the entire contribution, do not report the

contribution on Form 8606. In either case, attach a statement to your return explaining the recharacterization. If the recharacterization occurred in 2004, include the amount transferred from the traditional IRA on Form 1040, line 15a; Form 1040A, line 11a; or Form 1040NR, line 16a. If the recharacterization occurred in 2005, report the amount transferred only in the attached statement.

Example. You are single, covered by a retirement plan, and you contributed $3,000 to a new traditional IRA on May 28, 2004. On February 24, 2005, you determine that your 2004 modified AGI will limit your traditional IRA deduction to $1,000. The value of your traditional IRA on that date is $3,300. You decide to recharacterize $2,000 of the traditional IRA contribution as a Roth IRA contribution, and have $2,200 ($2,000 contribution plus $200 related earnings) transferred from your traditional IRA to a Roth IRA in a trustee-to-trustee transfer. You deduct the $1,000 traditional IRA contribution on Form 1040. You are not required to file Form 8606, but you must attach a statement to your return explaining the recharacterization. The statement indicates that you contributed $3,000 to a traditional IRA on May 28, 2004; recharacterized $2,000 of that contribution on February 24, 2005, by transferring $2,000 plus $200 of related earnings from your traditional IRA to a Roth IRA in a trustee-to-trustee transfer; and that all $1,000 of the remaining traditional IRA contribution is deducted on Form 1040. You do not report the $2,200 distribution from your traditional IRA on your 2004 Form 1040 because the distribution occurred in 2005. You do not report the distribution on your 2005 Form 1040 because the recharacterization related to 2004 and was explained in an attachment to your 2004 return.

3. You made a contribution to a Roth IRA and later recharacterized part or all of it to a traditional IRA. Report the nondeductible traditional IRA portion, if any, on Form 8606, Part I. If you did not recharacterize the entire contribution, do not report the remaining Roth IRA portion of the contribution on Form 8606. Attach a statement to your return explaining the recharacterization. If the recharacterization occurred in 2004, include the amount transferred from

the Roth IRA on Form 1040, line 15a; Form 1040A, line 11a; or Form 1040NR, line 16a. If the recharacterization occurred in 2005, report the amount transferred only in the attached statement, and not on your 2004 or 2005 tax return.

Example. You are single and contributed $3,000 to a new Roth IRA on June 14, 2004. On December 27, 2004, you determine that your 2004 modified AGI will allow a full traditional IRA deduction. You decide to recharacterize the Roth IRA contribution as a traditional IRA contribution and have $3,200, the balance in the Roth IRA account ($3,000 contribution plus $200 related earnings), transferred from your Roth IRA to a traditional IRA in a trustee-to-trustee transfer. You deduct the $3,000 traditional IRA contribution on Form 1040. You are not required to file Form 8606, but you must attach a statement to your return explaining the recharacterization. The statement indicates that you contributed $3,000 to a new Roth IRA on June 14, 2004; recharacterized that contribution on December 27, 2004, by transferring $3,200, the balance in the Roth IRA, to a traditional IRA in a trustee-to-trustee transfer; and that $3,000 of the traditional IRA contribution is deducted on Form 1040. You include the $3,200 distribution on your 2004 Form 1040, line 15a.

Return of IRA Contributions

If, in 2004, you made traditional IRA contributions or Roth IRA contributions for 2003 or 2004 and you had those contributions returned to you with any related earnings (or less any loss) by the due date (including extensions) of your 2004 tax return, the returned contributions are treated as if they were never contributed. Do not report the contribution or distribution on Form 8606 or take a deduction for the contribution. However, you must report the distribution and any related earnings on your 2004 Form 1040, lines 15a and 15b; Form 1040A, lines 11a and 11b; or Form 1040NR, lines 16a and 16b. Attach a statement explaining the distribution. You cannot deduct any loss that occurred (see Pub. 590 for an exception if you withdrew the entire amount in all your traditional or Roth IRAs). Also, if you

were under age 59½ at the time of a distribution with related earnings, you generally are subject to the additional 10% tax on early distributions (see Form 5329, Additional Taxes on Qualified Plans (Including IRAs) and Other Tax-Favored Accounts).

If you timely filed your 2004 tax return without withdrawing a contribution that you made in 2004, you can still have the contribution returned to you within 6 months of the due date of your 2004 tax return, excluding extensions. If you do, file an amended return with "Filed pursuant to section 301.9100-2" written at the top. Report any related earnings on the amended return and include an explanation of the withdrawal. Make any other necessary changes on the amended return (for example, if you reported the contributions as excess contributions on your original return, include an amended Form 5329 reflecting that the withdrawn contributions are no longer treated as having been contributed).

In most cases, the related earnings that you must withdraw are figured by your IRA trustee or custodian. If you need to figure the related earnings on IRA contributions that were made in 2003 or 2004 and were returned to you, use Notice 2000-39, section 1.408A-5, A-2(c), or Worksheet 1-4 in Pub. 590. You can find Notice 2000-39 on page 132 of Internal Revenue Bulletin 2000-30 at *www.irs.gov/pub/irs-irbs/irb00-30.pdf.* Notice 2000-39 permits the earnings or loss to be determined by allocating to the contribution a pro-rata share of the earnings that accrued in the IRA during the period the IRA held the contribution. If there are no intervening contributions or distributions, the earnings (or loss) is equal to the contribution multiplied by the net change in the value of the IRA divided by the value of the IRA immediately after the contribution was made. The net change in the value of the IRA is equal to the value of the IRA immediately prior to the distribution minus the value of the IRA immediately after the contribution was made. See the example below. If you made a contribution or distribution while the IRA held the returned contribution, see Notice 2000-39.

If you made a contribution in 2003 and you had it returned to you in 2004 as described above, do not report the distribution on your 2004

tax return. Instead, report it on your 2003 original or amended return in the manner described above. Likewise, report on your 2005 tax return any distribution made in 2005 that is a return of contributions that were made in 2005 for 2004 (but be sure that your original or amended 2004 tax return reflects that the contribution is treated as not having been contributed).

Example. On May 31, 2004, you contributed $3,000 to your traditional IRA. The value of the IRA was $18,000 prior to the contribution. On December 29, 2004, when you are age 57 and the value of the IRA is $22,600, you realize you cannot make the entire contribution because your taxable compensation for the year will be only $2,000. You decide to have $1,000 of the contribution returned to you and withdraw $1,076 from your IRA ($1,000 contribution plus $76 earnings). You did not make any other withdrawals or contributions. The earnings were figured according to Notice 2000-39 by first dividing the $1,600 increase in the value of the IRA by $21,000 (the value of the IRA immediately after the contribution) and multiplying the result by $1,000 (the amount being returned). You are not required to file Form 8606. You deduct the $2000 remaining contribution on Form 1040. You include $1,076 on Form 1040, line 15a, and $76 on line 15b. You attach a statement to your tax return explaining the distribution. Because you properly removed the excess contribution with the related earnings by the due date of your tax return, you are not subject to the additional 6% tax on excess contributions. However, because you were under age 59½ at the time of the distribution, the $76 of earnings is subject to the additional 10% tax on early distributions. You include $7.60 on Form 1040, line 59.

Return of Excess Traditional IRA Contributions

The return (distribution) in 2004 of excess traditional IRA contributions for years prior to 2004 is not taxable if all three of the following apply.

1. The distribution was made after the due date, including extensions, of your tax return for the year for which the contribution was made (if the distribution was made earlier, see

Return of IRA Contributions on page 4).

2. The total contributions (excluding rollovers and conversions) to your traditional and SEP IRAs for the year for which the excess contribution was made did not exceed:

a. $3,000 ($3,500 if age 50 or older at the end of 2003) for 2003,

b. $3,000 ($3,500 if age 50 or older at the end of 2002) for 2002,

c. $2,000 for years after 1996 and before 2002, or

d. $2,250 for years before 1997.

If your total IRA contributions for the year included employer contributions to a SEP IRA, increase the $3,000 ($3,500, if applicable), $2,000, or $2,250 by the smaller of the employer contributions or $40,000 ($35,000 for 2001, or $30,000 for years before 2001).

3. No deduction was allowable (without regard to the modified AGI limitation) or taken for the excess contributions.

Include the total amount distributed on Form 1040, line 15a; Form 1040A, line 11a; or Form 1040NR, line 16a; and attach a statement to your return explaining the distribution. See the example below.

If you meet the above conditions and are otherwise required to file Form 8606:
• Do not take into account the amount of the withdrawn contributions in figuring line 2 and
• Do not include the amount of the withdrawn contributions on line 7.

Example. You are single, you retired in 2001, and you had no taxable compensation after 2001. However, you made traditional IRA contributions (that you did not deduct) of $2,000 in 2002 and $3,000 in 2003. In November 2004, a tax practitioner informed you that you had made excess contributions for those years because you had no taxable compensation. You withdrew the $5,000 and filed amended returns for 2002 and 2003 reflecting the additional 6% tax on excess contributions on Form 5329. You include the $5,000 distribution on your 2004 Form 1040, line 15a, enter -0- on line 15b, and attach a statement to your return explaining the distribution, including the fact that you filed amended returns for 2002 and 2003 and paid the additional 6% tax on the excess contributions for those years. The statement indicates

that the distribution is not taxable because (a) it was made after the due dates of your 2002 and 2003 tax returns, including extensions, (b) your total IRA contributions did not exceed $3,000 ($3,500 if age 50 or older at the end of 2002) for 2002 or $3,000 ($3,500 if age 50 or older at the end of 2003) for 2003, and (c) you did not take a deduction for the contributions, and no deduction was allowable because you did not have any taxable compensation for those years. The statement also indicates that the distribution reduced your excess contributions to -0-, as reflected on your 2004 Form 5329 and it indicates your adjusted basis in nondeductible contributions.

Amending Form 8606

After you file your return, you can change a nondeductible contribution to a traditional IRA to a deductible contribution or vice versa. You also may be able to make a recharacterization (see page 3). If necessary, complete a new Form 8606 showing the revised information and file it with Form 1040X, Amended U.S. Individual Income Tax Return.

Penalty for Not Filing

If you are required to file Form 8606 to report a nondeductible contribution to a traditional IRA for 2004, but do not do so, you must pay a $50 penalty, unless you can show reasonable cause.

Overstatement Penalty

If you overstate your nondeductible contributions, you must pay a $100 penalty, unless you can show reasonable cause.

What Records Must I Keep?

To verify the nontaxable part of distributions from your IRAs, including Roth IRAs, keep a copy of the following forms and records until all distributions are made.
• Page 1 of Forms 1040 (or Forms 1040A, 1040NR, or 1040-T) filed for each year you made a nondeductible contribution to a traditional IRA.
• Forms 8606 and any supporting statements, attachments, and worksheets for all applicable years.
• Forms 5498 or similar statements you received each year showing contributions you made to a traditional IRA or Roth IRA.

• Forms 5498 or similar statements you received showing the value of your traditional IRAs for each year you received a distribution.
• Forms 1099-R or W-2P you received for each year you received a distribution.

Note. Forms 1040-T and W-2P are forms that were used in prior years.

Specific Instructions

Name and social security number (SSN). If you file a joint return, enter only the name and SSN of the spouse whose information is being reported on Form 8606. If both you and your spouse are required to file Form 8606, file a separate Form 8606 for each of you.

Part I—Nondeductible Contributions to Traditional IRAs and Distributions From Traditional, SEP, and SIMPLE IRAs

Line 1

If you used the IRA Deduction Worksheet in the Form 1040 or 1040A instructions, subtract line 10 of the worksheet (or the amount you chose to deduct on Form 1040, line 25, or Form 1040A, line 17, if less) from the smaller of line 8 or line 9 of the worksheet. Enter the result on line 1 of Form 8606. You cannot deduct the amount included on line 1.

If you used the worksheet Figuring Your Reduced IRA Deduction for 2004 in Pub. 590, enter on line 1 of Form 8606 any nondeductible contributions from the appropriate lines of that worksheet.

If you did not have any deductible contributions, you can make nondeductible contributions up to your contribution limit. Enter on line 1 of Form 8606 your nondeductible contributions.

Do not include on line 1 contributions that you had returned to you with the related earnings (or less any loss). See page 4.

Line 2

If this is the first year you are required to file Form 8606, enter -0-. Otherwise, use the chart below to find the amount to enter on line 2.

However, you may need to enter an amount other than -0- or adjust the amount from the chart if your basis changed because of any of the following.
• You had a return of excess traditional IRA contributions (see page 4).
• Incident to divorce, you transferred or received part or all of a traditional IRA (see *Distributions that are incident to divorce* on this page).
• You rolled over any nontaxable portion of your qualified employer plan to a traditional or SEP IRA. Include the nontaxable portion on line 2.

IF the last Form 8606 you filed was for...	THEN enter on line 2...
2003, 2002, or 2001	The amount from line 14 of that Form 8606
A year after 1992 and before 2001	The amount from line 12 of that Form 8606
A year after 1988 and before 1993	The amount from line 14 of that Form 8606
1988	The total of the amounts on lines 7 and 16 of that Form 8606
1987	The total of the amounts on lines 4 and 13 of that Form 8606

Line 4

If you made contributions to traditional IRAs for 2004 in 2004 and 2005 and you have both deductible and nondeductible contributions, you can choose to treat the contributions made in 2004 first as nondeductible contributions and then as deductible contributions, or vice versa. But the amount on line 4 cannot be less than the excess, if any, of the amount on line 1 over the contributions you actually made in 2004.

Example. You made contributions for 2004 of $1,500 in May 2004 and $1,500 in January 2005, of which $2,000 are deductible and $1,000 are nondeductible. You choose $1,000 of your contribution in 2004 to be nondeductible. You enter the $1,000 on line 1, but not line 4, and it becomes part of your basis for 2004.

Although the contributions to traditional IRAs for 2004 that you

made from January 1, 2005, through April 15, 2005, can be treated as nondeductible, they are not included in figuring the nontaxable part of any distributions you received in 2004.

Line 6

Enter the total value of all your traditional, SEP, and SIMPLE IRAs as of December 31, 2004, plus any outstanding rollovers. A statement should be sent to you by January 31, 2005, showing the value of each IRA on December 31, 2004. However, if you recharacterized any amounts, enter on line 6 the total value taking into account all recharacterizations, including recharacterizations made after December 31, 2004.

For line 6, a rollover is a tax-free distribution from one traditional, SEP, or SIMPLE IRA that is contributed to another traditional, SEP, or SIMPLE IRA. The rollover must be completed within 60 days of receiving the distribution from the first IRA. An outstanding rollover is any amount distributed within 60 days before the end of 2004 (from November 2 through December 31) that was rolled over after December 31, 2004, but within the 60-day rollover period.

The IRS may waive the 60-day requirement if failing to waive it would be against equity or good conscience, such as situations where a casualty, disaster, or other events beyond your reasonable control prevented you from meeting the 60-day requirement. Also, the 60-day period may be extended if you had a frozen deposit. See Pub. 590 for details.

Note. Do not include a rollover from a traditional or SEP IRA to a qualified employer plan even if it was an outstanding rollover.

Line 7

 If you received a distribution in 2004 from a traditional, SEP, or SIMPLE IRA and you also made contributions for 2004 to a traditional IRA that may not be fully deductible because of the income limits, you must make a special computation before completing the rest of this form. For details, including how to complete Form 8606, see Are Distributions Taxable? in Chapter 1 of Pub. 590.

Do not include any of the following on line 7.
• Distributions that you converted to a Roth IRA.
• Recharacterizations.

• Distributions that you rolled over by December 31, 2004, and any outstanding rollovers included on line 6.
• Distributions you rolled over to a qualified employer plan.
• Distributions that are treated as a return of contributions under *Return of IRA Contributions* on page 4.
• Distributions that are treated as a return of excess contributions under *Return of Excess Traditional IRA Contributions* on page 4.
• Distributions of excess contributions due to incorrect rollover information. If an excess contribution in your traditional IRA is the result of a rollover from a qualified retirement plan and the excess occurred because the information the plan was required to give you was incorrect, the distribution of the excess contribution is not taxable. Attach a statement to your return explaining the distribution and include the amount of the distribution on Form 1040, line 15a; Form 1040A, line 11a; or Form 1040NR, line 16a. See Pub. 590 for more details.
• Distributions that are incident to divorce. The transfer of part or all of your traditional, SEP, or SIMPLE IRA to your spouse under a divorce or separation agreement is not taxable to you or your spouse. If this transfer results in a change in the basis of the traditional IRA of either spouse, both spouses must file Form 8606 and show the increase or decrease in the amount of basis on line 2. Attach a statement explaining this adjustment. Include in the statement the character of the amounts in the traditional IRA, such as the amount attributable to nondeductible contributions. Also, include the name and social security number of the other spouse.

Line 8

If, in 2004, you converted any amounts from traditional, SEP, or SIMPLE IRAs to a Roth IRA, enter on line 8 the net amount you converted. To figure that amount, subtract from the total amount converted in 2004 any portion that you recharacterized back to traditional, SEP, or SIMPLE IRAs in 2004 or 2005 (see *Recharacterizations* on page 3). Do not take into account related earnings that were transferred with the recharacterized amount or any loss that occurred while the amount was in the Roth IRA. See item 1 under *Reporting recharacterizations* on page 3 for details.

Basis in Regular Roth IRA Contributions—Line 22

IF the most recent year prior to 2004 in which you took a Roth IRA distribution* was...	THEN enter on Form 8606, line 22, this amount...	PLUS the total of all your regular contributions** to Roth IRAs for...
2003 (you had an amount on your 2003 Form 8606, line 19)	The excess of your 2003 Form 8606, line 20, over line 19 of that Form 8606.	2004
2002 (you had an amount on your 2002 Form 8606, line 19)	The excess of your 2002 Form 8606, line 20, over line 19 of that Form 8606.	2003 and 2004
2001 (you had an amount on your 2001 Form 8606, line 19)	The excess of your 2001 Form 8606, line 20, over line 19 of that Form 8606.	2002 through 2004
2000 (you had an amount on your 2000 Form 8606, line 17)	The excess of your 2000 Form 8606, line 18d, over line 17 of that Form 8606	2001 through 2004
1999 (you had an amount on your 1999 Form 8606, line 17)	The excess of your 1999 Form 8606, line 18d, over line 17 of that Form 8606	2000 through 2004
1998 (you had an amount on your 1998 Form 8606, line 18)	The excess of your 1998 Form 8606, line 19c, over line 18 of that Form 8606	1999 through 2004
Did not take a Roth IRA distribution* prior to 2004	$0	1998 through 2004

*Excluding rollovers, recharacterizations, and contributions that you had returned to you.

**Excluding rollovers, conversions, Roth IRA contributions that were recharacterized, and any contributions that you had returned to you.

Line 15

If you were under age 59½ at the time you received distributions from your traditional, SEP, or SIMPLE IRA, there generally is an additional 10% tax on the portion of the distribution that is included in income (25% for a distribution from a SIMPLE IRA during the first 2 years). See the Instructions for Form 1040, line 59.

Part II—2004 Conversions From Traditional, SEP, or SIMPLE IRAs to Roth IRAs

Complete Part II if you converted part or all of your traditional, SEP, or SIMPLE IRAs to a Roth IRA in 2004, excluding any portion you recharacterized. See item 1 under *Reporting recharacterizations* on page 3 for details.

Limit on number of conversions. If you converted an amount from a traditional, SEP, or SIMPLE IRA to a Roth IRA in 2004 and then recharacterized the amount back to a traditional, SEP, or SIMPLE IRA, you cannot reconvert that amount until the later of January 1, 2005, or 30 days after the recharacterization. See Pub. 590 for details.

⚠ **CAUTION** *You cannot convert any amount to Roth IRAs in 2004 if (a) your modified AGI for Roth IRA purposes (see page 2) is more than $100,000 or (b) your filing status is married filing separately and you lived with your spouse at any time in 2004. If you erroneously made a conversion, you must recharacterize the converted amount. See Recharacterizations on page 3.*

Line 16

If you did not complete line 8, see the instructions for that line. Then, enter on line 16 the amount you would

have entered on line 8 had you completed it.

Line 17

If you did not complete line 11, enter on line 17 the amount from line 2 (or the amount you would have entered on line 2 if you had completed that line) plus any contributions included on line 1 that you made before the conversion.

Part III—Distributions From Roth IRAs

Complete Part III to figure the taxable part, if any, of your 2004 Roth IRA distributions.

Line 19

Do not include on line 19 any of the following.
• Distributions that you rolled over, including distributions made in 2004 and rolled over after December 31, 2004 (outstanding rollovers).
• Recharacterizations.
• Distributions that are a return of contributions under *Return of IRA Contributions* on page 4.
• Distributions made on or after age 59½ if you made a contribution (including a conversion) for 1998 or 1999.
• Distributions made upon death or due to disability if you made a contribution (including a conversion) for 1998 or 1999.
• Distributions that are incident to divorce. The transfer of part or all of your Roth IRA to your spouse under a divorce or separation agreement is not taxable to you or your spouse.

If, after considering the items above, you do not have an amount to enter on line 19, do not complete Part III; your Roth IRA distribution(s) is not taxable. Instead, include your total Roth IRA distribution(s) on Form 1040, line 15a; Form 1040A, line 11a; or Form 1040NR, line 16a.

Line 20

If you had a qualified first-time homebuyer distribution from your Roth IRA and you made a contribution (including a conversion) to a Roth IRA for 1998 or 1999, enter the amount of your qualified first-time homebuyer expenses on line 20, but do not enter more than $10,000.

Line 22

Figure the amount to enter on line 22 as follows.
• If you did not take a Roth IRA distribution before 2004 (other than

Basis in Roth IRA Conversions—Line 24

IF the most recent year prior to 2004 in which you had a distribution* in excess of your basis in contributions was...	THEN enter on Form 8606, line 24, this amount...	PLUS the sum of the amounts on the following lines...
2003 (you had an amount on your 2003 Form 8606, line 21)	The excess, if any, of your 2003 Form 8606, line 22, over line 21 of that Form 8606.	Line 16 of your 2004 Form 8606
2002 (you had an amount on your 2002 Form 8606, line 21)	The excess, if any, of your 2002 Form 8606, line 22, over line 21 of that Form 8606	Line 16 of your 2003 and 2004 Forms 8606
2001 (you had an amount on your 2001 Form 8606, line 21)	The excess, if any, of your 2001 Form 8606, line 22, over line 21 of that Form 8606	Line 16 of your 2002 through 2004 Forms 8606
2000 (you had an amount on your 2000 Form 8606, line 19)	The excess, if any, of your 2000 Form 8606, line 25, over line 19 of that Form 8606	Line 16 of your 2001 through 2004 Forms 8606
1999 (you had an amount on your 1999 Form 8606, line 19)	The excess, if any, of your 1999 Form 8606, line 25, over line 19 of that Form 8606	Line 14c of your 2000 Form 8606 and line 16 of your 2001 through 2004 Forms 8606
1998 (you had an amount on your 1998 Form 8606, line 20)	The excess, if any, of your 1998 Form 8606, line 14c, over line 20 of that Form 8606	Line 14c of your 1999 and 2000 Forms 8606 and line 16 of your 2001 through 2004 Forms 8606
Did not have such a distribution in excess of your basis in contributions	The amount from your 2004 Form 8606, line 16	Line 14c of your 1998, 1999, and 2000 Forms 8606 and line 16 of your 2001 through 2003 Forms 8606

*Excluding rollovers, recharacterizations, and contributions that you had returned to you.

an amount rolled over or recharacterized or a returned contribution), enter on line 22 the total of all your regular contributions to Roth IRAs for 1998 through 2004 (excluding rollovers and any contributions that you had returned to you), adjusted for any recharacterizations.
• If you did take such a distribution before 2004, use the chart on page 7 to figure the amount to enter.
• Increase or decrease the amount on line 22 by any basis transferred or received incident to divorce. Also attach a statement similar to the one explained under *Distributions that are incident to divorce* on page 6.

Line 23

Generally, there is an additional 10% tax on 2004 distributions from a Roth IRA that are shown on line 23. The additional tax is figured on Form 5329, Part I. See the instructions for Form 5329, line 1, for details and exceptions. However, do not complete Form 5329 if you have an amount on line 20 that is equal to or more than the amount on line 23; you do not owe the additional 10% tax.

Line 24

Figure the amount to enter on line 24 as follows.
• If you have never made a Roth IRA conversion, enter -0- on line 24.
• If you took a Roth IRA distribution (other than an amount rolled over or recharacterized or a returned contribution) before 2004 in excess of

your basis in regular Roth IRA contributions, use the chart on this page to figure the amount to enter on line 24.
• If you did not take such a distribution before 2004, enter on line 24 the total of all your conversions to Roth IRAs (other than amounts recharacterized). These amounts are shown on line 14c of your 1998, 1999, and 2000 Forms 8606 and line 16 of your 2001 through 2004 Forms 8606.
• Increase or decrease the amount on line 24 by any basis transferred or received incident to divorce. Also attach a statement similar to the one explained under *Distributions that are incident to divorce* on page 6.

Paperwork Reduction Act Notice. We ask for the information on this form to carry out the Internal Revenue laws of the United States. You are required to give us the information. We need it to ensure that you are complying with these laws and to allow us to figure and collect the right amount of tax.

You are not required to provide the information requested on a form that is subject to the paperwork reduction act unless the form displays a valid OMB control number. Books or records relating to a form or its instructions must be retained as long as their contents may become material in the administration of any Internal Revenue law. Generally, tax returns and return information are confidential, as required by section 6103.

The time needed to complete and file this form will vary depending on individual circumstances. The estimated average time is:

Recordkeeping . . . . 1 hr., 4 min.
Learning about the law or the form . . . . 1 hr., 12 min.
Preparing the form . . . . . 53 min.
Copying, assembling, and sending the form to the IRS . . . . 47 min.

If you have comments concerning the accuracy of these time estimates or suggestions for making this form simpler, we would be happy to hear from you. See the instructions for the tax return with which this form is filed.

Revenue Ruling 2002-62

Part I

Section 72.—Annuities; Certain Proceeds of Endowment and Life Insurance Contracts

SECTION 1. PURPOSE AND BACKGROUND

.01 The purpose of this revenue ruling is to modify the provisions of Q&A-12 of Notice 89-25, 1989-1 C.B. 662, which provides guidance on what constitutes a series of substantially equal periodic payments within the meaning of 72(t)(2)(A)(iv) of the Internal Revenue Code from an individual account under a qualified retirement plan. Section 72(t) provides for an additional income tax on early withdrawals from qualified retirement plans (as defined in 4974(c)). Section 4974(c) provides, in part, that the term "qualified retirement plan" means (1) a plan described in 401 (including a trust exempt from tax under 501(a)), (2) an annuity plan described in 403(a), (3) a tax-sheltered annuity arrangement described in 403(b), (4) an individual retirement account described in 408(a), or (5) an individual retirement annuity described in 408(b).

.02 (a) Section 72(t)(1) provides that if an employee or IRA owner receives any amount from a qualified retirement plan before attaining age 59½, the employee's or IRA owner's income tax is increased by an amount equal to 10-percent of the amount that is includible in the gross income unless one of the exceptions in 72(t)(2) applies.

(b) Section 72(t)(2)(A)(iv) provides, in part, that if distributions are part of a series of substantially equal periodic payments (not less frequently than annually) made for the life (or life expectancy) of the employee or the joint lives (or joint life expectancy) of the employee and beneficiary, the tax described in 72(t)(1) will not be applicable. Pursuant to 72(t)(5), in the case of distributions from an IRA, the IRA owner is substituted for the employee for purposes of applying this exception.

(c) Section 72(t)(4) provides that if the series of substantially equal periodic payments that is otherwise excepted from the 10-percent tax is subsequently modified (other than by reason of death or disability) within a 5-year period beginning on the date of the first payment, or, if later, age 59½, the exception to the 10-percent tax does not apply, and the taxpayer's tax for the year of modification shall be increased by an amount which, but for the exception, would have been imposed, plus interest for the deferral period.

Revenue Ruling 2002-62 (continued)

(d) Q&A-12 of Notice 89-25 sets forth three methods for determining whether payments to individuals from their IRAs or, if they have separated from service, from their qualified retirement plans constitute a series of substantially equal periodic payments for purposes of 72(t)(2)(A)(iv).

(e) Final Income Tax Regulations that were published in the April 17, 2002, issue of the Federal Register under 401(a)(9) provide new life expectancy tables for determining required minimum distributions.

SECTION 2. METHODS

.01 General rule. Payments are considered to be substantially equal periodic payments within the meaning of 72(t)(2)(A)(iv) if they are made in accordance with one of the three calculations described in paragraphs (a) - (c) of this subsection (which is comprised of the three methods described in Q&A-12 of Notice 89-25).

(a) The required minimum distribution method. The annual payment for each year is determined by dividing the account balance for that year by the number from the chosen life expectancy table for that year. Under this method, the account balance, the number from the chosen life expectancy table and the resulting annual

payments are redetermined for each year. If this method is chosen, there will not be deemed to be a modification in the series of substantially equal periodic payments, even if the amount of payments changes from year to year, provided there is not a change to another method of determining the payments.

(b) The fixed amortization method. The annual payment for each year is determined by amortizing in level amounts the account balance over a specified number of years determined using the chosen life expectancy table and the chosen interest rate. Under this method, the account balance, the number from the chosen life expectancy table and the resulting annual payment are determined once for the first distribution year and the annual payment is the same amount in each succeeding year.

(c) The fixed annuitization method. The annual payment for each year is determined by dividing the account balance by an annuity factor that is the present value of an annuity of $1 per year beginning at the taxpayer's age and continuing for the life of the taxpayer (or the joint lives of the individual and beneficiary). The annuity factor is derived using the mortality table ... and using the chosen inter-

Revenue Ruling 2002-62 (continued)

est rate. Under this method, the account balance, the annuity factor, the chosen interest rate and the resulting annual payment are determined once for the first distribution year and the annual payment is the same amount in each succeeding year.

.02 Other rules. The following rules apply for purposes of this section.

(a) Life expectancy tables. The life expectancy tables that can be used to determine distribution periods are: (1) the uniform lifetime table in Appendix A*, or (2) the single life expectancy table in 1.401(a)(9)-9, Q&A-1 of the Income Tax Regulations* or (3) the joint and last survivor table in 1.401(a)(9)-9, Q&A-3*. The number that is used for a distribution year is the number shown from the table for the employee's (or IRA owner's) age on his or her birthday in that year. If the joint and survivor table is being used, the age of the beneficiary on the beneficiary's birthday in the year is also used. In the case of the required minimum distribution method, the same life expectancy table that is used for the first distribution year must be used in each following year. Thus, if the taxpayer uses the single life expectancy table for the required minimum distribution method in the first distribution year, the same table must be used in subsequent distribution years.

(b) Beneficiary under joint tables. If the joint life and last survivor table in 1.401(a)(9)-9, Q&A-3, is used, the survivor must be the actual beneficiary of the employee with respect to the account for the year of the distribution. If there is more than one beneficiary, the identity and age of the beneficiary used for purposes of each of the methods described in section 2.01 are determined under the rules for determining the designated beneficiary for purposes of 401(a)(9). The beneficiary is determined for a year as of January 1 of the year, without regard to changes in the beneficiary in that year or beneficiary determinations in prior years. For example, if a taxpayer starts distributions from an IRA in 2003 at age 50 and a 25-year-old and 55-year-old are beneficiaries on January 1, the 55-year-old is the designated beneficiary and the number for the taxpayer from the joint and last survivor tables (age 50 and age 55) would be 38.3, even though later in 2003 the 55-year-old is eliminated as a beneficiary. However, if that beneficiary is eliminated or dies in 2003, under the required minimum distribution method, that individual

* You can find these tables in Appendix B of this book.

Revenue Ruling 2002-62 (continued)

would not be taken into account in future years. If, in any year there is no beneficiary, the single life expectancy table is used for that year.

(c) Interest rates. The interest rate that may be used is any interest rate that is not more than 120 percent of the federal mid-term rate (determined in accordance with 1274(d) for either of the two months immediately preceding the month in which the distribution begins). The revenue rulings that contain the 1274(d) federal mid-term rates may be found at www.irs.gov\tax_regs\fedrates.html.

(d) Account balance. The account balance that is used to determine payments must be determined in a reasonable manner based on the facts and circumstances. For example, for an IRA with daily valuations that made its first distribution on July 15, 2003, it would be reasonable to determine the yearly account balance when using the required minimum distribution method based on the value of the IRA from December 31, 2002 to July 15, 2003. For subsequent years, under the required minimum distribution method, it would be reasonable to use the value either on the December 31 of the prior year or on a date within a reasonable period before that year's distribution.

(e) Changes to account balance. Under all three methods, substantially equal periodic payments are calculated with respect to an account balance as of the first valuation date selected in paragraph (d) above. Thus, a modification to the series of payments will occur if, after such date, there is (i) any addition to the account balance other than gains or losses, (ii) any nontaxable transfer of a portion of the account balance to another retirement plan, or (iii) a rollover by the taxpayer of the amount received resulting in such amount not being taxable.

.03 Special rules. The special rules described below may be applicable.

(a) Complete depletion of assets. If, as a result of following an acceptable method of determining substantially equal periodic payments, an individual's assets in an individual account plan or an IRA are exhausted, the individual will not be subject to additional income tax under 72(t)(1) as a result of not receiving substantially equal periodic payments and the resulting cessation of payments will not be treated as a modification of the series of payments.

(b) One-time change to required minimum distribution method. An indi-

Revenue Ruling 2002-62 (continued)

vidual who begins distributions in a year using either the fixed amortization method or the fixed annuitization method may in any subsequent year switch to the required minimum distribution method to determine the payment for the year of the switch and all subsequent years and the change in method will not be treated as a modification within the meaning of 72(t)(4). Once a change is made under this paragraph, the required minimum distribution method must be followed in all subsequent years. Any subsequent change will be a modification for purposes of 72(t)(4).

SECTION 3. EFFECTIVE DATE AND TRANSITIONAL RULES

The guidance in this revenue ruling replaces the guidance in Q&A-12 of Notice 89-25 for any series of payments commencing on or after January 1, 2003, and may be used for distributions commencing in 2002. If a series of payments commenced in a year prior to 2003 that satisfied 72(t)(2)(A)(iv), the method of calculating the payments in the series is permitted to be changed at any time to the required minimum distribution method described in section 2.01(a) of this guidance, including use of a different life expectancy table.

SECTION 4. EFFECT ON OTHER DOCUMENTS

Q&A-12 of Notice 89-25 is modified.

SECTION 5. REQUEST FOR COMMENTS

The Service and Treasury invite comments with respect to the guidance provided in this revenue ruling. Comments should reference Rev. Rul. 2002-62. Comments may be submitted to CC:ITA:RU (Rev. Rul. 2002-62), room 5226, Internal Revenue Service, POB 7604 Ben Franklin Station, Washington, DC 20044. Comments may be hand delivered between the hours of 8:30 a.m. and 5 p.m. Monday to Friday to: CC:ITA:RU (Rev. Rul. 2002-62), Courier's Desk, Internal Revenue Service, 1111 Constitution Avenue NW., Washington, D.C. Alternatively, comments may be submitted via the Internet at Notice. Comments@irscounsel.treas.gov. All comments will be available for public inspection and copying.

Drafting Information

The principal author of this revenue ruling is Michael Rubin of the Employee Plans, Tax Exempt and Government Entities Division. For further information regarding this revenue ruling, please contact Mr. Rubin at 1-202-283-9888 (not a toll-free number).

Appendix B

Life Expectancy Tables

Table I: Single Life Expectancy

Age	Divisor	Age	Divisor	Age	Divisor	Age	Divisor
0	82.4	29	54.3	58	27.0	87	6.7
1	81.6	30	53.3	59	26.1	88	6.3
2	80.6	31	52.4	60	25.2	89	5.9
3	79.7	32	51.4	61	24.4	90	5.5
4	78.7	33	50.4	62	23.5	91	5.2
5	77.7	34	49.4	63	22.7	92	4.9
6	76.7	35	48.5	64	21.8	93	4.6
7	75.8	36	47.5	65	21.0	94	4.3
8	74.8	37	46.5	66	20.2	95	4.1
9	73.8	38	45.6	67	19.4	96	3.8
10	72.8	39	44.6	68	18.6	97	3.6
11	71.8	40	43.6	69	17.8	98	3.4
12	70.8	41	42.7	70	17.0	99	3.1
13	69.9	42	41.7	71	16.3	100	2.9
14	68.9	43	40.7	72	15.5	101	2.7
15	67.9	44	39.8	73	14.8	102	2.5
16	66.9	45	38.8	74	14.1	103	2.3
17	66.0	46	37.9	75	13.4	104	2.1
18	65.0	47	37.0	76	12.7	105	1.9
19	64.0	48	36.0	77	12.1	106	1.7
20	63.0	49	35.1	78	11.4	107	1.5
21	62.1	50	34.2	79	10.8	108	1.4
22	61.1	51	33.3	80	10.2	109	1.2
23	60.1	52	32.3	81	9.7	110	1.1
24	59.1	53	31.4	82	9.1	111+	1.0
25	58.2	54	30.5	83	8.6		
26	57.2	55	29.6	84	8.1		
27	56.2	56	28.7	85	7.6		
28	55.3	57	27.9	86	7.1		

Table II: Joint Life and Last Survivor Expectancy

AGES	30	31	32	33	34	35	36	37	38	39
30	60.2	59.7	59.2	58.8	58.4	58.0	57.6	57.3	57.0	56.7
31	59.7	59.2	58.7	58.2	57.8	57.4	57.0	56.6	56.3	56.0
32	59.2	58.7	58.2	57.7	57.2	56.8	56.4	56.0	55.6	55.3
33	58.8	58.2	57.7	57.2	56.7	56.2	55.8	55.4	55.0	54.7
34	58.4	57.8	57.2	56.7	56.2	55.7	55.3	54.8	54.4	54.0
35	58.0	57.4	56.8	56.2	55.7	55.2	54.7	54.3	53.8	53.4
36	57.6	57.0	56.4	55.8	55.3	54.7	54.2	53.7	53.3	52.8
37	57.3	56.6	56.0	55.4	54.8	54.3	53.7	53.2	52.7	52.3
38	57.0	56.3	55.6	55.0	54.4	53.8	53.3	52.7	52.2	51.7
39	56.7	56.0	55.3	54.7	54.0	53.4	52.8	52.3	51.7	51.2
40	56.4	55.7	55.0	54.3	53.7	53.0	52.4	51.8	51.3	50.8
41	56.1	55.4	54.7	54.0	53.3	52.7	52.0	51.4	50.9	50.3
42	55.9	55.2	54.4	53.7	53.0	52.3	51.7	51.1	50.4	49.9
43	55.7	54.9	54.2	53.4	52.7	52.0	51.3	50.7	50.1	49.5
44	55.5	54.7	53.9	53.2	52.4	51.7	51.0	50.4	49.7	49.1
45	55.3	54.5	53.7	52.9	52.2	51.5	50.7	50.0	49.4	48.7
46	55.1	54.3	53.5	52.7	52.0	51.2	50.5	49.8	49.1	48.4
47	55.0	54.1	53.3	52.5	51.7	51.0	50.2	49.5	48.8	48.1
48	54.8	54.0	53.2	52.3	51.5	50.8	50.0	49.2	48.5	47.8
49	54.7	53.8	53.0	52.2	51.4	50.6	49.8	49.0	48.2	47.5
50	54.6	53.7	52.9	52.0	51.2	50.4	49.6	48.8	48.0	47.3
51	54.5	53.6	52.7	51.9	51.0	50.2	49.4	48.6	47.8	47.0
52	54.4	53.5	52.6	51.7	50.9	50.0	49.2	48.4	47.6	46.8
53	54.3	53.4	52.5	51.6	50.8	49.9	49.1	48.2	47.4	46.6
54	54.2	53.3	52.4	51.5	50.6	49.8	48.9	48.1	47.2	46.4
55	54.1	53.2	52.3	51.4	50.5	49.7	48.8	47.9	47.1	46.3
56	54.0	53.1	52.2	51.3	50.4	49.5	48.7	47.8	47.0	46.1
57	54.0	53.0	52.1	51.2	50.3	49.4	48.6	47.7	46.8	46.0
58	53.9	53.0	52.1	51.2	50.3	49.4	48.5	47.6	46.7	45.8
59	53.8	52.9	52.0	51.1	50.2	49.3	48.4	47.5	46.6	45.7

Table II: Joint Life and Last Survivor Expectancy (continued)

AGES	30	31	32	33	34	35	36	37	38	39
60	53.8	52.9	51.9	51.0	50.1	49.2	48.3	47.4	46.5	45.6
61	53.8	52.8	51.9	51.0	50.0	49.1	48.2	47.3	46.4	45.5
62	53.7	52.8	51.8	50.9	50.0	49.1	48.1	47.2	46.3	45.4
63	53.7	52.7	51.8	50.9	49.9	49.0	48.1	47.2	46.3	45.3
64	53.6	52.7	51.8	50.8	49.9	48.9	48.0	47.1	46.2	45.3
65	53.6	52.7	51.7	50.8	49.8	48.9	48.0	47.0	46.1	45.2
66	53.6	52.6	51.7	50.7	49.8	48.9	47.9	47.0	46.1	45.1
67	53.6	52.6	51.7	50.7	49.8	48.8	47.9	46.9	46.0	45.1
68	53.5	52.6	51.6	50.7	49.7	48.8	47.8	46.9	46.0	45.0
69	53.5	52.6	51.6	50.6	49.7	48.7	47.8	46.9	45.9	45.0
70	53.5	52.5	51.6	50.6	49.7	48.7	47.8	46.8	45.9	44.9
71	53.5	52.5	51.6	50.6	49.6	48.7	47.7	46.8	45.9	44.9
72	53.5	52.5	51.5	50.6	49.6	48.7	47.7	46.8	45.8	44.9
73	53.4	52.5	51.5	50.6	49.6	48.6	47.7	46.7	45.8	44.8
74	53.4	52.5	51.5	50.5	49.6	48.6	47.7	46.7	45.8	44.8
75	53.4	52.5	51.5	50.5	49.6	48.6	47.7	46.7	45.7	44.8
76	53.4	52.4	51.5	50.5	49.6	48.6	47.6	46.7	45.7	44.8
77	53.4	52.4	51.5	50.5	49.5	48.6	47.6	46.7	45.7	44.8
78	53.4	52.4	51.5	50.5	49.5	48.6	47.6	46.6	45.7	44.7
79	53.4	52.4	51.5	50.5	49.5	48.6	47.6	46.6	45.7	44.7
80	53.4	52.4	51.4	50.5	49.5	48.5	47.6	46.6	45.7	44.7
81	53.4	52.4	51.4	50.5	49.5	48.5	47.6	46.6	45.7	44.7
82	53.4	52.4	51.4	50.5	49.5	48.5	47.6	46.6	45.6	44.7
83	53.4	52.4	51.4	50.5	49.5	48.5	47.6	46.6	45.6	44.7
84	53.4	52.4	51.4	50.5	49.5	48.5	47.6	46.6	45.6	44.7
85	53.3	52.4	51.4	50.4	49.5	48.5	47.5	46.6	45.6	44.7
86	53.3	52.4	51.4	50.4	49.5	48.5	47.5	46.6	45.6	44.6
87	53.3	52.4	51.4	50.4	49.5	48.5	47.5	46.6	45.6	44.6
88	53.3	52.4	51.4	50.4	49.5	48.5	47.5	46.6	45.6	44.6
89	53.3	52.4	51.4	50.4	49.5	48.5	47.5	46.6	45.6	44.6

AGES	30	31	32	33	34	35	36	37	38	39
Table II: Joint Life and Last Survivor Expectancy (continued)										
90	53.3	52.4	51.4	50.4	49.5	48.5	47.5	46.6	45.6	44.6
91	53.3	52.4	51.4	50.4	49.5	48.5	47.5	46.6	45.6	44.6
92	53.3	52.4	51.4	50.4	49.5	48.5	47.5	46.6	45.6	44.6
93	53.3	52.4	51.4	50.4	49.5	48.5	47.5	46.6	45.6	44.6
94	53.3	52.4	51.4	50.4	49.5	48.5	47.5	46.6	45.6	44.6
95	53.3	52.4	51.4	50.4	49.5	48.5	47.5	46.5	45.6	44.6
96	53.3	52.4	51.4	50.4	49.5	48.5	47.5	46.5	45.6	44.6
97	53.3	52.4	51.4	50.4	49.5	48.5	47.5	46.5	45.6	44.6
98	53.3	52.4	51.4	50.4	49.5	48.5	47.5	46.5	45.6	44.6
99	53.3	52.4	51.4	50.4	49.5	48.5	47.5	46.5	45.6	44.6
100	53.3	52.4	51.4	50.4	49.5	48.5	47.5	46.5	45.6	44.6
101	53.3	52.4	51.4	50.4	49.5	48.5	47.5	46.5	45.6	44.6
102	53.3	52.4	51.4	50.4	49.5	48.5	47.5	46.5	45.6	44.6
103	53.3	52.4	51.4	50.4	49.5	48.5	47.5	46.5	45.6	44.6
104	53.3	52.4	51.4	50.4	49.5	48.5	47.5	46.5	45.6	44.6
105	53.3	52.4	51.4	50.4	49.4	48.5	47.5	46.5	45.6	44.6
106	53.3	52.4	51.4	50.4	49.4	48.5	47.5	46.5	45.6	44.6
107	53.3	52.4	51.4	50.4	49.4	48.5	47.5	46.5	45.6	44.6
108	53.3	52.4	51.4	50.4	49.4	48.5	47.5	46.5	45.6	44.6
109	53.3	52.4	51.4	50.4	49.4	48.5	47.5	46.5	45.6	44.6
110	53.3	52.4	51.4	50.4	49.4	48.5	47.5	46.5	45.6	44.6
111	53.3	52.4	51.4	50.4	49.4	48.5	47.5	46.5	45.6	44.6
112	53.3	52.4	51.4	50.4	49.4	48.5	47.5	46.5	45.6	44.6
113	53.3	52.4	51.4	50.4	49.4	48.5	47.5	46.5	45.6	44.6
114	53.3	52.4	51.4	50.4	49.4	48.5	47.5	46.5	45.6	44.6
115+	53.3	52.4	51.4	50.4	49.4	48.5	47.5	46.5	45.6	44.6

Table II: Joint Life and Last Survivor Expectancy (continued)

AGES	40	41	42	43	44	45	46	47	48	49
40	50.2	49.8	49.3	48.9	48.5	48.1	47.7	47.4	47.1	46.8
41	49.8	49.3	48.8	48.3	47.9	47.5	47.1	46.7	46.4	46.1
42	49.3	48.8	48.3	47.8	47.3	46.9	46.5	46.1	45.8	45.4
43	48.9	48.3	47.8	47.3	46.8	46.3	45.9	45.5	45.1	44.8
44	48.5	47.9	47.3	46.8	46.3	45.8	45.4	44.9	44.5	44.2
45	48.1	47.5	46.9	46.3	45.8	45.3	44.8	44.4	44.0	43.6
46	47.7	47.1	46.5	45.9	45.4	44.8	44.3	43.9	43.4	43.0
47	47.4	46.7	46.1	45.5	44.9	44.4	43.9	43.4	42.9	42.4
48	47.1	46.4	45.8	45.1	44.5	44.0	43.4	42.9	42.4	41.9
49	46.8	46.1	45.4	44.8	44.2	43.6	43.0	42.4	41.9	41.4
50	46.5	45.8	45.1	44.4	43.8	43.2	42.6	42.0	41.5	40.9
51	46.3	45.5	44.8	44.1	43.5	42.8	42.2	41.6	41.0	40.5
52	46.0	45.3	44.6	43.8	43.2	42.5	41.8	41.2	40.6	40.1
53	45.8	45.1	44.3	43.6	42.9	42.2	41.5	40.9	40.3	39.7
54	45.6	44.8	44.1	43.3	42.6	41.9	41.2	40.5	39.9	39.3
55	45.5	44.7	43.9	43.1	42.4	41.6	40.9	40.2	39.6	38.9
56	45.3	44.5	43.7	42.9	42.1	41.4	40.7	40.0	39.3	38.6
57	45.1	44.3	43.5	42.7	41.9	41.2	40.4	39.7	39.0	38.3
58	45.0	44.2	43.3	42.5	41.7	40.9	40.2	39.4	38.7	38.0
59	44.9	44.0	43.2	42.4	41.5	40.7	40.0	39.2	38.5	37.8
60	44.7	43.9	43.0	42.2	41.4	40.6	39.8	39.0	38.2	37.5
61	44.6	43.8	42.9	42.1	41.2	40.4	39.6	38.8	38.0	37.3
62	44.5	43.7	42.8	41.9	41.1	40.3	39.4	38.6	37.8	37.1
63	44.5	43.6	42.7	41.8	41.0	40.1	39.3	38.5	37.7	36.9
64	44.4	43.5	42.6	41.7	40.8	40.0	39.2	38.3	37.5	36.7
65	44.3	43.4	42.5	41.6	40.7	39.9	39.0	38.2	37.4	36.6
66	44.2	43.3	42.4	41.5	40.6	39.8	38.9	38.1	37.2	36.4
67	44.2	43.3	42.3	41.4	40.6	39.7	38.8	38.0	37.1	36.3
68	44.1	43.2	42.3	41.4	40.5	39.6	38.7	37.9	37.0	36.2
69	44.1	43.1	42.2	41.3	40.4	39.5	38.6	37.8	36.9	36.0

Table II: Joint Life and Last Survivor Expectancy (continued)

AGES	40	41	42	43	44	45	46	47	48	49
70	44.0	43.1	42.2	41.3	40.3	39.4	38.6	37.7	36.8	35.9
71	44.0	43.0	42.1	41.2	40.3	39.4	38.5	37.6	36.7	35.9
72	43.9	43.0	42.1	41.1	40.2	39.3	38.4	37.5	36.6	35.8
73	43.9	43.0	42.0	41.1	40.2	39.3	38.4	37.5	36.6	35.7
74	43.9	42.9	42.0	41.1	40.1	39.2	38.3	37.4	36.5	35.6
75	43.8	42.9	42.0	41.0	40.1	39.2	38.3	37.4	36.5	35.6
76	43.8	42.9	41.9	41.0	40.1	39.1	38.2	37.3	36.4	35.5
77	43.8	42.9	41.9	41.0	40.0	39.1	38.2	37.3	36.4	35.5
78	43.8	42.8	41.9	40.9	40.0	39.1	38.2	37.2	36.3	35.4
79	43.8	42.8	41.9	40.9	40.0	39.1	38.1	37.2	36.3	35.4
80	43.7	42.8	41.8	40.9	40.0	39.0	38.1	37.2	36.3	35.4
81	43.7	42.8	41.8	40.9	39.9	39.0	38.1	37.2	36.2	35.3
82	43.7	42.8	41.8	40.9	39.9	39.0	38.1	37.1	36.2	35.3
83	43.7	42.8	41.8	40.9	39.9	39.0	38.0	37.1	36.2	35.3
84	43.7	42.7	41.8	40.8	39.9	39.0	38.0	37.1	36.2	35.3
85	43.7	42.7	41.8	40.8	39.9	38.9	38.0	37.1	36.2	35.2
86	43.7	42.7	41.8	40.8	39.9	38.9	38.0	37.1	36.1	35.2
87	43.7	42.7	41.8	40.8	39.9	38.9	38.0	37.0	36.1	35.2
88	43.7	42.7	41.8	40.8	39.9	38.9	38.0	37.0	36.1	35.2
89	43.7	42.7	41.7	40.8	39.8	38.9	38.0	37.0	36.1	35.2
90	43.7	42.7	41.7	40.8	39.8	38.9	38.0	37.0	36.1	35.2
91	43.7	42.7	41.7	40.8	39.8	38.9	37.9	37.0	36.1	35.2
92	43.7	42.7	41.7	40.8	39.8	38.9	37.9	37.0	36.1	35.1
93	43.7	42.7	41.7	40.8	39.8	38.9	37.9	37.0	36.1	35.1
94	43.7	42.7	41.7	40.8	39.8	38.9	37.9	37.0	36.1	35.1
95	43.6	42.7	41.7	40.8	39.8	38.9	37.9	37.0	36.1	35.1
96	43.6	42.7	41.7	40.8	39.8	38.9	37.9	37.0	36.1	35.1
97	43.6	42.7	41.7	40.8	39.8	38.9	37.9	37.0	36.1	35.1
98	43.6	42.7	41.7	40.8	39.8	38.9	37.9	37.0	36.0	35.1
99	43.6	42.7	41.7	40.8	39.8	38.9	37.9	37.0	36.0	35.1

AGES	40	41	42	43	44	45	46	47	48	49
Table II: Joint Life and Last Survivor Expectancy (continued)										
100	43.6	42.7	41.7	40.8	39.8	38.9	37.9	37.0	36.0	35.1
101	43.6	42.7	41.7	40.8	39.8	38.9	37.9	37.0	36.0	35.1
102	43.6	42.7	41.7	40.8	39.8	38.9	37.9	37.0	36.0	35.1
103	43.6	42.7	41.7	40.8	39.8	38.9	37.9	37.0	36.0	35.1
104	43.6	42.7	41.7	40.8	39.8	38.8	37.9	37.0	36.0	35.1
105	43.6	42.7	41.7	40.8	39.8	38.8	37.9	37.0	36.0	35.1
106	43.6	42.7	41.7	40.8	39.8	38.8	37.9	37.0	36.0	35.1
107	43.6	42.7	41.7	40.8	39.8	38.8	37.9	37.0	36.0	35.1
108	43.6	42.7	41.7	40.8	39.8	38.8	37.9	37.0	36.0	35.1
109	43.6	42.7	41.7	40.7	39.8	38.8	37.9	37.0	36.0	35.1
110	43.6	42.7	41.7	40.7	39.8	38.8	37.9	37.0	36.0	35.1
111	43.6	42.7	41.7	40.7	39.8	38.8	37.9	37.0	36.0	35.1
112	43.6	42.7	41.7	40.7	39.8	38.8	37.9	37.0	36.0	35.1
113	43.6	42.7	41.7	40.7	39.8	38.8	37.9	37.0	36.0	35.1
114	43.6	42.7	41.7	40.7	39.8	38.8	37.9	37.0	36.0	35.1
115+	43.6	42.7	41.7	40.7	39.8	38.8	37.9	37.0	36.0	35.1

Table II: Joint Life and Last Survivor Expectancy (continued)

AGES	50	51	52	53	54	55	56	57	58	59
50	40.4	40.0	39.5	39.1	38.7	38.3	38.0	37.6	37.3	37.1
51	40.0	39.5	39.0	38.5	38.1	37.7	37.4	37.0	36.7	36.4
52	39.5	39.0	38.5	38.0	37.6	37.2	36.8	36.4	36.0	35.7
53	39.1	38.5	38.0	37.5	37.1	36.6	36.2	35.8	35.4	35.1
54	38.7	38.1	37.6	37.1	36.6	36.1	35.7	35.2	34.8	34.5
55	38.3	37.7	37.2	36.6	36.1	35.6	35.1	34.7	34.3	33.9
56	38.0	37.4	36.8	36.2	35.7	35.1	34.7	34.2	33.7	33.3
57	37.6	37.0	36.4	35.8	35.2	34.7	34.2	33.7	33.2	32.8
58	37.3	36.7	36.0	35.4	34.8	34.3	33.7	33.2	32.8	32.3
59	37.1	36.4	35.7	35.1	34.5	33.9	33.3	32.8	32.3	31.8
60	36.8	36.1	35.4	34.8	34.1	33.5	32.9	32.4	31.9	31.3
61	36.6	35.8	35.1	34.5	33.8	33.2	32.6	32.0	31.4	30.9
62	36.3	35.6	34.9	34.2	33.5	32.9	32.2	31.6	31.1	30.5
63	36.1	35.4	34.6	33.9	33.2	32.6	31.9	31.3	30.7	30.1
64	35.9	35.2	34.4	33.7	33.0	32.3	31.6	31.0	30.4	29.8
65	35.8	35.0	34.2	33.5	32.7	32.0	31.4	30.7	30.0	29.4
66	35.6	34.8	34.0	33.3	32.5	31.8	31.1	30.4	29.8	29.1
67	35.5	34.7	33.9	33.1	32.3	31.6	30.9	30.2	29.5	28.8
68	35.3	34.5	33.7	32.9	32.1	31.4	30.7	29.9	29.2	28.6
69	35.2	34.4	33.6	32.8	32.0	31.2	30.5	29.7	29.0	28.3
70	35.1	34.3	33.4	32.6	31.8	31.1	30.3	29.5	28.8	28.1
71	35.0	34.2	33.3	32.5	31.7	30.9	30.1	29.4	28.6	27.9
72	34.9	34.1	33.2	32.4	31.6	30.8	30.0	29.2	28.4	27.7
73	34.8	34.0	33.1	32.3	31.5	30.6	29.8	29.1	28.3	27.5
74	34.8	33.9	33.0	32.2	31.4	30.5	29.7	28.9	28.1	27.4
75	34.7	33.8	33.0	32.1	31.3	30.4	29.6	28.8	28.0	27.2
76	34.6	33.8	32.9	32.0	31.2	30.3	29.5	28.7	27.9	27.1
77	34.6	33.7	32.8	32.0	31.1	30.3	29.4	28.6	27.8	27.0
78	34.5	33.6	32.8	31.9	31.0	30.2	29.3	28.5	27.7	26.9
79	34.5	33.6	32.7	31.8	31.0	30.1	29.3	28.4	27.6	26.8

Table II: Joint Life and Last Survivor Expectancy (continued)

AGES	50	51	52	53	54	55	56	57	58	59
80	34.5	33.6	32.7	31.8	30.9	30.1	29.2	28.4	27.5	26.7
81	34.4	33.5	32.6	31.8	30.9	30.0	29.2	28.3	27.5	26.6
82	34.4	33.5	32.6	31.7	30.8	30.0	29.1	28.3	27.4	26.6
83	34.4	33.5	32.6	31.7	30.8	29.9	29.1	28.2	27.4	26.5
84	34.3	33.4	32.5	31.7	30.8	29.9	29.0	28.2	27.3	26.5
85	34.3	33.4	32.5	31.6	30.7	29.9	29.0	28.1	27.3	26.4
86	34.3	33.4	32.5	31.6	30.7	29.8	29.0	28.1	27.2	26.4
87	34.3	33.4	32.5	31.6	30.7	29.8	28.9	28.1	27.2	26.4
88	34.3	33.4	32.5	31.6	30.7	29.8	28.9	28.0	27.2	26.3
89	34.3	33.3	32.4	31.5	30.7	29.8	28.9	28.0	27.2	26.3
90	34.2	33.3	32.4	31.5	30.6	29.8	28.9	28.0	27.1	26.3
91	34.2	33.3	32.4	31.5	30.6	29.7	28.9	28.0	27.1	26.3
92	34.2	33.3	32.4	31.5	30.6	29.7	28.8	28.0	27.1	26.2
93	34.2	33.3	32.4	31.5	30.6	29.7	28.8	28.0	27.1	26.2
94	34.2	33.3	32.4	31.5	30.6	29.7	28.8	27.9	27.1	26.2
95	34.2	33.3	32.4	31.5	30.6	29.7	28.8	27.9	27.1	26.2
96	34.2	33.3	32.4	31.5	30.6	29.7	28.8	27.9	27.0	26.2
97	34.2	33.3	32.4	31.5	30.6	29.7	28.8	27.9	27.0	26.2
98	34.2	33.3	32.4	31.5	30.6	29.7	28.8	27.9	27.0	26.2
99	34.2	33.3	32.4	31.5	30.6	29.7	28.8	27.9	27.0	26.2
100	34.2	33.3	32.4	31.5	30.6	29.7	28.8	27.9	27.0	26.1
101	34.2	33.3	32.4	31.5	30.6	29.7	28.8	27.9	27.0	26.1
102	34.2	33.3	32.4	31.4	30.5	29.7	28.8	27.9	27.0	26.1
103	34.2	33.3	32.4	31.4	30.5	29.7	28.8	27.9	27.0	26.1
104	34.2	33.3	32.4	31.4	30.5	29.6	28.8	27.9	27.0	26.1
105	34.2	33.3	32.3	31.4	30.5	29.6	28.8	27.9	27.0	26.1
106	34.2	33.3	32.3	31.4	30.5	29.6	28.8	27.9	27.0	26.1
107	34.2	33.3	32.3	31.4	30.5	29.6	28.8	27.9	27.0	26.1
108	34.2	33.3	32.3	31.4	30.5	29.6	28.8	27.9	27.0	26.1
109	34.2	33.3	32.3	31.4	30.5	29.6	28.7	27.9	27.0	26.1

Table II: Joint Life and Last Survivor Expectancy (continued)

AGES	50	51	52	53	54	55	56	57	58	59
110	34.2	33.3	32.3	31.4	30.5	29.6	28.7	27.9	27.0	26.1
111	34.2	33.3	32.3	31.4	30.5	29.6	28.7	27.9	27.0	26.1
112	34.2	33.3	32.3	31.4	30.5	29.6	28.7	27.9	27.0	26.1
113	34.2	33.3	32.3	31.4	30.5	29.6	28.7	27.9	27.0	26.1
114	34.2	33.3	32.3	31.4	30.5	29.6	28.7	27.9	27.0	26.1
115+	34.2	33.3	32.3	31.4	30.5	29.6	28.7	27.9	27.0	26.1

Table II: Joint Life and Last Survivor Expectancy (continued)

AGES	60	61	62	63	64	65	66	67	68	69
60	30.9	30.4	30.0	29.6	29.2	28.8	28.5	28.2	27.9	27.6
61	30.4	29.9	29.5	29.0	28.6	28.3	27.9	27.6	27.3	27.0
62	30.0	29.5	29.0	28.5	28.1	27.7	27.3	27.0	26.7	26.4
63	29.6	29.0	28.5	28.1	27.6	27.2	26.8	26.4	26.1	25.7
64	29.2	28.6	28.1	27.6	27.1	26.7	26.3	25.9	25.5	25.2
65	28.8	28.3	27.7	27.2	26.7	26.2	25.8	25.4	25.0	24.6
66	28.5	27.9	27.3	26.8	26.3	25.8	25.3	24.9	24.5	24.1
67	28.2	27.6	27.0	26.4	25.9	25.4	24.9	24.4	24.0	23.6
68	27.9	27.3	26.7	26.1	25.5	25.0	24.5	24.0	23.5	23.1
69	27.6	27.0	26.4	25.7	25.2	24.6	24.1	23.6	23.1	22.6
70	27.4	26.7	26.1	25.4	24.8	24.3	23.7	23.2	22.7	22.2
71	27.2	26.5	25.8	25.2	24.5	23.9	23.4	22.8	22.3	21.8
72	27.0	26.3	25.6	24.9	24.3	23.7	23.1	22.5	22.0	21.4
73	26.8	26.1	25.4	24.7	24.0	23.4	22.8	22.2	21.6	21.1
74	26.6	25.9	25.2	24.5	23.8	23.1	22.5	21.9	21.3	20.8
75	26.5	25.7	25.0	24.3	23.6	22.9	22.3	21.6	21.0	20.5
76	26.3	25.6	24.8	24.1	23.4	22.7	22.0	21.4	20.8	20.2
77	26.2	25.4	24.7	23.9	23.2	22.5	21.8	21.2	20.6	19.9
78	26.1	25.3	24.6	23.8	23.1	22.4	21.7	21.0	20.3	19.7
79	26.0	25.2	24.4	23.7	22.9	22.2	21.5	20.8	20.1	19.5
80	25.9	25.1	24.3	23.6	22.8	22.1	21.3	20.6	20.0	19.3
81	25.8	25.0	24.2	23.4	22.7	21.9	21.2	20.5	19.8	19.1
82	25.8	24.9	24.1	23.4	22.6	21.8	21.1	20.4	19.7	19.0
83	25.7	24.9	24.1	23.3	22.5	21.7	21.0	20.2	19.5	18.8
84	25.6	24.8	24.0	23.2	22.4	21.6	20.9	20.1	19.4	18.7
85	25.6	24.8	23.9	23.1	22.3	21.6	20.8	20.1	19.3	18.6
86	25.5	24.7	23.9	23.1	22.3	21.5	20.7	20.0	19.2	18.5
87	25.5	24.7	23.8	23.0	22.2	21.4	20.7	19.9	19.2	18.4
88	25.5	24.6	23.8	23.0	22.2	21.4	20.6	19.8	19.1	18.3
89	25.4	24.6	23.8	22.9	22.1	21.3	20.5	19.8	19.0	18.3

Table II: Joint Life and Last Survivor Expectancy (continued)

AGES	60	61	62	63	64	65	66	67	68	69
90	25.4	24.6	23.7	22.9	22.1	21.3	20.5	19.7	19.0	18.2
91	25.4	24.5	23.7	22.9	22.1	21.3	20.5	19.7	18.9	18.2
92	25.4	24.5	23.7	22.9	22.0	21.2	20.4	19.6	18.9	18.1
93	25.4	24.5	23.7	22.8	22.0	21.2	20.4	19.6	18.8	18.1
94	25.3	24.5	23.6	22.8	22.0	21.2	20.4	19.6	18.8	18.0
95	25.3	24.5	23.6	22.8	22.0	21.1	20.3	19.6	18.8	18.0
96	25.3	24.5	23.6	22.8	21.9	21.1	20.3	19.5	18.8	18.0
97	25.3	24.5	23.6	22.8	21.9	21.1	20.3	19.5	18.7	18.0
98	25.3	24.4	23.6	22.8	21.9	21.1	20.3	19.5	18.7	17.9
99	25.3	24.4	23.6	22.7	21.9	21.1	20.3	19.5	18.7	17.9
100	25.3	24.4	23.6	22.7	21.9	21.1	20.3	19.5	18.7	17.9
101	25.3	24.4	23.6	22.7	21.9	21.1	20.2	19.4	18.7	17.9
102	25.3	24.4	23.6	22.7	21.9	21.1	20.2	19.4	18.6	17.9
103	25.3	24.4	23.6	22.7	21.9	21.0	20.2	19.4	18.6	17.9
104	25.3	24.4	23.5	22.7	21.9	21.0	20.2	19.4	18.6	17.8
105	25.3	24.4	23.5	22.7	21.9	21.0	20.2	19.4	18.6	17.8
106	25.3	24.4	23.5	22.7	21.9	21.0	20.2	19.4	18.6	17.8
107	25.2	24.4	23.5	22.7	21.8	21.0	20.2	19.4	18.6	17.8
108	25.2	24.4	23.5	22.7	21.8	21.0	20.2	19.4	18.6	17.8
109	25.2	24.4	23.5	22.7	21.8	21.0	20.2	19.4	18.6	17.8
110	25.2	24.4	23.5	22.7	21.8	21.0	20.2	19.4	18.6	17.8
111	25.2	24.4	23.5	22.7	21.8	21.0	20.2	19.4	18.6	17.8
112	25.2	24.4	23.5	22.7	21.8	21.0	20.2	19.4	18.6	17.8
113	25.2	24.4	23.5	22.7	21.8	21.0	20.2	19.4	18.6	17.8
114	25.2	24.4	23.5	22.7	21.8	21.0	20.2	19.4	18.6	17.8
115+	25.2	24.4	23.5	22.7	21.8	21.0	20.2	19.4	18.6	17.8

Table II: Joint Life and Last Survivor Expectancy (continued)

AGES	70	71	72	73	74	75	76	77	78	79
70	21.8	21.3	20.9	20.6	20.2	19.9	19.6	19.4	19.1	18.9
71	21.3	20.9	20.5	20.1	19.7	19.4	19.1	18.8	18.5	18.3
72	20.9	20.5	20.0	19.6	19.3	18.9	18.6	18.3	18.0	17.7
73	20.6	20.1	19.6	19.2	18.8	18.4	18.1	17.8	17.5	17.2
74	20.2	19.7	19.3	18.8	18.4	18.0	17.6	17.3	17.0	16.7
75	19.9	19.4	18.9	18.4	18.0	17.6	17.2	16.8	16.5	16.2
76	19.6	19.1	18.6	18.1	17.6	17.2	16.8	16.4	16.0	15.7
77	19.4	18.8	18.3	17.8	17.3	16.8	16.4	16.0	15.6	15.3
78	19.1	18.5	18.0	17.5	17.0	16.5	16.0	15.6	15.2	14.9
79	18.9	18.3	17.7	17.2	16.7	16.2	15.7	15.3	14.9	14.5
80	18.7	18.1	17.5	16.9	16.4	15.9	15.4	15.0	14.5	14.1
81	18.5	17.9	17.3	16.7	16.2	15.6	15.1	14.7	14.2	13.8
82	18.3	17.7	17.1	16.5	15.9	15.4	14.9	14.4	13.9	13.5
83	18.2	17.5	16.9	16.3	15.7	15.2	14.7	14.2	13.7	13.2
84	18.0	17.4	16.7	16.1	15.5	15.0	14.4	13.9	13.4	13.0
85	17.9	17.3	16.6	16.0	15.4	14.8	14.3	13.7	13.2	12.8
86	17.8	17.1	16.5	15.8	15.2	14.6	14.1	13.5	13.0	12.5
87	17.7	17.0	16.4	15.7	15.1	14.5	13.9	13.4	12.9	12.4
88	17.6	16.9	16.3	15.6	15.0	14.4	13.8	13.2	12.7	12.2
89	17.6	16.9	16.2	15.5	14.9	14.3	13.7	13.1	12.6	12.0
90	17.5	16.8	16.1	15.4	14.8	14.2	13.6	13.0	12.4	11.9
91	17.4	16.7	16.0	15.4	14.7	14.1	13.5	12.9	12.3	11.8
92	17.4	16.7	16.0	15.3	14.6	14.0	13.4	12.8	12.2	11.7
93	17.3	16.6	15.9	15.2	14.6	13.9	13.3	12.7	12.1	11.6
94	17.3	16.6	15.9	15.2	14.5	13.9	13.2	12.6	12.0	11.5
95	17.3	16.5	15.8	15.1	14.5	13.8	13.2	12.6	12.0	11.4
96	17.2	16.5	15.8	15.1	14.4	13.8	13.1	12.5	11.9	11.3
97	17.2	16.5	15.8	15.1	14.4	13.7	13.1	12.5	11.9	11.3
98	17.2	16.4	15.7	15.0	14.3	13.7	13.0	12.4	11.8	11.2
99	17.2	16.4	15.7	15.0	14.3	13.6	13.0	12.4	11.8	11.2

Table II: Joint Life and Last Survivor Expectancy (continued)

AGES	70	71	72	73	74	75	76	77	78	79
100	17.1	16.4	15.7	15.0	14.3	13.6	12.9	12.3	11.7	11.1
101	17.1	16.4	15.6	14.9	14.2	13.6	12.9	12.3	11.7	11.1
102	17.1	16.4	15.6	14.9	14.2	13.5	12.9	12.2	11.6	11.0
103	17.1	16.3	15.6	14.9	14.2	13.5	12.9	12.2	11.6	11.0
104	17.1	16.3	15.6	14.9	14.2	13.5	12.8	12.2	11.6	11.0
105	17.1	16.3	15.6	14.9	14.2	13.5	12.8	12.2	11.5	10.9
106	17.1	16.3	15.6	14.8	14.1	13.5	12.8	12.2	11.5	10.9
107	17.0	16.3	15.6	14.8	14.1	13.4	12.8	12.1	11.5	10.9
108	17.0	16.3	15.5	14.8	14.1	13.4	12.8	12.1	11.5	10.9
109	17.0	16.3	15.5	14.8	14.1	13.4	12.8	12.1	11.5	10.9
110	17.0	16.3	15.5	14.8	14.1	13.4	12.7	12.1	11.5	10.9
111	17.0	16.3	15.5	14.8	14.1	13.4	12.7	12.1	11.5	10.8
112	17.0	16.3	15.5	14.8	14.1	13.4	12.7	12.1	11.5	10.8
113	17.0	16.3	15.5	14.8	14.1	13.4	12.7	12.1	11.4	10.8
114	17.0	16.3	15.5	14.8	14.1	13.4	12.7	12.1	11.4	10.8
115+	17.0	16.3	15.5	14.8	14.1	13.4	12.7	12.1	11.4	10.8

Table II: Joint Life and Last Survivor Expectancy (continued)

AGES	80	81	82	83	84	85	86	87	88	89
80	13.8	13.4	13.1	12.8	12.6	12.3	12.1	11.9	11.7	11.5
81	13.4	13.1	12.7	12.4	12.2	11.9	11.7	11.4	11.3	11.1
82	13.1	12.7	12.4	12.1	11.8	11.5	11.3	11.0	10.8	10.6
83	12.8	12.4	12.1	11.7	11.4	11.1	10.9	10.6	10.4	10.2
84	12.6	12.2	11.8	11.4	11.1	10.8	10.5	10.3	10.1	9.9
85	12.3	11.9	11.5	11.1	10.8	10.5	10.2	9.9	9.7	9.5
86	12.1	11.7	11.3	10.9	10.5	10.2	9.9	9.6	9.4	9.2
87	11.9	11.4	11.0	10.6	10.3	9.9	9.6	9.4	9.1	8.9
88	11.7	11.3	10.8	10.4	10.1	9.7	9.4	9.1	8.8	8.6
89	11.5	11.1	10.6	10.2	9.9	9.5	9.2	8.9	8.6	8.3
90	11.4	10.9	10.5	10.1	9.7	9.3	9.0	8.6	8.3	8.1
91	11.3	10.8	10.3	9.9	9.5	9.1	8.8	8.4	8.1	7.9
92	11.2	10.7	10.2	9.8	9.3	9.0	8.6	8.3	8.0	7.7
93	11.1	10.6	10.1	9.6	9.2	8.8	8.5	8.1	7.8	7.5
94	11.0	10.5	10.0	9.5	9.1	8.7	8.3	8.0	7.6	7.3
95	10.9	10.4	9.9	9.4	9.0	8.6	8.2	7.8	7.5	7.2
96	10.8	10.3	9.8	9.3	8.9	8.5	8.1	7.7	7.4	7.1
97	10.7	10.2	9.7	9.2	8.8	8.4	8.0	7.6	7.3	6.9
98	10.7	10.1	9.6	9.2	8.7	8.3	7.9	7.5	7.1	6.8
99	10.6	10.1	9.6	9.1	8.6	8.2	7.8	7.4	7.0	6.7
100	10.6	10.0	9.5	9.0	8.5	8.1	7.7	7.3	6.9	6.6
101	10.5	10.0	9.4	9.0	8.5	8.0	7.6	7.2	6.9	6.5
102	10.5	9.9	9.4	8.9	8.4	8.0	7.5	7.1	6.8	6.4
103	10.4	9.9	9.4	8.8	8.4	7.9	7.5	7.1	6.7	6.3
104	10.4	9.8	9.3	8.8	8.3	7.9	7.4	7.0	6.6	6.3
105	10.4	9.8	9.3	8.8	8.3	7.8	7.4	7.0	6.6	6.2
106	10.3	9.8	9.2	8.7	8.2	7.8	7.3	6.9	6.5	6.2
107	10.3	9.8	9.2	8.7	8.2	7.7	7.3	6.9	6.5	6.1
108	10.3	9.7	9.2	8.7	8.2	7.7	7.3	6.8	6.4	6.1
109	10.3	9.7	9.2	8.7	8.2	7.7	7.2	6.8	6.4	6.0

AGES	80	81	82	83	84	85	86	87	88	89
Table II: Joint Life and Last Survivor Expectancy (continued)										
110	10.3	9.7	9.2	8.6	8.1	7.7	7.2	6.8	6.4	6.0
111	10.3	9.7	9.1	8.6	8.1	7.6	7.2	6.8	6.3	6.0
112	10.2	9.7	9.1	8.6	8.1	7.6	7.2	6.7	6.3	5.9
113	10.2	9.7	9.1	8.6	8.1	7.6	7.2	6.7	6.3	5.9
114	10.2	9.7	9.1	8.6	8.1	7.6	7.1	6.7	6.3	5.9
115+	10.2	9.7	9.1	8.6	8.1	7.6	7.1	6.7	6.3	5.9

Table II: Joint Life and Last Survivor Expectancy (continued)

AGES	90	91	92	93	94	95	96	97	98	99
90	7.8	7.6	7.4	7.2	7.1	6.9	6.8	6.6	6.5	6.4
91	7.6	7.4	7.2	7.0	6.8	6.7	6.5	6.4	6.3	6.1
92	7.4	7.2	7.0	6.8	6.6	6.4	6.3	6.1	6.0	5.9
93	7.2	7.0	6.8	6.6	6.4	6.2	6.1	5.9	5.8	5.6
94	7.1	6.8	6.6	6.4	6.2	6.0	5.9	5.7	5.6	5.4
95	6.9	6.7	6.4	6.2	6.0	5.8	5.7	5.5	5.4	5.2
96	6.8	6.5	6.3	6.1	5.9	5.7	5.5	5.3	5.2	5.0
97	6.6	6.4	6.1	5.9	5.7	5.5	5.3	5.2	5.0	4.9
98	6.5	6.3	6.0	5.8	5.6	5.4	5.2	5.0	4.8	4.7
99	6.4	6.1	5.9	5.6	5.4	5.2	5.0	4.9	4.7	4.5
100	6.3	6.0	5.8	5.5	5.3	5.1	4.9	4.7	4.5	4.4
101	6.2	5.9	5.6	5.4	5.2	5.0	4.8	4.6	4.4	4.2
102	6.1	5.8	5.5	5.3	5.1	4.8	4.6	4.4	4.3	4.1
103	6.0	5.7	5.4	5.2	5.0	4.7	4.5	4.3	4.1	4.0
104	5.9	5.6	5.4	5.1	4.9	4.6	4.4	4.2	4.0	3.8
105	5.9	5.6	5.3	5.0	4.8	4.5	4.3	4.1	3.9	3.7
106	5.8	5.5	5.2	4.9	4.7	4.5	4.2	4.0	3.8	3.6
107	5.8	5.4	5.1	4.9	4.6	4.4	4.2	3.9	3.7	3.5
108	5.7	5.4	5.1	4.8	4.6	4.3	4.1	3.9	3.7	3.5
109	5.7	5.3	5.0	4.8	4.5	4.3	4.0	3.8	3.6	3.4
110	5.6	5.3	5.0	4.7	4.5	4.2	4.0	3.8	3.5	3.3
111	5.6	5.3	5.0	4.7	4.4	4.2	3.9	3.7	3.5	3.3
112	5.6	5.3	4.9	4.7	4.4	4.1	3.9	3.7	3.5	3.2
113	5.6	5.2	4.9	4.6	4.4	4.1	3.9	3.6	3.4	3.2
114	5.6	5.2	4.9	4.6	4.3	4.1	3.9	3.6	3.4	3.2
115+	5.5	5.2	4.9	4.6	4.3	4.1	3.8	3.6	3.4	3.1

Table II: Joint Life and Last Survivor Expectancy (continued)

AGES	100	101	102	103	104	105	106	107	108	109
100	4.2	4.1	3.9	3.8	3.7	3.5	3.4	3.3	3.3	3.2
101	4.1	3.9	3.7	3.6	3.5	3.4	3.2	3.1	3.1	3.0
102	3.9	3.7	3.6	3.4	3.3	3.2	3.1	3.0	2.9	2.8
103	3.8	3.6	3.4	3.3	3.2	3.0	2.9	2.8	2.7	2.6
104	3.7	3.5	3.3	3.2	3.0	2.9	2.7	2.6	2.5	2.4
105	3.5	3.4	3.2	3.0	2.9	2.7	2.6	2.5	2.4	2.3
106	3.4	3.2	3.1	2.9	2.7	2.6	2.4	2.3	2.2	2.1
107	3.3	3.1	3.0	2.8	2.6	2.5	2.3	2.2	2.1	2.0
108	3.3	3.1	2.9	2.7	2.5	2.4	2.2	2.1	1.9	1.8
109	3.2	3.0	2.8	2.6	2.4	2.3	2.1	2.0	1.8	1.7
110	3.1	2.9	2.7	2.5	2.3	2.2	2.0	1.9	1.7	1.6
111	3.1	2.9	2.7	2.5	2.3	2.1	1.9	1.8	1.6	1.5
112	3.0	2.8	2.6	2.4	2.2	2.0	1.9	1.7	1.5	1.4
113	3.0	2.8	2.6	2.4	2.2	2.0	1.8	1.6	1.5	1.3
114	3.0	2.7	2.5	2.3	2.1	1.9	1.8	1.6	1.4	1.3
115+	2.9	2.7	2.5	2.3	2.1	1.9	1.7	1.5	1.4	1.2

Table II: Joint Life and Last Survivor Expectancy (continued)

AGES	110	111	112	113	114	115	
110	1.5	1.4	1.3	1.2	1.1	1.1	
111	1.4	1.2	1.1	1.1	1.0	1.0	
112	1.3	1.1	1.0	1.0	1.0	1.0	
113	1.2	1.1	1.0	1.0	1.0	1.0	
114	1.1	1.0	1.0	1.0	1.0	1.0	
115+	1.1	1.0	1.0	1.0	1.0	1.0	

Table III: Uniform Lifetime Table							
Age	Applicable Divisor	Age	Applicable Divisor	Age	Applicable Divisor
70	27.4	86	14.1	101	5.9
71	26.5	87	13.4	102	5.5
72	25.6	88	12.7	103	5.2
73	24.7	89	12.0	104	4.9
74	23.8	90	11.4	105	4.5
75	22.9	91	10.8	106	4.2
76	22.0	92	10.2	107	3.9
77	21.2	93	9.6	108	3.7
78	20.3	94	9.1	109	3.4
79	19.5	95	8.6	110	3.1
80	18.7	96	8.1	111	2.9
81	17.9	97	7.6	112	2.6
82	17.1	98	7.1	113	2.4
83	16.3	99	6.7	114	2.1
84	15.5	100	6.3	115+	1.9
85	14.8				

1st yr.

$$\frac{\text{IRA Amt. (by 12-31)}}{27.4} = \text{required minimum distribution)}$$

2nd yr.

$$\frac{\text{IRA amt.(after subtracting 1st distribution)}}{26.5} =$$

3rd yr.

$$\frac{\text{IRA amt.(after subtracting 2nd dist.)}}{25.6} =$$

Table IV: Survivor Benefit Limits

Excess of Employee's Age Over Beneficiary's Age	Applicable Percentage	Excess of Employee's Age Over Beneficiary's Age	Applicable Percentage
10 years or less	100%	28	62%
11	96%	29	61%
12	93%	30	60%
13	90%	31	59%
14	87%	32	59%
15	84%	33	58%
16	82%	34	57%
17	79%	35	56%
18	77%	36	56%
19	75%	37	55%
20	73%	38	55%
21	72%	39	54%
22	70%	40	54%
23	68%	41	53%
24	67%	42	53%
25	66%	43	53%
26	64%	44 and greater	52%
27	63%		

Index

Your comments make a big difference in the development and revision of Nolo books and software. Please take a few minutes and register your Nolo product—and your comments—with us. Not only will your input make a difference, you'll receive special offers available only to registered owners of Nolo products on our newest books and software. Register now by:

PHONE
1-800-728-3555

FAX
1-800-645-0895

EMAIL
cs@nolo.com

or **MAIL** us
this registration card

fold here

Nolo
in the
NEWS

"Nolo helps lay people perform legal tasks without the aid—or fees—of lawyers."

—USA TODAY

Nolo books are ..."written in plain language, free of legal mumbo jumbo, and spiced with witty personal observations."

—ASSOCIATED PRESS

"...Nolo publications...guide people simply through the how, when, where and why of law."

—WASHINGTON POST

"Increasingly, people who are not lawyers are performing tasks usually regarded as legal work... And consumers, using books like Nolo's, do routine legal work themselves."

—NEW YORK TIMES

"...All of [Nolo's] books are easy-to-understand, are updated regularly, provide pull-out forms...and are often quite moving in their sense of compassion for the struggles of the lay reader."

—SAN FRANCISCO CHRONICLE

- - - - - - - - - - - - - - - fold here -

Place
stamp here

Nolo
950 Parker Street
Berkeley, CA 94710-9867

Attn: RET 7.0